Indian Fiscal Federalism

Indian Fiscal Federalism

Y.V. Reddy
G.R. Reddy

OXFORD
UNIVERSITY PRESS

OXFORD

UNIVERSITY PRESS

Oxford University Press is a department of the University of Oxford.
It furthers the University's objective of excellence in research, scholarship,
and education by publishing worldwide. Oxford is a registered trademark of
Oxford University Press in the UK and in certain other countries.

Published in India by
Oxford University Press
2/11 Ground Floor, Ansari Road, Daryaganj, New Delhi 110 002, India

First Edition published in 2019

ISBN-13 (print edition): 978-0-19-949362-3
ISBN-10 (print edition): 0-19-949362-6

ISBN-13 (eBook): 978-0-19-909704-3
ISBN-10 (eBook): 0-19-909704-6

Typeset in Berling LT Std 9.5/13
by Tranistics Data Technologies, Kolkata 700 091
Printed in India by Replika Press Pvt. Ltd

To Dr Babasaheb Bhimrao Ambedkar,
a scholar and a statesman,
with gratitude

TABLE OF CONTENTS

LIST OF TABLES, FIGURES, AND BOX

TABLES

FIGURES

BOX

ACKNOWLEDGEMENTS

WE EXPRESS OUR DEEP GRATITUDE to Professor M. Govinda Rao, but for whose encouragement, constant advice, and guidance, this book would not have been completed. Dr Pinaki Chakraborty was gracious with his time and advice. He went through all the chapters meticulously and offered valuable suggestions.

In the process of writing the book, we consulted a number of friends and experts. Among those who have been of great help to us in select chapters are Arigapudi Premchand, V. Bhaskar, C. Narendra Reddy, Rammanohar Reddy, and V. Senthil.

The valuable opinion of the referees also benefited us immensely.

We would like to thank Angoor Vinayak for his excellent support in putting together and analysing the statistical information in this book.

We also thank Sunil Nagpal, ably assisted by B. Sudhakar Reddy, for their help on this book.

We express our gratitude to Oxford University Press India for guiding us at every step with professionalism and dedication, and for their untiring efforts in bringing out this book in an expeditious manner.

Y.V. Reddy acknowledges with love his wife Geetha, and his children and grandchildren for tolerating his obsession with writing this book. G.R. Reddy acknowledges the encouragement and warm support of his wife Devi, daughters Vijaya and Vani, and, in particular, his granddaughter Pallavi for her excitement in looking forward to this book.

ABBREVIATIONS

ADE	Additional Duty of Excise
AIBP	Accelerated Irrigation Benefit Programme
BE	Budget Estimate
CENVAT	Central Value Added Tax
CGST	Central Goods and Services Tax
CRF	Calamity Relief Fund
CSS	Centrally Sponsored Schemes
EAP	Externally Aided Projects
EC	Empowered Committee
FRBM Act	Fiscal Responsibility and Budget Management Act
GBS	Gross Budgetary Support
GDP	Gross Domestic Product
GSDP	Gross State Domestic Product
GST	Goods and Services Tax
GSTC	Goods and Services Tax Council
IATP	Income Adjusted Total Population
IGST	Integrated Goods and Services Tax
ISC	Inter-State Council
ITC	Input Tax Credit

MODVAT	Modified Value Added Tax
NCCF	National Calamity Contingency Fund
NDA	National Democratic Alliance
NDC	National Development Council
NDMA	National Disaster Management Authority
NDMF	National Disaster Mitigation Fund
NDRF	National Disaster Response Fund
NEIDS	North Eastern Industrial Development Scheme
NER	North Eastern Region
NITI Aayog	National Institution for Transforming India
NSSF	National Small Savings Fund
PRIs	Panchayat Raj Institutions
RBI	Reserve Bank of India
SDGs	Sustainable Development Goals
SDRF	State Disaster Response Fund
SFCs	State Finance Commissions
SGST	State Goods and Services Tax
SRC	States Reorganisation Commission
ToR	Terms of Reference
UGST	Union Territories Goods and Services Tax
VAT	Value Added Tax

INTRODUCTION

FISCAL FEDERALISM IN INDIA CAN be viewed, in practice, as a game in politics, economics, and public finance played between the Union and States. It can also be seen as an interplay of ideologies or beliefs, intentions or objectives, individuals, institutions, and instruments. A study of these underlying factors could lead us to an appreciation of where fiscal federalism stands now in the country, and where it may be headed.

In the federal system, powers and responsibilities are divided between the Union and States. (Though the word 'Centre' does not figure in the Constitution, the words 'Union' and 'Centre' are used interchangeably in the literature on Indian fiscal federalism and in common parlance.) Tax-raising powers and expenditure responsibilities are also shared between the two. Such a division results in imbalance in revenue powers and expenditure responsibilities between the Centre and States. While the Centre has a larger share of the revenue, the States have greater responsibilities, especially in economic and social services. This is a source of vertical imbalance in fiscal management that has to be corrected through tax sharing or through fiscal transfers.

The States incur over 60 per cent of the total Government expenditure (that is, including both Centre and States), but their share in revenue collection is just about 40 per cent. Borrowings also fund the expenditure of the States or Centre; however, borrowing by a State is subject to approval by the Union Government when the former is indebted to the latter. This is, in a manner of speaking, a game of Union versus States.

The gaps between capacity to collect revenue and expenditure needs vary significantly from State to State. The mechanisms of tax sharing and transfers attempt to address these imbalances. Consequently, per capita transfers are higher to States with lower per capita incomes. However, transfers do not fully offset the revenue disabilities of poorer States. More affluent States may incur significantly higher per capita expenditures than their poorer counterparts, but feel that they should be enabled to perform better. The States compete among themselves to obtain a higher share of the overall fund corpus from the Centre. Thus, we have a game of competing States confronting the Centre together, a phenomenon that can be described as Union versus competing States of India.

Inter-State disparities in per capita incomes (Gross State Domestic Product, GSDP) are inevitable. The per capita revenues of the States closely follow variations in per capita GSDP. Per capita revenues vary with per capita incomes predominantly because of variations in revenue capacity. At the same time, there is an expectation that all citizens of a country should be entitled to a nationally acceptable minimum standard of living, or at least to minimum standards of governmental services, such as roads, street lights, security, education, and health. These considerations affect any arrangements that deal with fiscal imbalances.

The vertical and horizontal imbalances and the manner of managing them have varied over the years, partly because of developments in the economy and partly from political economy considerations. A chronological account of some of these is attempted in the book. Our Constitution mandates the appointment of a Finance Commission once every five years by the President of India to resolve these imbalances.

The Commission makes recommendations on tax devolution and grants-in-aid of revenues. The objectives and functioning of the Finance Commission have had elements of continuity and change. Its functioning has always been, and will continue to be, critical. The Government of India has also been exercising its freedom to transfer beyond what is recommended by the Finance Commission. The relative shares of Finance Commission and non-Finance Commission transfers have also been a bone of contention between the Union and States. A major part of the book is devoted to this theme. In addition to explicit transfers to States through multiple channels, there are implicit and hidden transfers. These transfers are mainly in the form of Central Government investments in public enterprises, administered prices, industrial incentives, tax exportation, priority sector lending, and interest subventions. A study (Rao 1997) revealed the regressive nature of these invisible transfers. Though the extent of invisible transfers is important in fiscal federalism, because of the complexities in assessing the magnitude and impact, this aspect is not analysed in the book.

Transfers from the Central Government to States can take the form of general-purpose or specific-purpose transfers. They can be formula based or discretionary. The mix has been changing, and neither can we discern any specific pattern nor can we attribute any specific reasons for the varying mix.

The States collectively seek a higher level of non-discretionary funds but they are reluctant to give up their claims to discretionary grants. Many of the grants from the Centre require a matching contribution from States, and the States would prefer minimizing their share.

There are also vertical and horizontal imbalances in access to public debt. The aggregate borrowing limits are set by macroeconomic conditions. The Union Government has privileged access to debt-financing due to both Constitutional provisions and financial market perceptions. Among the States, the poorer ones perceive that disadvantages in their access and cost of borrowing are not taken into account in the prevailing fiscal federal relations.

INTERPLAY OF FACTORS AFFECTING FISCAL FEDERALISM

Many feel that preserving the unity of the country requires elements of centralization. The contrary view is that recognizing and promoting decentralization would strengthen unity, as illustrated by the formation of linguistic States. Equally, while some may argue that the Centre has national interests alone or that at the very least such interests should be uppermost, others hold that a one-size-fits-all approach by the Centre in a country with vast diversity is inefficient and intrusive. The former school would argue that the standards of governance at the Centre are better than in most, if not all, States. There are those who advocate strengthening local units at the sub-State level to achieve true decentralization. Others believe that we should stick to the original intent of the Constitution, namely, organize a Union of States under a dual polity system with the Union at the Centre and the State Governments at the periphery. Some argue that the Directive Principles of State Policy are binding on the Union while others believe that these are equally binding on all tiers. The study of the past attempted in the book hopefully gives insights into how these conflicting considerations have been dealt with at various points in time.

The objectives of arrangements for fiscal transfers and related policies may be narrow or broad. They may aim to merely correct the fiscal imbalances (defined as revenues not fully meeting current expenditures in the normal course of business). Current expenditure may be limited to non-Plan expenditure, or include all current expenditure but not capital needs. It could be very broad to promote balanced growth and to ensure equity. Its intermediate or more realistic objectives may be to provide for or enable the provision of similar standards of social or economic services by State Governments. A more realistic objective may be the provision of specified minimum standards of defined public services to every citizen, regardless of where he or she lives. There may also be political objectives such as holding the country together by favouring certain States with more transfers; to incentivize the States to improve performance in the delivery of public services; or to undertake reforms in the national interest.

Fiscal federalism cannot be viewed on a stand-alone basis as a technical exercise. It is to be seen in a context in which individuals also matter. Judicial interpretations of Constitutional provisions as well as political economy considerations underlie many of the tensions as well as resolutions in fiscal relations between the Union and States.

Some of the institutional changes have had a significant impact on fiscal relations between the States and with the Centre. For example, the anti-defection law and party discipline undermine the capacity of the elected members of the Rajya Sabha who represent the views of the States that have elected them. The electoral process in which the prime ministerial candidates promise to deliver on subjects relevant to the States also influence inter-State relations. Above all, personalities matter. Pandit Nehru, as Prime Minister, used to write letters to the Chief Ministers sharing with them his thoughts on various subjects in the Union List. The concept of dual polity was respected. The leadership of Indira Gandhi was characterized by the strengthening of the Union. Rajiv Gandhi did not change much, except that he emphasized decentralization, which had the effect of undermining the position of the States vis-à-vis the Union. Later, P.V. Narasimha Rao steered a broad-based reform of the Indian economy. Having served both in the Union and State Cabinets and having been Chief Minister of a State, Rao was fully aware of the States' point of view in the Union–State dynamics. He was in a position to build consensus-based Union–State relations. The tradition was continued faithfully by Atal Behari Vajpayee. A lasting contribution made under Manmohan Singh, a technocrat Prime Minister, relates to the framing of the Terms of Reference (ToR) of the Fourteenth Finance Commission. Although ToR for the Commission are issued in the presidential notification, in effect, it is the executive that frames them. Singh's tenure in the Planning Commission, both as member Secretary and Deputy Chairman, had a salutary effect on his approach to Union–State relations. Narendra Modi, as the Prime Minister, committed himself to a new framework of federalism. His long innings as Chief Minister influenced his enthusiastic acceptance of the recommendations of the Fourteenth Finance Commission. However, in actual implementation, and in the framing of the ToR of the Fifteenth

Finance Commission, there are indications of a shift towards centralization. Over the years, there have been increased attempts to influence the recommendations of the Commission (which is supposed to be neutral between the Centre and States), with directives nudging it towards adopting asymmetric approaches in the treatment of the Centre and States. This can be seen distinctly in the case of the Fifteenth Finance Commission, which will be discussed later.

This book records the working of institutions such as the Finance Commission and the Planning Commission and of certain events, but does not deal with the complete subject of the role of individuals. An exception has been made in the chapter on asymmetric federalism, which narrates the puzzles relating to special-category status for Andhra Pradesh.

The practice of fiscal federalism depends on the Constitutional provisions relating to fiscal imbalances. The Constitution of India envisages a Finance Commission, an institution that has played a critical role in our fiscal federalism, and thus in resolving fiscal imbalances. A large part of the book is devoted to the working of the various Finance Commissions and their recommendations. A separate chapter is devoted to an analysis of the ToR of the Fifteenth Finance Commission, the latest one constituted in 2017, in view of the controversies surrounding it.

Acting on an enabling provision in the Constitution, and after the Commission on Centre–State Relations chaired by Justice R.S. Sarkaria made its recommendation, an Inter-State Council to discuss policies and disputes was established in 1990. The body, however, remains almost dormant. Besides, as the Council is placed under the Union Home Ministry, it lost the required status of neutrality—and the confidence of the States. Similarly, the Constitution was amended in 1992 to introduce a third tier, local self-governments. The Amendment provided a role for the Union Finance Commission to support local bodies based on the recommendations of Finance Commissions at State levels. A separate chapter is devoted to this subject.

The Planning Commission, an extra-Constitutional body created by a Cabinet Resolution to undertake development planning in 1950, played a crucial role in fiscal federalism. Its replacement by NITI (National Institution for Transforming India) Aayog raises more questions than answers about its contribution. A chapter on NITI Aayog focuses on what it could do in the future.

The National Development Council (NDC) and its successor, the Governing Council of NITI Aayog, find a passing mention because both, formed by an administrative order, are virtually non-functional, if not irrelevant.

Borrowing is critical to financing the capital needs of both the Union and States, and of late, revenue expenditure needs as well. The interface between the Union and the States with regard to public debt is because of inter-governmental implications of fiscal deficit over time. The States' access to public debt is thus important in Centre–State relations. Its evolution and interface with the Union and the Finance Commission, and the current status are narrated in this book.

The narratives in many chapters indicate the range of instruments available to manage vertical and horizontal imbalances. Most important among these are tax devolution and grants on the recommendations of the Finance Commission, and loans and additional grants by the Union to States. The grants could be discretionary and purpose-specific, or untied. There may be incentives or rewards built into the flow of funds to States. The use or usefulness of these instruments in relation to the objectives can be discerned from the activities of institutions.

WHERE DO WE STAND?

The record of the practice of fiscal federalism in India and its current status has to be viewed in the Constitutional and political context, and also in terms of economic management, including of the external sector.

First, soon after Independence, India had to simultaneously design the units that would constitute the new federation while setting in motion the process to form the Union. That unprecedented task was performed well. It is remarkable that national integration in India has been facilitated by the Union, which recognized and accepted diversity as it emerged and asserted from time to time. This is reflected in the process of the States' reorganization on a linguistic basis since 1956 and the adoption of asymmetric federalism.

Second, in regard to the political context, India can boast of a peaceful change of political regimes in a regular and systematic manner at the Union and State levels, with few exceptional episodes. The credit for that goes as much to the States as to the Union. All elections, Parliamentary as well as to State Legislatures, are conducted wholly by bureaucracy from different States under the aegis of the Central Election Commission. The Union Government has no administrative machinery of its own to conduct such operations, and the Election Commission operates through the State Governments.

Third, in terms of economic management, many, if not all, States have improved their capabilities to plan, allocate resources, and implement policies and programmes. The gap between expertise at the Union level and at the State level in many cases has narrowed in recent years for several reasons, the most important being technological development and globalization. In fact, many States legitimately claim that almost all flagship schemes of the Union Government in recent years had been, in fact, initiated by some States. The schemes were initially viewed with disfavour by the Union Government. But in recent years, the debate has not been so much between the Mahalanobis and the Bramhananda models as between the Tamil Nadu, Bihar, and Gujarat models. More recently, the one-nation-one-policy model being popularized has caused some discomfort.

Fourth, as per Article 293 of the Constitution, the borrowing programme of a State has to be approved by the Union as long as it is in debt to the Union. This helps the States exercise restraint on borrowings. There have been cases of States bypassing the Central restriction by borrowing through their enterprises by extending guarantees. The Reserve Bank of India (RBI) is debt manager for both the Union and the States. The involvement of RBI as a banker and debt manager provides a degree of comfort to the financial markets.

Fifth, Constitutional provisions prohibit external borrowings by States. This ensures that problems in the external sector do not arise on account of States incurring external liabilities beyond sustainable levels. Many other developing countries have faced problems on this account.

Sixth, in terms of arrangements for fiscal transfers to sub-national governments, the Indian system differs from that of other federations among emerging economies, such as South Africa, China, Brazil, and Indonesia. The arrangements for transfer in most of these countries permit far greater discretion to the federal government than India. The primary mode of transfers in these countries is grants from the higher to lower level of government, and such transfers are mostly discretionary. These countries do not have a Constitutional provision for sharing of national-level taxes, unlike in the case of India and Pakistan. Of course, in most federations there are separate taxes, or both levels have tax powers. In India, the arrangements for transfer to local bodies have undergone changes in recent years, but arrangements for Union–State transfers have continued.

In our Constitution, the Finance Commission was devised as a mechanism for providing predictability in the fiscal federal relations for five years. The Commission has the flexibility to review and revise the relations after the five-year term. The Planning Commission was an innovation of the Union Government, and not derived from the Constitution. It not only had the expertise but its functioning also gave flexibility to accommodate fiscal needs arising out of socio-political developments from time to time. (It had the freedom to take outside experts in different domains to assist it. In addition, it had a number of sector-specific divisions headed by advisers to regularly work on those issues. Some of its members were well-known subject-matter experts.) This body has since been replaced by NITI Aayog on 1 January 2015. The most significant institutional innovation in the history of fiscal federalism in India, however, is the Goods and Services Tax Council (GSTC), a new Constitutional body. The GSTC is responsible for the entire architecture of the Goods and Services Tax (GST). Since there is no exclusive tax base for the Union or States in respect of a number of indirect taxes post GST, the operation of the GSTC is key to the success of fiscal federalism in the country.

We have every reason to be proud of our success in the practice of fiscal federalism as it has evolved over the years. In the context of economic reforms at the national level since 1991, Union–State fiscal relations have been incidental, while the developments since 2015 represent game changers. There are emerging signs now, however, of what may be described as fiscal federalism being at a crossroads.

AT A CROSSROADS

Several developments in recent years point to the emergence of a new era in fiscal federalism, the contours of which are still unfolding.

First, the establishment of the GSTC on a statutory basis, which is emerging as the most significant body in fiscal federalism since Independence. Decisions regarding the major indirect taxes are now decided jointly by the Union and States through the mechanism of the GSTC, where the Union has a de facto veto. As far as the States are concerned, this marks a significant erosion of their fiscal autonomy, and this is particularly significant as the sales tax/VAT, which was transformed into GST, was the only broad-based tax assigned to them. However, the reform has to be seen as a trade-off between the benefits of tax harmonization and the loss of the States' fiscal autonomy and, to an extent, that of the Centre.

Second, the Planning Commission, which played an uninterrupted critical role in fiscal transfers from the Union to States from 1950 onwards, was wound up in 2014 and replaced by NITI Aayog. Similarly, the NDC, a body of Chief Ministers, functioning since 1952, has been replaced by a Governing Council that has the Prime Minister as the Chairperson, a Vice Chairman, full-time members of NITI Aayog, Chief Ministers of all the States, the Lieutenant Governor of Andaman and Nicobar Islands, and Union Ministers (who are the ex-officio members of NITI Aayog). The NDC in any case was meeting infrequently. Another change that has been made is that the distinction between Plan and non-Plan has been removed. The consequences of the new arrangements are yet to be fully appreciated.

Third, the recommendations of the Fourteenth Finance Commission were accepted as game changers in February 2015. The basic approach was to reduce discretion in making transfers to States. But the ToR of the Fifteenth Finance Commission constituted in 2017 seem to not just reverse some of the recommendations of the previous Commission but give greater discretion than ever before to the Union Government. The outcomes of this are unclear.

Fourth, the ToR of the Fifteenth Finance Commission have become contentious, with some States making a joint appeal to the President. The politicization of the ToR, by itself, poses unprecedented challenges to the Commission.

Fifth, the access of States to the borrowing programme has also become a bone of contention between the Union and States. The issue relating to vertical and horizontal imbalances that was so far confined to revenues and expenditures has now extended to public debt. Public debt has provided fiscal support of large magnitudes to States, but the Union is granting access to borrowings with discretionary conditionalities despite rules governing fiscal deficits.

Sixth, competing State-wise models of development, a matter of pride in 2014, have now been replaced with a one-nation-one-policy model.

Finally, there are several instances where the States resent what they perceive as intrusion of the Centre into their domain. These include the Prime Minister or Union Ministers addressing State Chief Secretaries and Secretaries and deploying Central Government officials for village outreach programmes to evaluate the working of schemes funded by the Centre. There is resentment that these contravene the spirit of the Constitution, and it is felt in some quarters that a cooperative and competitive federalism is being replaced with coercive federalism.

A PRACTITIONERS' PERSPECTIVE

The authors, by virtue of being associated with fiscal federalism in the Planning and Finance departments in States and the Union Government and several Finance Commissions as practitioners, decided to write a book that facilitates an appreciation of fiscal federalism as it evolved since Independence. This book is a historical and analytical account; in some cases, however, data has been used to illustrate and indicate. It explores the likely developments in the future as well.

Indian fiscal federalism is continuously evolving and changing. This book seeks to explore how India has coped with these changes; how institutions such as the Finance Commission have adapted to these changes; and how Indian fiscal federalism has stood the test of time. Despite these changes, the Union–State fiscal relations are facing challenges and are at a crossroads now. An attempt is made to present the broad contours of a way forward that could simultaneously address institutional as well as policy challenges.

SELECT REFERENCE

Rao, M. Govinda. 1997. 'Invisible Transfers in Indian Federalism', *Public Finance/Finances Publiques*, 52 (3–4).

1

ORIGINS OF FISCAL FEDERALISM

THE CONSTITUTION OF INDIA (ARTICLE 1) states that India, that is Bharat, shall be a 'Union of States'. What are these States, their composition, and their background? Historically, the States that constitute the Union of India were, for the major part, successors to Provinces in British India and the erstwhile Princely States. The Provinces of British India themselves were successors to Presidencies, which had been created by the East India Company.

At the time of Independence, India had nine Provinces and over 500 Princely States. The Princely States accounted for 40 per cent of the territory and 30 per cent of the population, and were diverse in size, character, systems, and in the nature of their relations with British India. They were integrated with India after Independence, and the Union of States came into existence on 26 January 1950. The diverse systems of Princely States and corresponding diversity in their links with British India were replaced by the system prevalent in the Provinces in British India.

Many of the features of fiscal federalism in India have their origins in this history. The East India Company was a creation of the British Crown. It was granted a Charter of incorporation by Queen Elizabeth in 1600 CE. Under the Charter, the Company was given the exclusive right of trading with India. It was later given the right to impose punishments for offenses committed by its servants. Although it initially derived authority from the Crown, the Company later jointly exercised the power to govern its most prized colony.

The Company set up a number of factories and trading centres at various places in India. Of these, Bombay, Madras, and Calcutta became the main settlements and were declared as Presidencies.

The semblance of a government was set up under the Act of 1773 in the Calcutta Presidency with full powers over the Presidencies of Madras and Bombay, but a Central fiscal authority with the Presidencies as constituent units was enshrined only 60 years later, in the Charter Act of 1833. It vested the financial and legislative powers in India solely in the Governor-General of Bengal, who was designated the Governor-General of India. The entire administration became centralized, with the Presidencies becoming administrative units. With the assumption of direct control by the Crown in 1858, the current system of the financial year ending on 31 March, as in England, was adopted along with the principles of the English budget system.

The first budget under the new system was presented for the year 1860–1. The system, in a way, gave the rudiments of the Union, State, and Concurrent Lists prevalent in the Indian Constitution now. Revenue was classified into India, Provincial and Divided, as the system of divided heads of revenue evolved gradually. In 1904, the system of a quasi-permanent settlement was introduced by fixing the revenue assigned to a Province. This amount could not be altered by the Central Government except in case of extreme necessity or distortions. This period saw the evolution of the sharing of the fiscal burden between the Centre and States on account of natural calamities, and also the system of a five-year review of revenue sharing between the Centre and Provinces.

The Montague-Chelmsford reforms manifested in the Government of India Act, 1919 introduced a system of diarchy in which administrative subjects were divided into two categories, Central and Provincial. Provincial Subjects were further divided into Transferred Subjects, administered by the Governor and his ministers responsible to the Legislative Council, and Reserved Subjects, administered by the Governor and his Executive Council without the involvement of the Legislative Council. Thus, under the Act, Provinces got power by way of delegation and the Central Legislature retained the power to legislate for the entire country relating to any subject. The sources of revenue were also divided between the Centre and Provinces.

The Simon Commission appointed in 1927 to review the working of the Act of 1919 favoured the establishment of a federation of Indian States and Provinces. The word 'States' refers to Princely States and the word 'Provinces' to the administrative divisions of the British Government in the subcontinent.

An expert committee with Lord Viscount Peel as Chairman was appointed in 1931 to examine the fiscal relations between the Centre and Provinces. The Committee felt that the distribution of taxes based on origin, population, and collection was not equitable. It suggested that any system of distribution should be simple and provide ease of administration. Income tax should be shared between the Centre and Provinces. The share of Provinces should be fixed, subject to a revision every five years. The Centre should have the power to levy surcharges on any tax levied and collected by it. Central grants should be distributed to Provinces on the basis of population. It is not difficult to notice the similarities between these recommendations and the current framework of Constitutional provisions relating to vertical and horizontal balance.

Based on these recommendations, a federal system with Provinces and Indian States as two distinct constituent units was established under the Government of India Act, 1935. The Act delineated the relationship between the Federal Government and Provinces and between the Federal Government and Princely States in a contentious manner. Under the Act, the States were given the option to join the federation. A Princely State was deemed to have acceded to the federation if the ruler had executed the Instrument of Accession. As the States did not exercise this option, the federation envisaged by the Act did not become a reality.

Thus, the federal provisions of the Act which came into force on 1 April 1937 applied only to the Central Government and Provinces. The federal system that was formally launched in India in 1937 was an incomplete federal system, with 40 per cent of the territory outside the system. Very few were optimistic at that time about amicably resolving the issue relating to the Princely States.

The Act of 1935 distributed legislative powers under three lists, viz., Federal List, Provincial List, and the Concurrent List. The Governor-General was empowered to authorize either the Federal or the Provincial Legislature to enact a law for the subjects not listed in any of the three Lists. The Act made the revenues and finances of the Provincial Government distinct from those of the Federal Government. Levies could be collected and retained by the Federal Government or shared with the Provinces as stipulated in the Act. The Act spelt out the manner of distribution of financial resources and provided for grants-in-aid to Provinces which were in need of assistance. It also provided that such sums as prescribed by His Majesty in Council shall be charged on the revenues of the federation. In brief, the Government of India Act, 1935 established the basic structure of Indian fiscal federalism, one that survives even today.

Recommendations to operationalize the provisions of the 1935 Act went beyond sharing of taxes and included writing off the outstanding debt due to the Centre contracted before 1 April 1935 by the Provinces of Bengal, Bihar, Assam, the North Western Frontier Province, and Orissa. Introduced in 1936, this practice became somewhat common in Independent India with a number of Finance Commissions recommending such write-offs.

When Britain decided to grant independence to the country, it came to the conclusion that a Union of India comprising Provinces and Princely States was the basis of independence acceptable to prominent political parties. A Constituent Assembly was constituted in November 1946, with 292 members selected on the basis of an indirect election by members of Provincial Assemblies, 93 members representing the Princely States, and 4 members representing the Chief Commissioners' Provinces. At this stage, the design of the Indian federation did not envisage a partition and assumed the continuance of two categories of constituent units, namely, Provinces and States.

The Indian Constituent Assembly held its first meeting on 9 December 1946. Dr Rajendra Prasad was elected the President of the Assembly at the second session on 11 December 1946.

The troubling ambiguities of the positions of Princely States in the proposed independent India are clear from a Resolution (Government of India) moved by Pandit Jawaharlal Nehru on 13 December 1946, which states, inter alia, that

> 1) This Constituent Assembly declares its firm and solemn resolve to proclaim India as an Independent Sovereign Republic and to draw up for her future governance a Constitution; 2) wherein the territories that now comprise British India, the territories that now form the Indian States, and such other parts of India as are outside British India and the States as well as other territories as are willing to be constituted into the independent sovereign India shall be a Union of them all....

This resolution was unanimously adopted on 22 January 1947.

As Govinda Rao (2010) has observed:

> Although there were strong arguments for decentralisation before independence, and even though the Cabinet Mission sent by the imperial government envisaged limited powers for the Union in a three-tiered federal structure, the constitution that was eventually adopted by the Indian Republic closely followed the Government of India Act, 1935, with pronounced 'quasi-federal' features. The shift probably occurred for two reasons: First, once the Muslim majority areas opted out of India to form a separate country, the principal rationale for a loose federal structure no longer existed. Second, a strong Centre was found desirable to safeguard against fissiparous tendencies among constituent units particularly, the erstwhile Princely States. The federal framework provided by the founding fathers of Indian Constitution was an experiment in adopting the federal idea to a large and extremely diverse economic, cultural, social, and linguistic society.

Following the partition plan of 3 June 1947, a separate Constituent Assembly was constituted for Pakistan.

In sum, the budget practices in India were derived from the practices of Britain, with a unitary form of government. However, the federal framework evolved in India indigenously over a period. The final shape to the federal form of government and federal finance was incorporated in the Government of India Act, 1935. It had some features of a parliamentary system. The actual implementation, no doubt, had setbacks because of the Second World War and domestic political controversies, but the basic framework remained. The biggest problem that was envisaged in the run-up to Independence was the nature of the relationship between the proposed Federal Government and the Provinces of British India relative to that of the Princely States. This was resolved after Independence, but before the Constitution was adopted.

The Constituent Assembly approved a Union of States, removing the distinction between Provinces and States. However, the influence of the Act of 1935 on the design of the Union was itself a matter of debate in the Assembly. The journey to the Republic of India from independent India is a fascinating story, seen in the next chapter.

SELECT REFERENCES

1. Ambedkar, Bhimrao. 1923. *The Evolution of Provincial Finance in British India*. London: P.S. King & Son, Ltd.

2. Austin, Granville. 1966. *The Indian Constitution—Cornerstone of a Nation*. New Delhi: Oxford University Press.

3. Government of India. 1935. The Government of India Act, 1935. Available at www.legislation.gov.uk/ukpga/1935/2/pdfs/ukpga_19350002_en.pdf, viewed on 20 October 2018.

4. Government of India. *Constituent Assembly of India Debates Volume 1*. Available at www.164.100.47.194/Loksabha/Debates/cadebatefiles/C09121946.html, viewed on 20 October 2018.

5. Rao, M. Govinda. 2010. 'A Review of Indian Fiscal Federalism', a research study submitted to the Punchhi Commission on Centre–State Relations.

6. Thomas, P.J. 1939. *The Growth of Federal Finance in India*. Madras: Oxford University Press.

7. Munshi, K.M. (ed). 1967. *Indian Constitutional Documents—Munshi Papers, Volume II*. Bombay: Bharatiya Vidya Bhavan.

8. Government of India. 1930. *Report of the Indian Statutory Commission, Vols. I and II*, Calcutta: Central Publication Branch.

9. Ministry of Finance. Various Years. *Report of the Finance Commission*. New Delhi: Government of India.

10. Thompson, John Perronet. 1933. *India, the White Paper*. London: Macmillan and Co.

2

EVOLUTION OF FISCAL FEDERALISM

THE CONSTITUENT ASSEMBLY, WHEN FORMED, was confronted with two problems concerning the design of the system of governance for which no agreement was in sight. The Muslim League was insisting on provincial autonomy, a claim which the Indian National Congress was resisting. The diversity in the Princely States demanded a differential relationship between the Union and States. The first was resolved by the Partition. The second was solved by the integration of Princely States with a special and temporary provision of asymmetric arrangement for Jammu & Kashmir.

In the aftermath of the Partition, India emerged as a Federation with a strong Centre. This was clear from the report given by the Committee of the Constituent Assembly on Powers of Union, presided over by Pandit Nehru, followed by a second report on 5 July 1947. Pandit Nehru explained the momentous changes that had taken place since the submission of the first report. He indicated that in view of the changed circumstances (that is, the Partition), the Committee came to the unanimous view that 'it would be injurious to the interests of the country to provide for a weak Central authority which would be incapable of ensuring peace, of coordinating vital matters of common concern and of speaking effectively for the whole country in the international sphere' (Second Report of the Union Powers Committee 1947).

Pandit Nehru referred to the Committee's conclusion that the soundest framework for the Constitution was a federation with a strong Centre. In the matter of distributing powers between the Centre and the States, the Committee favoured drawing up three lists on the lines of the Government of India Act, 1935, namely, the Federal, the Provincial, and the Concurrent.

The influence of the 1935 Act on the Indian Constitution on fiscal matters was itself a matter of debate at that time. However, B.N. Rau, the Constitutional Adviser in defence of the draft Constitution, expressed the view that so long as the provisions of the Act were adapted to India's circumstances, it could not be construed as a defect.

The second problem related to the initial design that contemplated a federation of Provinces and States as two distinct categories. This was overcome with the integration of Princely States when the Constituent Assembly was in session.

In 1950, the Constitution contained a fourfold classification of the States of the Indian Union, into Parts A, B, C, and D. In all, they numbered 29. Part-A States comprised nine erstwhile Governor's Provinces of British India. Part-B States consisted of nine erstwhile Princely States with legislatures. Part-C States consisted of the former Chief Commissioner's Provinces of British India and some of the erstwhile Princely States. These Part-C States, ten in number, were administered by the Centre. The Andaman and Nicobar Islands were kept as the solitary Part-D State.

The Government of India constituted the States Reorganisation Commission (SRC) in 1956. Based on the recommendations of the Commission, the States were reorganized according to language. By the States Reorganisation Act (1956) and the 7th Constitutional Amendment Act (1956), the distinction between Part-A and Part-B States was done away with, while Part-C and Part-D States were abolished. Some of them were merged with adjacent States and some others were designated as Union Territories. We now have 29 States and seven Union territories, the latest addition to the list of States being Telangana, formed on 2 June 2014.

The Indian Constitution distributes legislative and financial powers between the Union and the States. All residual powers that are not part of Lists I and II (the Union and State Lists) of the Seventh Schedule are vested with the Union. The Parliament and the Legislatures of States have been vested with the power to make laws with respect to any of the matters given in List III, which is the Concurrent List. However, if a law made by a State Legislature on a subject included in the Concurrent List is inconsistent with a previous law passed by the Parliament, the State concerned has to obtain the assent of the President of India. If approved, such law shall prevail in that State only. The functions assigned to the Union and the States broadly follow the system in other federations. The Union is assigned subjects such as defence, maintenance of macroeconomic stability, international relations and trade, atomic energy and space, and matters having implications for more than one State. The important subjects assigned to States are law and order, land, agriculture, irrigation, education, health, industries, etc., which directly touch upon the lives of the people. The distribution of financial powers is mostly based on the principle of separation, i.e., a tax is assigned either to the Union or the States with exclusive jurisdiction. Most broad-based taxes are assigned to the Union. Though the States are assigned numerous taxes, the only tax buoyant among them is the tax on sale or purchase of goods.

Owing to the vertical imbalance between the financial powers and functional responsibilities assigned to the Union and the States, suitable provisions were made for sharing the proceeds of certain Union taxes with the States. The tax sharing was under three heads, namely, duties to be levied by the Union but collected and appropriated by the States; taxes levied and collected by the Union but assigned to States; and taxes levied and collected by the Union and distributed between the Union and the States. The distribution of the proceeds of taxes was initially in terms of a fixed mandate, but thereafter was based on the recommendations of the Finance Commission.

The Constitution provides for grants-in-aid to the States that the Parliament deems to be in need of assistance, and different sums may be fixed for different States. The Constitution included a provision conferring power on the Union to levy surcharges on certain duties and taxes for the purpose of the Union.

UNION–STATE FISCAL RELATIONS: THE FRAMEWORK

The Constitution envisaged the sharing of taxes between the Union and States and grants-in-aid from the Union to States as per the recommendations of the Finance Commission from time to time. However, transfers outside this framework were made under the enabling provisions of Article 282, whereby the Union or a State may make a grant for any public purpose. These transfers were made mainly through recommendations of the Planning Commission. Until 1969, the total assistance offered as well as the grant–loan components were decided on the basis of projects approved. However, with the States complaining about the arbitrariness and subjectivity of such an arrangement, a formula was evolved by the then Deputy Chairman of the Planning Commission D.R. Gadgil, which was adopted by the NDC. Over the years, with some modifications introduced by Pranab Mukherjee when he was the Deputy Chairman of the Planning Commission, the formula came to be known as the Gadgil–Mukherjee formula. With the Plan grants becoming formula-based, the Ministries of the Union Government introduced various schemes. Thus, the Plan assistance had two components, namely, formalized (normal Plan assistance) and scheme-based. With the abolition of the Planning Commission, normal Plan assistance has ceased to be operational.

The Union Government exercised its discretion in giving access to debt to each State based on the overall size of the Plan. Such access to a State has to be approved under Article 293 (3) of the Constitution if the State has any outstanding amounts against loans previously extended to it by the Government of India. The access to a State was not based on any formula until the enactment of fiscal responsibility legislations at the State level. The nationalization of banks in 1969 opened up another source of finance for public policy. Access to credit was allocated partly as per public policy. While there were sectoral allocations, there were no State-wise allocations of credit.

THE FINANCE COMMISSION

An important provision relating to resource transfers to States is the constitution of a Finance Commission within two years from the commencement of the Constitution, and thereafter at the expiration of every fifth year or at such other time as the President considers necessary. It is the responsibility of the Commission to make recommendations to the President on the distribution of the net proceeds of taxes between the Union and States, and the allocation between the States of the respective shares of such proceeds; the principles which should govern the grants-in-aid to States out of the revenues of India; and any other matter referred to the Commission by the President in the interest of sound finance. It is useful to note that the Finance Commission as envisaged by the Constitution does not prohibit its continuous functioning, except that it has to be reconstituted before the expiry of every five years.

The Constitution also provides that the Commission shall determine its own procedure and shall have such powers in the performance of its functions as the Parliament may confer on it by law. In compliance with the provisions of the Constitution and an enabling Act of Parliament, there have been fourteen Finance Commissions so far and the fifteenth has been constituted in 2017. The Commissions generally take one to two years to submit their reports.

THE PLANNING COMMISSION: A JUXTAPOSITION

Prompted by the commitment of Prime Minister Nehru, the government's intention of constituting a Planning Commission was announced in the Finance Minister's budget speech in February 1950. The Commission was established on 15 March 1950 through a Cabinet resolution. While there was a virtual consensus in favour of planning as an approach for the reconstruction and development of the economy, there was disagreement about the need for an institution like the Planning Commission, with strong opposition even from within the Cabinet. John Mathai, then the Finance Minister, resigned, stating that his objection was not merely to the idea of a Planning Commission but also to the method of its working. Following the Finance Minister's resignation, a number of Ministers expressed their opposition to the Commission. There were also serious concerns about the role of the Planning Commission in governance at the Union level and in Union–State relations. There were apprehensions that it would be an extra-Constitutional authority. Some felt that any financial transfer outside the Finance Commission was not envisaged in the Constitution.

The Prime Minister had always been an ex-officio Chairman of the Planning Commission, with a Deputy Chairman in the rank of a Cabinet Minister nominated by the Prime Minister. Some select Cabinet Ministers acted as ex-officio Members of the Commission. The full-time Members nominated by the Prime Minister were subject experts. Thus, the membership of the Planning Commission was virtually coterminous with that of the Prime Minister. It is very clear that the Planning Commission has been a body of the Union Government and its composition coincided with political cycles.

The NDC was established in 1952, also by a resolution of the Cabinet on the basis of a recommendation in the draft outline of the First Five-Year Plan. It was chaired by the Prime Minister and had as members the Deputy Chairman and Members of the Commission, the Cabinet Ministers of the Union Government, Chief Ministers of all the States, and representatives of Union Territories. As the number of Members exceeded 50, a Standing Committee was established in November 1954 with only nine Chief Ministers and fewer Union Ministers to improve its effectiveness. The functions of the NDC related to the formulation of the national Plan; reviewing the working of the Plan; and considering important questions of social and economic policy affecting national development. In a way, therefore, the Planning Commission was to be guided by the NDC, but the decisions on convening the NDC, its remit, and its effectiveness were largely determined by the Prime Minister.

The broad functions of the Planning Commission in practice remained the same since its inception. These were formulating medium- to long-term Plans; advising on the allocation of funds to Ministries in the Union Government through the annual budget; approving the Plan of each State and allocating transfers of funds from Union to States, both untied and tied to activities or schemes under the Plan; monitoring, evaluating, etc., incidental to Planning; and assisting the NDC on these matters.

The Five-Year Plan had a medium-term outlook and strategy, while Annual Plans focused on the allocation of funds. The Annual Plans of the Union and States were expected to be prepared within the framework of the Five-Year Plan and operationalized mainly through the Plan components of their respective Annual Budgets. The Planning Commission virtually determined the distribution of Plan assistance between the Union Government and the States, and among the States inter se. Plan outlays were generally equated with public investments and capital outlays of budgets.

The Planning Commission persuaded the States to establish Planning Boards at the State level. The experience with the State-level Planning Boards had been varied across States and over time. However, they had generally been less central to the process of policy than the Planning Commission was at the national level.

A notable function of the Planning Commission that contributed to its importance was dispensing Plan assistance to the States; it thus became a juxtaposition in fiscal federalism. The Government of India accepted a note of dissent of the Member-Secretary of the Third Finance Commission and ruled that the Finance Commission should confine itself to non-Plan revenue expenditure requirements of the States. From the Fourth Finance Commission, the ToR in the presidential order appointing the Commission excluded the consideration of the Plan requirements of the States by the Finance Commission, and the Planning Commission became an important parallel channel of transfers.

Initially, the Plan assistance—its volume as well as grant-loan components to the States—was decided on the basis of the projects approved, but in 1969, with demands from States, the NDC adopted the Gadgil formula for distribution. According to the formula, 30 per cent of the total assistance was to be earmarked for special-category States (deserving special fiscal support from the Centre), which were to receive 90 per cent of the assistance by way of grants and the remaining 10 per cent as loans. The pattern of assistance to general-category States was set as 30 per cent grant and 70 per cent loan. The distribution among the States inter se was done with the predominant weightage assigned to population and factors such as backwardness, fiscal performance, and special problems faced by them.

Often, when some of the States complained about the adverse impact of the norms adopted by the Finance Commission, the Planning Commission stepped in to give some additional discretionary assistance to meet their non-Plan revenue expenditure requirements as well.

In the initial years, particularly the 1960s, and to some extent in the 1970s, the State Governments had the benefit of understanding the planning techniques and the associated processes from the Planning Commission. Thus, the Commission exercised soft power over the States, and the States also often viewed it as a body representing their interests in the Union Government. In the 1970s, perceptions began to change as States started to feel that the Planning Commission was becoming a political instrument of the party in power in the Union Government. The State Governments also felt more confident about their capacity to do their own planning. Further, the NDC meetings became less frequent, and it functioned less as a discussion forum and more as what might be called a posture forum. In recent years, State Governments have expressed resentment about the role of the Planning Commission in the transfer of funds from the Union Government to the State Governments outside the awards of the Finance Commission.

There was also a perception among analysts that the Planning Commission was encouraging fiscal profligacy in both Union and State Governments through the advocacy of new investments and an ever-increasing Plan size. There was also a perception that non-Plan expenditure for the maintenance and upkeep of assets and, more importantly, those relating to general services, such as police and judiciary, were not receiving the attention they deserved. There was also considerable resentment among the Union Ministries about the growing importance of the Planning Commission in public investments, including projects involving public–private partnership.

Whether the Planning Commission's advice contributed to accelerated growth is a matter on which there have been genuine differences of opinion. However, the actual outcome of most Five-Year Plans and Annual Plans generally fell short of the targets indicated. The implementation agencies blamed the Planning Commission for wrong design, while the Planning Commission blamed the implementation agencies for poor implementation. Both of them blamed the political leadership, which in turn pointed to the role of bureaucracy.

In 2009, the then Prime Minister Manmohan Singh suggested that the Planning Commission be reformed, but apparently no serious reform really occurred. On 15 August 2014, Prime Minister Modi announced the decision to wind up the Planning Commission. It was replaced by NITI Aayog in 2015, with a composition not entirely dissimilar to its predecessor. But it has more of an advisory mandate to the Union Government and, to some extent, the States, and a less active role in fund allocations. The distinction between Plan and non-Plan in the Union Budget was given up from 2017–18.

THE INTER-STATE COUNCIL

Besides the Finance Commission, the Constitution provides for the establishment of an Inter-State Council (ISC) (Article 263) with a mandate to advise upon disputes which may arise between the States, and for investigating and discussing subjects in which some or all of the States or the Union and one or more of the States have a common interest. The Council could also make recommendations on any subject affecting the States, in particular, recommendations for better coordination of policy and action with respect to that subject. The ISC was set up in 1990 following the recommendation of the Sarkaria Commission on Centre–State Relations, which submitted its report in 1988. However, the ISC has met only eleven times so far and has remained ineffective in providing a forum to the States to sort out issues with the Union. More importantly, as it was made a part of the Home Ministry, it has not been seen as a neutral institution but as a part of the Union Government.

DISCRETIONARY TRANSFERS VERSUS FORMULA-BASED TRANSFERS

The Constitution envisaged sharing of taxes as the major source of funds for the States, and grants-in-aid were meant to take care of inadequacies of formula-based sharing (which itself had to be guided by the principles recommended by the Finance Commission). The adoption of Planning implied some centralization of financial resources and implementation, and transfers were effected initially through scheme-based assistance to States and later by the Gadgil-formula-based normal Plan assistance. Normal Plan assistance remained a significant channel of resource transfers to States outside the Finance Commission until there was a proliferation of centrally sponsored schemes (CSS), mainly in the area of State subjects. These schemes involved discretionary transfers on the recommendation of the Planning Commission, an institution of the Union Government.

By the end of the Third Five-Year Plan, there were as many as 92 CSS. The modalities for the implementation of these schemes by the States, including the staffing pattern, were prescribed by the Union Ministries concerned. A sub-committee of the NDC constituted in 1967 recommended that the number of CSS be reduced, with only a limited number of schemes in the areas of national policy to be implemented, such as family planning, resettlement of agricultural labourers, and those relating to specialized research and training of national importance. In 1968, the NDC took a decision that no more than one-sixth of Central Plan assistance should be outside the Gadgil-formula-based normal Central assistance. Basically, the Gadgil formula covered only a part of the Plan transfers to States. Over a period of time, the share of non-formula-based discretionary transfers increased to the detriment of formula-based transfers. These transfers also required matching financial contributions from the States, thereby altering their own priorities in allocation. This has been a source of tension.

Despite a number of committees re-examining the proliferation of CSS and recommending their reduction, Union Ministries continued to introduce new schemes with periodic restructuring. In July 2013, the Planning Commission restructured the existing 147 CSS, mapping them into 66 by bringing them under certain umbrella heads. Another change was earmarking at least 10 per cent of the outlay of each CSS as flexi-fund to impart flexibility to States in implementation. There was another restructuring of CSS in 2016 based on the recommendations of the Sub-Group of Chief Ministers. This Committee divided all the schemes into three categories: core of the core schemes, core schemes, and optional schemes. This brought all CSS under 28 umbrella schemes with no effective reduction in their number, but gave some flexibility to States with regard to the components of a scheme. Except for the northeastern and other hilly States, these schemes also reduced the share of contribution of the Union Government to 60 per cent, with a corresponding increase in the States' share. The component of flexi-funds was raised to 25 per cent in the case of States and to 30 per cent in the case of Union Territories. A third channel of transfers, additional Central assistance, emerged over the years to fund specific-purpose schemes. These schemes were no different from the Central sector schemes.

The shift in emphasis from formula-based normal Central assistance to discretionary transfers persisted. In 2014–15, the share of normal Plan assistance was a mere 11.64 per cent of the total Central Plan assistance. From 2015–16, formula-based normal Central assistance ceased with the abolition of the Planning Commission, and with the Fourteenth Finance Commission subsuming Plan grants in tax devolution. The practice of approval of State Plans by the Planning Commission, which many Chief Ministers resented, also ended. However, the CSS and Central sector schemes continued unabated through restructuring.

In sum, the main transfer system, as it has emerged over time, consists of formula-based tax devolution, principle-based grants-in-aid by the Finance Commission, and discretionary transfers through the Central Sector and CSS. Though the Central Sector and CSS have some criteria, these are not explicit and relate to the activities being funded.

A THIRD TIER IN GOVERNANCE: AN IMPOSITION

While introducing the draft Constitution in the Constituent Assembly on 4 November 1948, B.R. Ambedkar explained the form of the Constitution proposed. He explained that '[though] the country and the people may be divided into different States for convenience of administration the country is one integral whole, its people a single people living under a single imperium derived from a single source'. In essence, the Indian Constitution is a flexible federation but with a centripetal bias. Such a bias is also reflected in the provisions relating to fiscal relations between the Union and States. The distribution of resources and functions to local bodies was left to the States.

Though the Directive Principles of State Policy (Article 40 of the Constitution) laid down that the State shall take steps to organize village Panchayats and endow them with such powers and authority as may be necessary to enable them to function as units of self-government, they may in no sense be considered as a third layer as there is no reference to urban local bodies. The Panchayati Raj system evolved out of a recommendation made by the Balwant Rai Mehta Committee to synchronize democratic decentralization, with decentralization of development administration. The Panchayati Raj set-up is not confined to villages but is a form of local self-government for rural areas within each State, at District, Taluk, Block, and Village levels. It was left to each State to set up a Panchayati Raj system by its own legislative process. The Union, through the Planning process, started bypassing States by directing the flow of funds to District-level bodies directly.

The Union Government took the stand in the 1980s that it was necessary to enshrine certain basic features of Panchayat institutions in the Constitution itself to strengthen them as units of self-government. This resulted in the 73rd Amendment to the Constitution. There was a similar concern with regard to the working of the urban local bodies and culminated in the enactment of the 74th Amendment. With these Amendments, it is widely believed that a third tier has been incorporated in India's federal set-up. However, Entry 5 in the State List in the Seventh Schedule puts local government squarely in the domain of States.

Most States consider the Constitutional Amendments an imposition of a uniform model. In practice, the implementation of the third tier varies across the country as the system has to be implemented through the laws of the States concerned. Apart from mandating periodic elections to Panchayats and urban local bodies, and reservations for schedules castes, scheduled tribes, and women, these Amendments also provide for the constitution of a State Election Commission to supervise the preparation of electoral rolls and conduct of elections. A replication of the Central Finance Commission is also mandated at the State level in the form of State Finance Commissions within one year of the commencement of these Amendments, and thereafter, after the expiration of every fifth year.

State Finance Commissions are mandated to make recommendations in regard to local bodies on lines somewhat similar to the Central Finance Commission. They are also mandated to recommend measures needed to improve the financial position of local bodies and on any other matter referred to them in the interest of sound finance of Panchayats or Municipalities. State Governments are mandated to lay before the Legislature of the State every recommendation made by their State Finance Commissions along with an explanatory memorandum as to the action taken thereon. The 73rd and 74th Constitutional Amendments resulted in the addition of the Eleventh and Twelfth Schedules listing out the subjects that the State Governments may devolve on the Panchayats and Municipalities respectively. However, there is no separate list of taxes assigned to them and the States may devolve powers to levy taxes on some bases which are localized and charges on some local services.

New provisos were subsequently inserted, mandating the Central Finance Commission to recommend measures needed to augment the Consolidated Fund of a State to supplement the resources of the Panchayats or Municipalities on the basis of the recommendations made by State Finance Commissions.

Even after nearly 25 years of the amendment to the Constitution, many States have failed to confer on the local bodies the responsibilities listed in the Eleventh and Twelfth Schedules. Similarly, their track record in transferring powers of taxation has been poor, with the exceptions being States such as Kerala and Karnataka. Many State Governments have failed to reconstitute their State Finance Commissions after every five years. Even when constituted, State Finance Commissions have not been following a uniform pattern in the preparation of their reports; their approach in assessing the revenues and needs of the local bodies; and in assessing the cushion available with a State to support those local bodies fiscally. This has made it difficult for the Central Finance Commission to take into account their recommendations.

In brief, most States seem to treat the third tier as an imposition by the Union even though it now has a place in the Constitution. And though it may be less than effective, it has some impact.

ENLARGEMENT OF THE CONCURRENT LIST AND REDUCING THE STATES' AUTHORITY

The enlargement and liberal or one-sided interpretation of the Concurrent List extended the scope of Union jurisdiction. For example, the 42nd Amendment to the Constitution (1976) shifted the Subjects of forests and education from the State List to the Concurrent List.

District-level agencies dealing with the development of small farmers, drought-prone areas, rural areas, and tribal areas were registered as entities outside the Government, but received funds from Governments and supplementary funds from nationalized banks. The amount directly transferred to implementing agencies in the States amounted to Rs 107,015 crore in 2013–14 (Revised Estimates, RE) (Government of India). These autonomous agencies at sub-State level sponsored by the Union Government undermined local self-governing institutions.

The practice of direct transfer of funds by Central Ministries to a number of CSS bypassing State Governments started in the mid-1990s. This practice evolved ostensibly on the grounds that the States were delaying transferring the money received from the Union to the autonomous implementing agencies. Even after improvements in State finances following the introduction of value added tax (VAT), higher economic growth, and fiscal responsibility and budget management legislations, the Union persisted with the practice. This only widened the trust deficit between the Union and the States. The High Level Expert Committee on Efficient Management of Public Expenditure chaired by C. Rangarajan observed in 2011 that under the system of direct transfers by the Centre, there was no certainty as to whether the money had been spent on the schemes and whether there was a proper account of the assets created by the implementing agencies. Even when the funds were released based on the utilization certificates furnished by the implementing agencies, it was observed that the money remained unspent in their bank accounts. Considering these infirmities, the Committee recommended transfer of funds through the treasury route. The practice of direct transfer of funds to the implementing agencies was dispensed with starting from the fiscal year 2014–15.

ERA OF ENTITLEMENT-BASED CENTRAL LEGISLATIONS

A telling example of the manner in which the Centre circumvented the States' authority is through the enactment of entitlement-based legislations by the Union, which was done without proper consultations with the States. Important among these legislations are the Mahatma Gandhi National Rural Employment Guarantee Act, 2005; Right of Children to Free and Compulsory Education Act, 2009; and National Food Security Act, 2013. Though these enactments may be justified on social security considerations, it has to be appreciated that the States' freedom in these areas has been curtailed while imposing additional commitments on them.

SIMPLIFICATION OF TAX SHARING

Until 2000, tax devolution to States was confined to income tax (which was to be compulsorily shared) and Union excise duty (the sharing of this was optional, based on the recommendations of the Finance Commission under Articles 270 and 272 of the Constitution). This resulted in a very high percentage of the proceeds from income tax being devolved to the States to the extent that the Union Government had very little stake in introducing any major reforms relating to this tax. Based mostly on the alternative scheme of devolution suggested by the Tenth Finance Commission, the 80th Amendment to the Constitution was enacted in 2000. Consequently, Article 270 of the Constitution was substituted in its place, providing for the inclusion of net proceeds of all taxes levied by the Union, with the exception of select taxes, and Article 272 was omitted.

CIRCUMVENTING TAX SHARING

The Constitution empowers the Union to levy any cess for a specific purpose and retain its proceeds. The Union can levy a surcharge on any tax levied by it. The proceeds of cesses and surcharges do not form part of the divisible pool of Union taxes and are therefore not shareable with States. Initially, cesses were levied sparingly and were mainly to meet the regulatory needs of certain commodities, such as tea, coffee, jute, mica, and bidis. In 1988, the levy of cesses was extended to petroleum products. This was followed by the levy of primary education cess on all major taxes in 2004–5 and secondary and higher education cess in 2006–7. In 2015–16, the Swachh Bharat cess was added to the list (but was abolished following the introduction of GST).

Currently, surcharges are levied on income tax, corporation tax, and in the form of special additional duty of customs and excise on petrol. The higher percentage of cesses and surcharges in the tax revenue of the Union had the effect of moderating somewhat the benefit of higher tax devolutions recommended by successive Finance Commissions. This increasing share of cesses and surcharges in the gross tax revenue of the Union and its adverse impact on the States' share of taxes has been pointed out by several Finance Commissions, but no action has been taken thereon.

RULE-BASED FISCAL MANAGEMENT

The Constitution enables the adoption of fiscal rules through the prescription of a ceiling on borrowings by the Union and the States.

During the discussions in the Constituent Assembly on 10 August 1949, it was expected that appropriate legislation would take place at the Union and State levels, but no such legislation was passed. Indirectly, however, a limit on borrowing has been brought about through the Fiscal Responsibility and Budgetary Management (FRBM) Act, 2003.

The FRBM Act, 2003 and relevant rules laid down a roadmap for the Union Government for the phased reduction of fiscal deficit to 3 per cent of the GDP and the elimination of revenue deficit by 31 March 2009. Rule-based fiscal control was also introduced in all the States (except West Bengal and Sikkim) in the year 2005–6, as per the recommendation of the Twelfth Finance Commission. The Thirteenth Finance Commission was given an additional ToR to suggest a revised roadmap for FRBM. It recommended shifting the timeline for bringing down fiscal deficit to 31 March 2014 and that of elimination of revenue deficit to 31 March 2015. The Central Government, however, amended the rules, and shifted the date for reducing fiscal deficit to March 2017. It introduced the concept of 'effective revenue deficit' and called for its elimination by March 2015, thus diluting the fiscal rules further.

The FRBM Review Committee chaired by N.K. Singh, in its report submitted in January 2017, recommended the enactment of a new Debt and Fiscal Responsibility Act, adopting a prudent medium-term target for the general government debt of 60 per cent of GDP (40 per cent for the Centre and 20 per cent for the States) to be achieved by no later than financial year 2023. It also recommended that fiscal deficit should be the key operational target consistent with the medium-term debt ceiling, and the Union Government should bring it down in a phased manner to 2.5 per cent while the revenue deficit should come down to 0.8 per cent of the GDP by 2023 as well.

A TAX THAT WAS NOT ENVISAGED

In the Constitution, service tax, introduced in 1994–5, is assigned neither to the Union nor the States. Because of the growing contribution of the services sector to the country's GDP, the Union Government, under the residuary powers vested with it, first levied the tax on three services, viz., general insurance, stock brokerage, and telecommunications. The tax was extended to cover over 70 services by 2004–5. In 2004, the Constitution was amended to confer powers to the Union to tax services. The Expert Group on Taxation of Services chaired by Govinda Rao recommended the extension of the tax to all services, with a small negative list and exemptions in 2001. However, the rationalization took place in the system of services taxation in the country in 2012–13, with the extension of service tax to all sectors except for those included in the negative list under 17 heads. With the proceeds of service tax forming part of the divisible pool of Central taxes, the States also benefited from the introduction of this tax.

The tax that was not envisaged has been subsumed in the new GST, an indirect tax levied jointly, also in parallel, by the Union and States on sale of goods and services. The two innovations that are noteworthy in the GST are its design and its new institutional arrangement, as the GST Council (see the chapter on GST for a detailed account). This, perhaps, is the best compromise between fiscal autonomy of the States and tax harmonization.

MARKETIZATION OF BORROWING BY STATES

As mentioned earlier, normal Plan assistance under the Gadgil formula contained a loan component. In effect, the Government of India was borrowing in order to lend to State Governments to finance their Plan expenditures. Borrowings were left out of the consideration by the First Finance Commission, a practice that was subsequently reinforced by the exclusion of the consideration of Plan expenditures. This is perhaps because it was envisaged that borrowings would be used for capital expenditures and pay for themselves.

The Twelfth Finance Commission recommended that the Union should not act as an intermediary and allow the States to approach the market directly. The Union Government decided to dispense with the loan component of normal Plan assistance and delegate such powers to the States.

Since States are not permitted to borrow from external sources, the Union Government borrows from institutions like World Bank and

Asian Development Bank and on-lends to State Governments. The Union was on-lending to States by passing on external assistance to general-category States in the form of 70 per cent loan and 30 per cent grant, and to special-category States in the form of 90 per cent grant and 10 per cent loan, without any regard to the loan component and terms of external assistance. Following the recommendation of the Twelfth Finance Commission, the Union introduced in 2015–16 the system of transferring external assistance to States on the same terms and conditions as attached to such assistance by external funding agencies or on back-to-back basis, thereby making the Government of India a financial intermediary without any gain or loss. However, external assistance to special-category States continues to be passed on in the grant–loan ratio of 90:10.

NITI AAYOG

On 1 January 2015, the Government of India announced its decision through a Cabinet Resolution to set up the National Institution for Transforming India (NITI Aayog) in place of the erstwhile Planning Commission. It was bring about institutional changes reflecting the changed dynamics of new India and the diminished role of centralized planning.

The Cabinet Resolution also listed the functions of NITI Aayog under 13 heads. Important among these are to evolve a shared vision of national priorities; foster cooperative federalism through structural support initiatives and mechanisms on a continuous basis; design strategic and long-term policy and programme frameworks and initiatives; offer advice; establish knowledge, innovation, and entrepreneurial support; offer a platform for resolution of inter-sectoral and inter-departmental issues; maintain a state-of-the-art resource centre; and actively monitor and evaluate the programmes and initiatives.

NITI Aayog has a Governing Council that is similar to the NDC's in its composition. Unlike the Planning Commission, it is purely an advisory body with no role in resource allocation. The Cabinet Resolution also provides for the formation of Regional Councils for a specified tenure to address specific issues and contingencies impacting more than one State or region. These Councils will be convened by the Prime Minister and chaired by him or her, or by a designated nominee.

THE GST COUNCIL: A UNIQUE AND SIGNIFICANT INSTITUTION

The Constitution (One Hundred and First Amendment) Act, 2016 paved the way for the introduction of the Goods and Services Tax in India. The new Article 279-A, inserted following the Constitutional Amendment provides for the creation of a GST Council by the President within 60 days of its commencement. As per this Article, the GST Council will be a joint forum of the Union and the States. Thus, a new Constitutional body has been added in the sphere of Indian fiscal federalism. The Council has been entrusted with the responsibility of making recommendations on GST rates, taxes, cesses, and surcharges to be subsumed under GST, exemptions under GST, etc. This is a unique and permanent institution which meets at regular intervals to decide on matters relating to GST, a common tax shared between the Union and the States.

THE FIFTEENTH FINANCE COMMISSION

The Fifteenth Finance Commission was appointed in November 2017. The considerations specified and additional matters referred to in its ToR evoked a number of controversies and apprehensions among the States. These controversies and apprehensions are mainly to do with six issues.

First, the Commission has been asked to examine whether revenue-deficit grants be provided at all (paragraph 5 of the ToR). This may be construed as asking the Commission to ignore Article 275 (1) of the Constitution, which provides for grants-in-aid of the revenues of such States as the Parliament may determine to be in need of assistance. This Article stipulates that after a Finance Commission has been constituted, no order shall be made except after considering the recommendations of the Finance Commission.

Second, the consideration regarding the use of the 2011 Census figures of the population in India has resulted in intense debate and controversy. What has caused the current controversy is the likely impact of the significant decline in the share of population of some southern States by one percentage point or more between the 1971 and 2011 population census.

Third, the Commission has been asked to take into account the impact of the fiscal situation of the Union Government owing to the substantially enhanced tax devolution to States following the recommendations of the Fourteenth Finance Commission, coupled with the continuing imperative of the National Development Programme, including New India 2022. If the requirements of national programmes get priority in the assessment of the needs of the Union, there is an apprehension that this will result in the Centre taking increasing recourse to such programmes. By implication, the States lose out.

Fourth, the consideration with regard to the conditions that the Government of India may impose on States' borrowings while providing consent under Article 293 (3) of the Constitution has caused great concern. The argument is that when the States' borrowings are subject to limits under fiscal responsibility legislations, there should be no conditions attached to such loans.

Fifth, the consideration stipulating that the Commission may consider proposing measurable, performance-based incentives for States is also controversial. These include, among others, progress made in the implementation of flagship programmes of the Government of India. The argument here is that such programmes with a one-size–fits-all approach may not be of equal importance to all States. There is no such consideration to be taken into account in regard to the performance of the Union Government.

Sixth, another consideration which has resulted in a lot of resentment from the States is the control, or lack of control, over incurring expenditure on populist measures. There are no objective criteria to categorize schemes into populist and non-populist. With India being so vast, the requirements differ from State to State, and even within a

State, from District to District. What is deemed a populist measure in one State may be a necessity in another.

▼▲▼

The federal framework of the Indian Constitution came into existence out of three chaotic events, namely, the reconstruction after the Second World War, the Partition of the country, and the integration of Princely States. The fiscal framework, however, was an extension of what existed before Independence. It was built on a dual policy, with elected governments at the Union and States. The civil services also operate at the State and Centre, except for a few from the All India Services. The tax powers are divided as well, as are the expenditure responsibilities, except that there are some subjects over which there is a Concurrent jurisdiction. In order to address the issue of fiscal imbalances in this federal set-up, the Constitution envisaged the institution of the Finance Commission. This institution continues to be a pillar of fiscal federalism in India.

The adoption of Planning with consequential centralizing tendencies necessitated the creation of the Planning Commission. The Planning Commission became a parallel institution for transfers from Union to States. While the focus of the Finance Commission was on revenue account, the focus of the Planning Commission was mostly on the capital account.

In parallel, at a political level, the NDC was established in 1952 to oversee the work of the Planning Commission. Over a period of time, it became less active. A similar body but with wider scope, the ISC, which was established in 1990 as enabled by the Constitution, continues to be inactive.

Fiscal federalism has been further complicated by the relative importance of discretionary and formula-based transfers from the Union to States. This was particularly contentious in regards to transfers outside the Finance Commission. A major part of the controversy related also to the increase in the number of Subjects in the Concurrent List, and thus under the jurisdiction of both the Union and the States. On the revenue side, a contentious issue has been the recourse taken by the

Union Government to implement cesses and surcharges and thus avoid sharing revenue with the States. All these issues continue to persist. The ToR of the Fifteenth Finance Commission have also generated controversies. Only the GST provides a unique example of cooperative fiscal federalism.

SELECT REFERENCES

1. Bagchi, Amaresh. 2003. 'Fifty Years of Fiscal Federalism in India—An Appraisal', working paper, National Institute of Public Finance and Policy, New Delhi.

2. Government of India. 2014. Union Budget 2014–15. Available at https://www.indiabudget.gov.in/budget2014-2015/ub2014-15/eb/stat18.pdf, viewed on 20 October 2018.

3. Rao, M. Govinda and Nirvikar Singh. 2005. *Political Economy of Federalism in India*, New Delhi: Oxford University Press.

4. Reddy, Y.V. 2018. 'Fiscal Federalism in India: Emerging Issues,' in Naseer Ahmed Khan (ed.), *Challenges and Issues in Indian Fiscal Federalism*. Springer.

5. Vithal, B.P.R. and M.L. Sastry. 2001. *Fiscal Federalism in India*. New Delhi: Oxford University Press.

6. 'Second Report of the Union Powers Committee', Constituent Assembly of India Debates (Proceedings), Volume V, 20 August 1947, http://164.100.47.194/loksabha/writereaddata/cadebatefiles/C20081947.html, viewed on 20 October 2018.

3

FINANCE COMMISSIONS
THEIR COMPOSITION AND FUNCTIONS

THE CONSTITUTION OF INDIA MANDATES that the President shall, within two years of the commencement of the Constitution and thereafter at the expiry of every fifth year or earlier, constitute a Finance Commission consisting of a Chairman and four other members. An Act of the Parliament (1951) gave effect to the provisions of the Constitution. The Chairman is selected from among persons who have had experience in public affairs. The remaining members are drawn from the judiciary or are officials with expertise or experience in finance and accounts of government, or in financial matters, administration, or economics. The functions are set forth as ToR in the Presidential order constituting the Commission. The considerations that the Commission should keep in view are also set forth in the relevant presidential orders.

We have had fourteen Finance Commissions so far, and the fifteenth was appointed in November 2017. What has been the experience up to this point? The composition of the Commissions has been changing, and the scope of the ToR has contracted in some ways and expanded in others.

GROWING DOMINANCE OF ECONOMISTS

Out of the first ten Finance Commissions, seven were headed by persons having experience in public affairs and with a political background, one by a former justice of the Supreme Court, one by a former Justice of a High Court, and one by a former Comptroller and Auditor General of India. The Eleventh, Twelfth, and Thirteenth Finance Commissions were headed by economists with experience in policymaking, while the Fourteenth Finance Commission was headed by an administrator with long experience in a State Government, the RBI, and the Government of India, and with an academic background in economics. The latter set of appointments coincided with a political consensus in favour of economic reforms consequent upon the balance-of-payments crisis in 1991. It also coincided with the longest spell of coalition governments at the Union level, and the emerging challenge to the concentration of economic power in Union. The Fifteenth Finance Commission has been constituted under the chairmanship of an administrator with long experience in the Union Government, in economic policy, and in political activity in recent years.

The composition of the members of Finance Commissions was a broad mixture of administrators, economists, people with experience in public affairs, and those from the legal profession. Until the Ninth Commission, one of the members was either a retired justice of the Supreme Court or a High Court, except when the Commission itself was headed by a former judge. Perhaps this was done to equip the Commissions with expertise in Constitutional and legal matters. In the Tenth Commission, there was no member with a background in law. The Eleventh Commission had a former Advocate General of a State as one of its members. The subsequent Commissions have had no members with a background in law.

One distinct feature of the Commissions was that they had a minimum of one or two economists of repute as members. The Thirteenth and Fourteenth Finance Commissions had more than one economist; the latter Commission had as many as three. The Fifteenth Finance Commission followed the pattern of its predecessor. This could be due to the fact that many additional matters referred to the recent Finance Commissions were economic in nature. Another development in the composition from the Sixth Finance Commission onwards until the Fourteenth was the induction of one of the members of the Planning Commission as a part-time member. This was done on the recommendations of the First Administrative Reforms Commission in 1969. This convention was breached in the case of the Tenth and Eleventh Commissions because of unforeseen developments. In the Fifteenth Finance Commission, since the Planning Commission has been replaced with NITI Aayog, one of its members has been appointed as a member of the Finance Commission.

There was in underlying rationale for this induction. It had been the norm for States to furnish two different sets of forecast of revenue and expenditure to the Planning and Finance Commissions, with the one to the latter presenting a lower forecast of revenue and higher forecast of expenditure. Therefore, better coordination between the two Commissions was considered necessary.

In brief, the composition of the Commissions reflected the growing importance of economic developments in the Union–State relations and the acceptability of a professional approach relative to political bargaining and entitlements.

ADDITION TO CORE FUNCTIONS

To appreciate the work of the Finance Commission, it is useful to differentiate between the core ToR, namely, sharing of taxes and grants-in-aid, as stipulated in the Constitution, and other terms. The core terms are common to all Commissions. Matters referred to each Commission at the discretion of the President in the interest of sound finance are contextual and are referred to as additional matters. These vary from time to time. The considerations that have to be taken into account that accompany the ToR are in the nature of guidelines to the Commissions.

The Finance Commission is the sole agency that deals with sharing of resources through devolution of taxes. This is a core reference, as are principles governing grants-in-aid. In practice, the stand taken by the Union Government is that it has powers to give grants to States independent of Finance Commission awards. Though these transfers are outside the recommendations of the Finance Commission, they cannot ignore the impact of these grants on Union–State relations.

The core functions of the Finance Commission as stipulated in the Constitution remained the same for the first ten Finance Commissions. These are to make recommendations on the distribution between the Union and States of the net proceeds of taxes which are to be, or may be, divided between them under the Constitution, and the allocation among the States of their respective shares of such proceeds; and the principles which should govern the grants-in-aid of the revenues of the States out of the Consolidated Fund of India.

The Eleventh Finance Commission's mandate was expanded (as a result of an amendment to Article 280 of the Constitution) to make recommendations on the measures needed to augment the Consolidated Fund of a State to supplement the resources of Panchayats and Municipalities in the State on the basis of the recommendations made by the Finance Commission of a State. The ToR of the Finance Commissions since the eleventh Commission included the expanded duties.

EXPANDING LIST OF ADDITIONAL MATTERS

In addition to the core functions, the President can refer to the Commission any other matter in the interests of sound finance. These are described as additional matters.

The additional matters referred to the First Finance Commission related to the sums to be prescribed as grants-in-aid of the revenues of the States of Assam, Bihar, Orissa, and West Bengal in lieu of the assignment of any share of the net proceeds in each year of the export duty on jute and jute products to these States. The Second Finance Commission was asked to make recommendations on the principles that should govern the distribution of net proceeds of estate duty and those of tax on railway fares, and the proceeds of additional duty of excise (ADE) on mill-made textiles, sugar, and tobacco. The additional matter with regard to ADE was included in the ToR following the tax rental agreement between the Centre and the States. This additional matter was referred up to the Eleventh Finance Commission. Following the 80th Amendment to the Constitution, all the taxes of the Union became shareable and the additional matter relating to ADE was dropped from the Twelfth Finance Commission onwards.

The additional matters referred to the Fifth Finance Commission were issues of broader concern, namely, the scope for raising revenue by States from taxes and duties, and the problem of unauthorized overdrafts of certain States with the RBI.

The Sixth Finance Commission was given a landmark term of reference, namely, reviewing the policy and arrangements for financing relief expenditure by States affected by natural calamities and the feasibility of establishing a National Fund. This additional matter was also included in the ToR of the Seventh Finance Commission. Since a Calamity Relief Fund was set up following the recommendations of the Ninth Commission, the Tenth Commission was asked to review its working and to make appropriate recommendations.

The Sixth Finance Commission also went beyond reviewing revenues and expenditures with the inclusion of the debt burden of States into its agenda. It was asked to make an assessment of the non-Plan capital gap of States on a uniform basis and to undertake a general review of the States' debt position based on such an assessment. A similar additional item was included in the ToR of the seventh Commission. The ninth and tenth Commissions were also asked to make an assessment of the debt position of States and suggest corrective measures.

The Ninth Commission's ToR included, for the first time, examining the feasibility of the merger of additional duties of excise in lieu of sales tax with basic duties and evolving a suitable formula for allocating a part of the duties of excise for distribution among States.

The Eleventh Finance Commission was mandated by an additional ToR after its constitution to draw up a monitorable fiscal reforms programme. This was to reduce the revenue deficit of States and to recommend the manner in which the grants to States to cover the assessed deficit in their non-Plan revenue account might be linked to their progress in implementing the programme. Thus, the problem of deficits on the revenue account came to the fore in the agenda of the Finance Commissions. It is interesting that the revenue deficit of the States was given attention, even though the Union had a similar problem.

The additional matters referred to the Twelfth Finance Commission reiterated the continued discomfort with the growing fiscal imbalances. These included reviewing the state of the finances of the Union and of the States and suggesting a plan of action by which the governments might collectively and severally restructure public finances, restore budgetary balance, and achieve macroeconomic stability and debt reduction along with equitable growth.

The issue of non-tax revenues was brought into the remit of the Twelfth Finance Commission's ToR. It was asked to look into whether non-tax revenue receivable by the Central Government out of the profit generated on account of the production of crude oil and natural gas from the fields awarded by the Central Government under a production-sharing contract should be shared with the States where mineral oils were produced, and if so, to what extent. Though non-tax revenues of the Union are not shareable with the States as per the Constitutional provisions, the inclusion of such a ToR was perhaps a reflection of the growing share of non-tax revenues by way of off-shore royalties, sale proceeds of spectrum and dividends from public sector undertakings, and the States' increasing demand for a share in such revenue.

The broader issue of fiscal balance dominated the macro-policy of the Thirteenth Finance Commission, and the additional items referred to included a review of the state of finances of the Union and the States, particularly keeping in view the operation of the States' Debt Consolidation and Relief Facility 2005–10 introduced on the basis of the recommendations of the Twelfth Finance Commission, and suggestions for a stable and sustainable fiscal environment consistent with equitable growth.

In the Fourteenth Finance Commission, the focus was on the working of rule-based fiscal management. Its remit was to review the state of the finances, deficit, and debt levels of the Union and the States in an integrated manner, keeping in view the fiscal consolidation roadmap, and to suggest measures for maintaining a stable and sustainable fiscal environment consistent with equitable growth, including suggestions to amend the Fiscal Responsibility and Budget Management Acts, then in force.

Following the reorganization of the State of Andhra Pradesh into successor States of Andhra Pradesh and Telangana in 2014, the Fourteenth Finance Commission was mandated by an additional ToR to take into account the resources available to the successor States and to make recommendations for them on all matters referred to in the ToR. Though there were reorganizations of States even in 2000, they were done after the Eleventh Finance Commission had already submitted its report. Thus, in these cases, it was left to the Union Government to allocate the respective shares in tax devolution and grants-in-aid to the newly created States. The new State of Telangana was formed while the Fourteenth Commission was still in office, and it is the first Commission to have been entrusted with such a mandate.

By an additional item in the ToR, the Fifteenth Commission has been mandated to review the current status of the finances of the Union and the States and recommend a fiscal consolidation roadmap for sound fiscal management. This needs to be done after taking into account the responsibility of the Central and State Governments to adhere to appropriate levels of debt and deficit while fostering higher inclusive growth in the country. The Commission has also been asked to examine whether revenue-deficit grants should be provided at all. While the former is in tune with the additional matters referred to the Eleventh Finance Commission onwards, the latter is totally new and unprecedented. Another additional matter referred to it is proposing measurable performance-based incentives for States at appropriate levels of government in as many as nine areas. These include achievements in the implementation of flagship programmes of the Government of India and control—or lack of it—in incurring expenditure on populist measures.

In brief, there has been a remarkable recognition of changing circumstances in the economy, warranting attention to areas that were not anticipated as integral to Union–State fiscal relations. The trust commanded by the Finance Commission and its awareness of emerging economic issues were taken advantage of by the President on matters of sound finance through the enabling provision in the Constitution. The expanding list, for the most part, helped fiscal federalism and the idea of sound finance that the Constitution envisaged.

STIPULATION OF CONSIDERATIONS: OVERREACHING

The stipulation of considerations that should govern the work of the Finance Commission was neither envisaged nor prohibited by the Constitution. The practice of inserting the considerations in the ToR of the Finance Commissions started from the second Commission. The ToR of the second and third Commissions stipulated that the grants-in-aid to States might be arrived at having regard, among other considerations, to the requirements of the Five-Year Plans and the efforts made by States to raise additional resources. There was an expansion to the considerations listed in the ToR of the Fourth Commission. These considerations were the revenue resources of the States based on the levels of taxation likely to be reached; the requirements to meet the committed expenditure on the maintenance and upkeep of Plan schemes; and the expenditure for servicing their debt. While the consideration with regard to assessment of revenue resources remained substantively the same as in the case of the fourth Commission, other considerations—such as the revenue requirements on the maintenance and upkeep of completed Plan schemes, and transfer of funds to local bodies as well as the scope for better fiscal management—were introduced in the ToR of the Fifth Finance Commission.

The considerations in making recommendations regarding grants-in-aid were further expanded for the sixth Commission to include the requirements of the States that were backward in the standards of general administration. This introduced an element of equalization and provision for emoluments of government employees, teachers, and local body employees as obtaining on a specified date.

There was a major shift in the nature and coverage of the considerations starting from the ToR of the Seventh Finance Commission. The considerations were listed in a separate paragraph (No. 5) of the ToR and these considerations applied to all the recommendations including those on tax devolution, grants-in-aid, and on other matters.

Most of the States in their memoranda submitted to the Seventh Finance Commission contended that their entitlement in the share of taxes had nothing to do with the considerations listed out in paragraph 5 of the ToR and that these considerations should be applied only for the purpose of determining grants-in-aid to them. Some of the States also contended that it was not proper on the part of the President to impose any considerations, as these were in the nature of constraints on the Commission. The Seventh Finance Commission (1978) in its report observed that

> [such] a view would be difficult to sustain, as we have to estimate the requirements of all States uniformly within the Constitutional framework of Centre–State financial relations.... The change in our terms of reference compared to those of the earlier Commissions is, in a sense, a purely formal one, recognizing the past practice. Further, tax shares and grants-in-aid under Art. 275 have always been inextricably linked in the scheme of transfer of the past Commissions. Actually, grants under Art. 275 were determined for the purpose of making up the revenue requirements of the States to the extent that the tax shares have not met them.

On the view of the States regarding the inappropriateness on the part of the President imposing constraints, the Commission observed:

> This view would have some validity if the considerations set out in the Order were in fact constraints, or prescribed procedures, which were already not inherent in the established practice.... It is, therefore, reasonable to take the view, which in fact we have taken, that the contents of paragraph 5 of the Presidential Order were not constraints on the Commission in any way.

This view endorsed the 'past practice' for future guidance.

The ToR of the Ninth Commission went a step further in terms of comprehensiveness and binding character and was actually in the nature of a directive. It stated that the Commission 'shall' adopt a normative approach in assessing the receipts and expenditure on the revenue account of the States and the Centre and have due regard to the need for providing adequate incentives for better resource mobilization and financial discipline. It required the Commission to take into account the need for speed, efficiency, and effectiveness of government functioning and of delivery systems for government programmes, and keep in view the objective of not only balancing the receipts and expenditure on revenue account of both the States and the Centre, but also generating surpluses for capital investment.

The inclusion of the word 'shall' resulted in a controversy, with States contending that it amounted to giving directions to the Commission. The word 'shall' is in contrast to the earlier practice of ToRs stating that the Commission 'shall have regard, among other considerations'. There were also reservations with regard to the adoption of a normative approach and the mandate to take into account all committed liabilities of the Centre and the absence of a similar mandate while assessing the revenue requirements of the States. Addressing the concerns of States, N.K.P. Salve, the Chairman of the Commission, wrote a letter to the Chief Ministers on 10 December 1987, stating that it was the prerogative of the Commission to adopt such approach and methods as it considered fit and appropriate with regard to tax devolution and grants-in-aid. The Chairman clarified that the Commission would apply a uniform, just, and equitable yardstick both to the Centre and the States.

Following the concern and perception of States that the word 'shall' amounted to a directive to the Commission, the Union Government reverted to the practice of using the wording, 'shall have regard, among other considerations', in the ToR of the Tenth Commission.

The tilt in favour of the Centre in the framing of considerations continued in the ToR of the Eleventh Commission. While in the case of the Centre, the Commission was asked to take into account its resources and the demand thereon, for States, it was required to take into account their resources on the basis of the levels of taxation possible to be achieved in 1998–9; targets set for additional resource mobilization for the Plan; potential for raising additional taxes; and the requirements of States for meeting non-Plan and Plan expenditure. The Commission was asked to keep in view the need for generating surplus for capital investment and for reducing fiscal deficit. The other considerations related to the maintenance and upkeep of capital assets and the maintenance expenditure of Plan schemes to be completed by

31 March 2000; the requirements of States for upgradation of standards in non-developmental sectors; and the need for ensuring reasonable returns on investments made by States in irrigation and power projects and other undertakings. By implication, these considerations were not applicable to the assessment of the Centre's resource position.

With regard to local bodies, the Eleventh Finance Commission was asked to take into account the recommendations of State Finance Commissions. Where the State Finance Commissions had not been constituted or submitted their report, the Commission was to make its own assessment taking into account a variety of requirements.

Significantly, an additional ToR was issued to the Eleventh Finance Commission to draw a monitorable fiscal reforms programme and to recommend the manner in which grants to States to cover the assessed deficit in their non-Plan revenue account might be linked to progress in implementing it. It was widely believed at that time that this was done at the instance of a Chief Minister. The fact that the additional ToR was issued on 28 April 2000, nearly two years after the constitution of the Commission and just two months before the submission of its final report, lends credence to this belief. The Commission was constituted on 3 July 1998 and its report was submitted on 28 June 2000.

The Eleventh Finance Commission submitted a supplementary report on the additional ToR on 30 August 2000. In this report, the Commission drew up a monitorable fiscal reforms programme by assigning equal weightage to raising revenue and control of non-Plan revenue expenditure. Within revenue-raising performance, the growth of tax and non-tax revenues were assigned a weightage of 30 per cent and 20 per cent respectively. The measures included for controlling non-Plan revenue expenditure were salaries and allowances, interest payments, and subsidies. While salaries and wages was assigned a weightage of 30 per cent, interest payments and reduction of subsidies were assigned a weightage of 10 per cent each. The Commission emphasized that the ultimate objective was to bring down the revenue deficit of the States to zero, in the aggregate, by 2004–5.

The Commission recommended the establishment of an incentive fund consisting of two parts, A and B. Part A of the fund would comprise 15 per cent of the revenue-deficit grants recommended by the

Commission. Part B of the fund would receive a contribution from the Central Government, equivalent to 15 per cent of the revenue-deficit grants recommended by the Commission. The size of the fund recommended by the Commission for the five-year period (2000–5) was Rs 10,607.72 crore. This fund was initially meant to be distributed among all the States in proportion to their population in 1971. However, the actual eligibility of a State would be in proportion to its performance in respect of a monitorable fiscal reforms programme in each year.

For the purpose of drawing up the fiscal reforms programme, the Commission recommended the constitution of a Monitoring Group consisting of representatives of the Planning Commission, Ministry of Finance, as well as representatives of the State Government for which the programme was to be worked out. The Group would also authorize the releases from the Incentive Fund.

Amaresh Bagchi, one of the members of the Commission, in a note of dissent, expressed the view that withholding a part of the revenue-deficit grant recommended in the main report was unjustifiable and was contrary to the spirit of Article 275. He also objected to the imposition of conditionalities attached to the release of grants-in-aid to meet revenue deficits. He further emphasized that another reason why deficit grants should not be withheld was that all States were not entitled to receive them.

However, the Government of India accepted the recommendations of the Commission on the additional ToR. This reinforced the concept of conditional grants related to fiscal performance.

The considerations given to the Twelfth Finance Commission mentioned the objective of balancing the receipts and expenditure and taxation efforts of the Centre and States. The consideration with regard to maintenance expenditure on Plan schemes to be completed by 31 March 2005 was limited to non-salary- and non-wage-related expenditure in regard to States only. As in the case of the previous Commission, the consideration with regard to commercial viability of irrigation and power projects applied only to States. Most of the States, in their memoranda to the Commission, expressed their strong objection to limiting the maintenance expenditure only to the non-salary component. The States' contention was that in the case of medical care, education, and other social services, most of the expenditure was salary related and of a recurring nature.

The considerations for the thirteenth Commission expanded with the addition of the impact of the proposed introduction of GST; the need to improve the quality of public expenditure; and the need to manage ecology, environment and climate change consistent with sustainable development. Though there were growing concerns with regard to the deterioration in the quality of expenditure and environment, this was perhaps one of the first attempts to mainstream environmental concerns in Indian fiscal federalism.

The new considerations in the ToR of the Fourteenth Finance Commission related to the level of sustainable subsidies and their equitable sharing between the Centre and the States, and insulating the pricing of public utility services from policy fluctuations. The consideration with regard to public enterprises was expanded to include the need for making them competitive and market-oriented, the requirements for listing and disinvestment, and for relinquishing non-priority enterprises.

Two new considerations in the ToR of the fifteenth Commission require the need to take into account the impact on the fiscal situation of the Union Government after the substantially enhanced tax devolution to States following the recommendations of the Fourteenth Finance Commission, coupled with the continuing imperative of the national development programme, including New India 2022, and any conditions that the Government of India may impose while providing consent under Article 293 (3) of the Constitution.

DEBATING THE PROPRIETY OF STIPULATIONS

A number of questions had been raised about the legality of the presidential orders listing out the considerations that the Commissions shall have to keep in mind while making their recommendations. This issue cropped up as the Finance Commission is a Constitutional body, with its mandate as well as its powers to determine its procedures set out in the Constitution itself. The Parliament has been empowered to prescribe only the powers of the Commission in discharging its duties.

There is some merit in this stand, but supporters of this practice point out that issues relating to fiscal federalism in an emerging and growing economy cannot be cast in stone. Though the main functions are listed out in the Constitution itself, there are many developments since the adoption of the Constitution which have a bearing on these functions. Therefore it is argued that it may not be inappropriate for the presidential order to list out some of these developments in the ToR and mandate the Finance Commission to take into account these, among others, while making recommendations.

Assuming that such listing out is not inappropriate, the considerations should undoubtedly apply uniformly to the Centre and States. In practice, however, the treatment was not even-handed. Most of the Commissions had been asked to take into account the revenues of the Centre; in the case of the States, they were asked to take into account the efforts made for raising additional resources. Also, while the considerations mentioned expenditure liabilities of the Centre, such considerations for States were mostly restricted to non-Plan expenditure. Further, while considerations specifying the emoluments of State Government and local body employees were to be taken as obtaining on a specified date, there was no such cut-off date in the case of the Centre. The Commissions were asked to take into account the need for ensuring reasonable returns on power and irrigation projects and other State public sector undertakings. There was no such consideration for assessing the Union finances.

As far as the revenue assessment of the Centre and States was concerned, until the 80th Amendment of the Constitution, only two Union taxes—income tax and Union excise duties—were under the purview of the Finance Commission. This gave rise to a perception among some analysts that the additional resource measures by the Central Government were not as relevant. But this perception ignored the fact that any improvement in the finances of the Union would facilitate higher transfers to States. The logic was that the assessment of resources of the Centre was mainly for the purpose of determining its capacity to devolve funds to the States. As the needs of each State were different, it called for a detailed assessment. But this does not justify assessing the resources of the Centre and States based on different considerations.

Starting from the seventh Commission, there has been a normative assessment of the resources of both the Centre and the States, whether the considerations specified such a basis or not.

To sum up, there has been an expansion in the considerations listed in the ToR of successive Finance Commissions. Though some of the considerations were biased in favour of the Centre, others reflected emerging developments, such as the deterioration in the quality of public expenditure, increase in the number as well as quantum of subsidies, environmental degradation, and the increasing drag of public enterprises on State as well as Central finances.

ACTION ON RECOMMENDATIONS

The issue as to who should consider, decide, act, and report on the recommendations of the Commission was discussed at length by several eminent personalities in the Constituent Assembly in August 1949. The debate finally resulted in the formulation of Article 281 of the Constitution of India. It states: 'The President shall cause every recommendation made by the Finance Commission under the provisions of this Constitution together with an explanatory memorandum as to the action taken thereon to be laid before each House of Parliament.'

The existing procedure and disclosure requirements include the presentation of an Action Taken Report by the President to the Parliament. The recommendations are submitted to the President by the Finance Commission and made available to the Union Government, which, in turn, assists the President in examining the recommendations and implementing them. The State Governments have no role in this exercise. There is also no evidence of any input from the State Governments to the President regarding the action taken on the Commissions' recommendations. The action taken by the President in regard to recommendations that are in the jurisdiction of the State Government is also not available in public domain.

The tradition has been that the recommendations of the Finance Commission in regard to the core items, namely, tax devolution and grants-in-aid, have been invariably accepted. It could be said that the Action Taken Report is incomplete, since it does not include actions relating to recommendations on non-core items. It has also been a tradition that the majority opinion which constitutes the decision of the Commission is accepted. There was only one instance where this was not done, in the case of the Third Finance Commission.

In regard to grants-in-aid as recommended by the Commission, there is no record of the releases made by the Government of India and savings thereon. In a way, the savings made from non-utilization of grants-in-aid, other than revenue-deficit grants, tend to benefit the Union Government.

TWO COMMISSIONS AT WORK

The Second Finance Commission (1957) devoted a separate section in its report to the interface between the Planning and Finance Commissions. The Commission observed:

> We had some difficulty in dovetailing our work with that of the Planning Commission owing to two factors. First, the second five year plan covers only the first four years of the quinquennium to which our recommendations will apply. Secondly, the plan does not distinguish between revenue expenditure and capital expenditure, while our main function under the Constitution is to make recommendations for the devolution of revenue resources.

The third Commission was asked to give its report covering the period of four years, 1962–6, so that the periods covered by the Fourth Finance Commission and the Fourth Plan could be coterminous (1966–71). But there was a delay in finalizing the Fourth Plan because of the war with China and consequently the Fourth Plan commenced from 1969–70.

A second attempt at synchronization was made by curtailing the period covered by the Fourth Commission by two years. The Fifth Commission's recommendation covered the period 1969–74, synchronous with the Fourth Plan. This synchronization continued until the Fifth Five-Year Plan. A third attempt to make the periods coterminous was done by asking the Ninth Finance Commission to give two reports, the first one covering the year 1989–90 and the second one covering the period 1990–5, which was coterminous with the proposed period for the Eighth Five-Year Plan. As the Eighth Plan commenced from 1992–3, the attempt at synchronization once again failed to materialize. Thereafter, no further attempt was made to make the periods covered by the Five-Year Plans and the awards of the Finance Commission coterminous.

The broader issue of coordination between the works of the two Commissions was raised periodically. In particular, the existence of two Commissions with overlapping mandates seems to have led the States to indulge in gaming the projections they submitted to the two Commissions. They used to under-project revenues and over-project non-Plan revenue expenditures to show large gaps with the hope of getting more transfers from the Finance Commission. In contrast, they used to show an optimistic projection of revenues and underestimate non-Plan revenue expenditures to submit an exaggerated Plan size to the Planning Commission. This issue was partly resolved with the induction of a serving member of the Planning Commission as a part-time member of the Finance Commission. There was also a view that representation of a member of the Planning Commission in the Finance Commission was inappropriate, as whoever represented the Union Government was an interested party in the matter of arbitration between the Union and States. It was also argued that memberships to the Planning Commission were political appointments by the Prime Minister of the day, while the Finance Commission was expected to be apolitical. However the practice continues, and a nominee of NITI Aayog is part of the Fifteenth Finance Commission.

At some point, a case was made for the merger of the Planning and Finance Commissions on the grounds that they were pulling public policy in opposite directions. For instance, the Planning Commission was traditionally more liberal towards increasing public debt, while the Finance Commission advocated fiscal prudence. Further, the Planning Commission tended to centralize decision-making more than the Finance Commission. Interestingly, the inter se allocations among States were more progressive in the awards given by the Finance Commission relative to Plan transfers. The duplication of work was another point in favour of the merger. Though this is not inconsistent with the Constitution, the Fourteenth Finance Commission's view (2014) was clear when it said:

> We believe that the option of entrusting the Finance Commission with responsibilities relating to all transfers from the Union to the States is not advisable. At the same time, we believe that a Finance Commission should take a comprehensive view of all fiscal transfers from the Union to the States. However, it should limit its own recommendations only to tax devolution, grants-in-aid to an extent, and any other matter referred to it in the interest of sound finance ... in our view the Union Government should continue to have fiscal space to provide grants to States for functions that are broadly in the nature of 'overlapping functions' and for area-specific interventions.

The Commission recommended the evolution of a new institutional arrangement to identify the sectors in the States that should be eligible for grants from the Union; indicate criteria for inter-State distribution; help design schemes with appropriate flexibility to the States; and identify and provide area-specific grants. It recommended that the schemes chosen for assistance should be designed by a committee comprising representatives from the Central and State Governments and domain experts.

With the abolition of the Planning Commission and its replacement by NITI Aayog, the tale of two Commissions has apparently ended. The abolition of the distinction between Plan and non-Plan has further diluted the debate. The normal Central assistance to State plans has been discontinued. Yet, the issue remains, namely, of the relative roles of the Finance Commission, which makes recommendations once in five years, providing assurance and stability in Union–State fiscal relations, and of an institution that recommends transfers outside the mechanism of the Finance Commission, providing continuous flexibility to meet unforeseen circumstances and also scope for much-needed political bargaining. It can be argued that in the absence of the latter, there is a danger of the Finance Commission being politicized.

▼▲▼

The mandate given to the President by the Constitution for the appointment of Finance Commissions has been fulfilled without break or material modifications. There has been virtually no controversy in regard to the appointment of the Chairman or Members of the Commission. However, there has been a growing dominance of economists, partly reflecting the rapid changes in the economy. There have been additions to core functions from Eleventh Finance Commission. In addition to these, the President has been referring to the Commission other matters in the interest of sound finance, and this list has been expanding. Similarly, there has been an overreach of the stipulation of considerations that should be kept in view by the Finance Commission. This stipulation of consideration amounts to giving an indication of the directions in which the Government of India would like the recommendations to be. Naturally, the stipulation of consideration has been a matter of controversy. The most critical event that affected the scope and effectiveness of the Finance Commissions was the establishment of the Planning Commission. Inevitably, the de-facto functions of the Commission were constrained by this development. As of 2015, the Planning Commission has been replaced by NITI Aayog.

Overall, there have been only two extraordinary events in this regard. First, the important recommendation of the Third Finance Commission in regard to Plan revenue expenditure of the majority was not accepted by the Central Government. Secondly, as mentioned, an additional ToR was issued to the Eleventh Finance Commission just two months before the submission of its final report to give due weightage to fiscal performance.

In conclusion, fiscal federalism is a work in progress and cannot remain oblivious to changing situations. Despite the tilt in considerations in favour of the Centre and the increase in the number of additional matters of contemporary importance referred to Finance Commissions, most of them made it clear that all the considerations were not equally binding. Some of the Finance Commissions have even made observations and suggestions outside their remit to maintain fiscal prudence and to maintain the sustainability of public finances in the country. Finance Commissions have, over time, generally demonstrated that they were truly national, equally fair to the Union and the States, apolitical and innovative, as needed.

SELECT REFERENCES

1. Bagchi, Amaresh. 2007. 'Role of Planning and the Planning Commission in the New Indian Economy: Case for a Review', *Economic and Political Weekly*, Vol 42, No. 44, 3–9 November.

2. Ministry of Finance. Various Years. *Report of the Finance Commission*. New Delhi: Government of India.

3. Reddy, Y.V. 2014. 'A Tale of Two Commissions and Missing Links', Presidential address delivered at the Ninety Seventh Conference of the Indian Economic Association, Mohanlal Sukhadia University, Udaipur, Rajasthan.

4

CONTINUITY AND CHANGE
APPROACHES OF FINANCE COMMISSIONS

THE APPROACHES OF SUCCESSIVE FINANCE COMMISSIONS have remained unchanged in several ways, even as there has been flexibility in introducing elements of change as warranted by circumstances. The basic approach and procedures set forth by the First Finance Commission have broadly been followed by the first fourteen Commissions. The three main considerations kept in view by the First Finance Commission while making its recommendations were the Centre's capacity to accommodate additional transfers without undue strain on its resources; uniformity in the application of the principles for the distribution of tax devolution and determination of grants-in-aid to all the States; and lessening the inequalities between the States. The Commission made it explicit that it was primarily concerned with the distribution of revenues between the Centre and the States and with the determination of grants, and that the capital needs of both the Centre and the States had to be met largely from borrowed funds. These considerations became a benchmark for all other Commissions.

The procedures adopted by the First Finance Commission, such as seeking the views of and information from States and holding discussions with Chief Ministers and other State officials, Union Ministries, the Comptroller and Auditor General (CAG) of India, industry bodies, and economists, as well as seeking public opinion became the standard operating practices for future Commissions.

While appreciating the needs of the States to meet their expanding responsibilities for the welfare and development of people, the Commission felt that the Centre's ability to assist them was equally important. Further, while drawing up the plan for a substantial transfer of resources, it relied more on the devolution of taxes. An important observation made by the Commission was that an increase in the number of divisible taxes would make it possible to diversify the basis of distribution and achieve a balanced scheme that would benefit the States.

The task of the second Commission became much wider because of the creation of the new State of Andhra in 1953; the reorganization of States in 1956; and the additional ToR with regard to estate duty and additional excise duties in lieu of sales tax. The Second Finance Commission broadly followed the approach of the First Finance Commission. Though it acknowledged that its task had been made easier by the general approach and procedures laid down by its predecessor, it also made some landmark observations and assumptions. The second Commission, while broadly accepting the approach of its predecessor that grants-in-aid should be a residual form of assistance, observed that such grants should be general and unconditional and that the eligibility of a State to grants-in-aid should depend on its fiscal need in a comprehensive sense. The Commission also observed that grants should subserve the objective of planned development and that the priorities of the Plan itself should determine the fiscal needs for development during a Plan period.

The Second Finance Commission had taken the view that it was the responsibility of the Planning Commission and the NDC to ensure equalization of standards of essential social services to the extent practicable. The Commission ruled out any grants in the field of social services. The landmark suggestion that the scheme of devolution recommended by it was an integrated one and should be honoured as such, and that any modification of an individual recommendation would upset the balance has been honoured since then, with very few exceptions. The suggestion that grants-in-aid should be unconditional, however, was breached by later Commissions.

The Third Finance Commission adopted the approach of its predecessors. The Commission raised a number of concerns with regard to the increasing dependence of States on the Centre; the competitive populism among them; and their laxity in raising resources secure in the knowledge that the gaps in their resources would be met by the devolution of Union resources and grants-in-aid, and the discretionary nature of transfers following the emergence of the Planning Commission as an apparatus of national planning. These observations generated debates about the perverse incentives that a gap-filling approach would entail and the emergence of the Planning Commission as a parallel channel of resource transfers to States.

Like the earlier Commissions, the ToR of the Third Finance Commission required it to assess the needs of the States without making a distinction between Plan and non-Plan. However, by that time, the Planning Commission had become prominent and wanted to have a say in determining the Plan requirements of the States. The Commission too recognized this factor and the majority recommendation took into account 75 per cent of the Plan expenditures while leaving the remaining to be adjusted by the Planning Commission. However, the Member-Secretary of the Commission wrote a note of dissent stating that the Finance Commission should stay clear of assessing the Plan revenue-expenditure requirements, and the assessment of the entire Plan expenditure requirements must be left to the Planning Commission. The Government of India rejected the recommendation of the majority and accepted the recommendation of the Member-Secretary. This is the only time in the history of the Finance Commission that the majority recommendation was rejected by the Government. The ToR of the subsequent Commissions until the Thirteenth Finance Commission restricted them to assess only non-Plan requirements. A notable exception was the Eleventh Finance Commission. It was the Fourteenth Finance Commission that broke from the past and went on to address the total revenue-expenditure requirements in its recommendations.

The Fourth Finance Commission took the view that that its function was not to simply recommend devolution and grants to fill the non-Plan revenue deficits as reported by States, but to reassess the States' estimates more comprehensively. Thus it was the first Commission which laid emphasis on the reassessment of the forecasts of revenue and expenditure presented by States. Second, the Commission departed from the criterion of relative financial weaknesses of the States for determining their share in the divisible pool of Union excise duties. It took the view that if any State was in need of specific assistance on account of large deficits that could not be covered by the uniform tax-sharing formula, such assistance should be given explicitly as grants rather than being disguised as a share in Central taxes. Third, the Commission decided not to consider the revenue component of Plan expenditure. This decision was not on the grounds of any Constitutional limitation but on practical considerations following the institutional arrangements relative to the Five-Year Plans. For the first time, the Finance Commission devoted a separate chapter articulating its approach. This became a standard practice for the Commissions that followed.

The Fifth Finance Commission made an important observation. It held that the task of Finance Commissions was to strike a dynamic balance between the competing claims of the two layers of government and to allocate the available resources to serve the needs of the country's welfare and development. The Commission expressed difficulties in taking a call on the propriety of the policies of States and of regulating grants on the basis of any judgment regarding specific policies that individual States had adopted. The Commission observed that all that could be done was to keep in view broad considerations that could be applied to all States as regards their total tax effort, overall expenditure levels, and returns from investments. This principle was violated by some of the subsequent Commissions owing to the introduction of incentives and disincentives in the scheme of allocation.

The Sixth Finance Commission felt the need to attempt new initiatives without disturbing the delicate framework that had evolved over the previous 25 years. The Commission observed that the emergence of the Planning Commission as a channel of resource transfers in no way detracted from the efficacy of provisions embodied in the Constitution. It took the view that the distribution of resources between the Centre and the States should be considered in dynamic terms and that the problem should be viewed as one of distribution of resources, as between the Subjects coming within the purview of the Centre and the States. The Commission indicated that in its scheme of devolution of resources, it had taken the view that the resources belonged to the entire nation and that they should be applied where they were most needed. The Commission (1973) further observed that '[w]hen the emphasis is on social justice, there is no escape from the realignment of resources in favour of the States, because services and programmes which are at the core of a more equitable social order come within the purview of the States in the Constitution'. Thus, the Commission, for the first time, brought to the fore the need for maintaining symmetry between functional responsibilities and resource availability. It took into account the regional disparities across States in its scheme of resource transfers, but held that a Finance Commission could not be expected to play a significant a role in addressing regional disparities as there were other agencies concerned with the allocation of Central resources and the formulation of Central policies. The Commission also made an important observation with regard to the need for regular consultations between the Centre and the States:

We would only like to point out that there could be a significant improvement in the climate of Centre–State financial relations, if decisions that affect the revenues of the States are taken after the widest possible measure of consultation. The spirit underlying Article 274 of the Constitution would also seem to call for such consultation. It is, perhaps, the absence of such consultation and the consequent lack of comprehension of the difficulties of the Centre that is largely responsible for the feeling of dissatisfaction among the States. If the process of consultation between the Centre and the States on fiscal issues is placed on a systematic basis and speedy decisions are taken in the light of these consultations, a good deal of this type of dissatisfaction would disappear.

This observation is valid even today.

With regard to the controversy arising out of the change introduced in the ToR (i.e., listing considerations separately and making them applicable to both grants and tax devolution), the Seventh Finance Commission observed that it considered the change as one of form, one that did not impose constraints on its working. Like the previous Finance Commissions, it refrained from considering the requirements of financing the Central and State Plans. It took a stand consistent with that taken by some of the previous Finance Commissions, that grants should be a residual item as far as possible.

The Seventh Finance Commission laid out a formal approach to grants-in-aid. It felt that they should cover the fiscal gaps after tax devolution; narrow differences in the administrative and social infrastructure between the developed and less-developed States to the extent feasible; and meet the special burdens of individual States because of their peculiar circumstances.

The eighth Commission made it clear that in considering competing claims on resources, the overriding consideration would be national interest. It leaned in favour of the backward States by making tax devolution more progressive. The Commission observed that an increase in administered prices (when used by the Centre to raise extra-budgetary resources) was justified if there was an increase in the cost of production. It held that if revenue was the sole consideration, the appropriate course would be to raise excise duties. On the issue of non-Plan revenue-deficit grants encouraging less-well-managed States to squander resources, the Commission observed that Finance Commissions did not accept the forecasts furnished by States at face value. Like its predecessor, it took the view that requirements of States on account of developmental needs should generally be met by the Planning Commission. Finally, it departed from the previous Commissions by setting apart 5 per cent of the net proceeds of shareable excise duties exclusively for non-Plan revenue-deficit States. The Commission allowed a 5 per cent rate of growth to grants to give them a measure of buoyancy.

The basic approach of the ninth Commission was guided by two considerations: the fair apportionment of revenue resources between the Centre and the States given their Constitutional responsibilities, and the promotion of fiscal autonomy of States while promoting fiscal responsibility on the part of both the Centre and States. The Commission expressed concern over the rapidly growing public debt on the one hand and the inadequate returns from borrowings on the other, and the burden of debt servicing. The Commission indicated that the basic objectives underlying its approach was to phase out revenue deficits to ensure vertical and horizontal equity in the distribution of resources, and the promotion of fiscal discipline. The Commission's approach was to phase out revenue deficits of the Centre and States to a relatively small figure by 31 March 1995. Thus, it was the first Commission to have brought attention to the issue of sustainability of public finances in the country.

The ninth Commission was also the first one to have been explicitly mandated to adopt a normative approach. The Commission (1989) took the view that its basic objective of fiscal sustainability had

> ... naturally led us to the normative approach according to which 'needs' and 'capacities' of different governments are assessed normatively and such normative assessments are then taken as the basis for determining the volume and pattern of federal transfers. This is the first basic departure this Commission made from the practice of the previous Commissions.

The Commission felt that the Gadgil formula had no linkage to the non-Plan revenue account position or the overall financial position of State Governments:

> As yet, there is no formal channel through which additional assistance could be extended to those States whose non-Plan revenue accounts have no surplus and whose shares of Gadgil formula grants are substantially less than their approved Plan revenue expenditures. Such States have to divert their borrowings to meet a good part of their revenue Plan requirements and this sets in motion a vicious circle which, ultimately, may invalidate the very concept of balanced regional development. We propose to introduce a mechanism to correct this basic flaw in the present system of federal fiscal transfers.

For operationalizing the proposed mechanism, it first worked out the non-Plan revenue deficits of States as was done by previous Commissions. Then the Gadgil formula assistance was estimated for each State assuming a growth rate of 10 per cent per annum with 1989–90 as base. To this estimated assistance, an amount equivalent to 40 per cent of the estimated non-Plan revenue surplus was added in the case of States having such surplus. This amount was then set off against the minimum revenue Plan expenditure for each State estimated by the Commission. For non-Plan revenue-deficit States, only the Gadgil formula assistance was applied. If a State had an estimated deficit in the revenue Plan expenditure after the above set-off, 50 per cent of that deficit was recommended under Article 275 grants. As a result of this mechanism, non-Plan revenue-deficit States, as well as other States whose revenue surplus and estimated Plan assistance could not meet the minimum Plan revenue as assessed by the Commission, received additional grants under Article 275.

The tenth Commission was appointed after the introduction of far-reaching economic reforms in the country following the twin crises of growing fiscal imbalances and the balance of payments. The Commission was mandated, as per the ToR, to not only balance the revenue accounts but also to generate surpluses for capital investment. Therefore, it had as its priority objective the task of restoring fiscal equilibrium in the country. The Commission favoured assessing the entire revenue account, but was constrained by another explicit ToR which mandated it to assess the non-Plan revenue account. It confined itself to recommending shares of States in income tax and Union excise duties in view of the Constitutional limitation, but proposed a historic alternative scheme of devolution that involved the pooling of all Union tax revenues. The Commission had indicated that its concern for equity had been built into the devolution formula and had recommended grants for upgrading services and addressing special problems. On the issue of growing debt levels, it felt that the solution did not lie in debt relief, but in taking corrective measures. Keeping these considerations in view, it recommended incentive-based debt relief. Though there was no specific ToR, the Commission recommended grants to local bodies for the first time, taking cognizance of the 73rd and 74th Amendments to the Constitution which became operational in April 1993 when the tenth Commission was in office.

The Eleventh Finance Commission was asked to review the state of finances of the Union and States and suggest ways and means whereby the governments, collectively and severally, might bring about a restructuring of the public finances to restore budgetary balances and maintain macroeconomic stability. It expressed concern over the worrisome feature of fiscal deficits being driven more and more by deficits on revenue account; a spurt in post-devolution deficits of all States in 1997–8 and 1998–9; and over the fact that both the Centre and States had resorted to borrowings over the last two decades to finance even a part of their revenue expenditure. It further observed that the most serious flaw in the system of federal transfers was the segmented flow of resources from the Centre to the States. It was also worried about the lack of regular consultation and policy coordination.

The Commission sought to rectify these deficiencies by addressing in particular the complications created by segmentation of transfer channels; reformulating the principles governing the transfers; and putting in place incentives for fiscal discipline and efficiency and activating inter-governmental consultations. It attempted to address these tasks by defining the goals in terms of budget outcomes and key budget variables, such as levels of revenue, expenditure, and deficits. The scheme recommended by the Commission sought to restore fiscal balance in the medium term by reducing the fiscal deficit substantially and eliminating the revenue deficits at the State level. This was based on the expectation that revenue and expenditure growth would be as per the projections made by the Commission.

The Eleventh Finance Commission was the first to recommend a notional ceiling on aggregate revenue account transfers to States at 37.5 per cent of the total revenue receipts of the Centre. It felt that this was necessary to underpin the parameters of revenue and expenditure of both levels of government as envisaged by it. The Commission argued that the prescribed normative approach was implicit in the projections of revenue and expenditure of previous Commissions and that it had tried to strengthen the approach to the extent feasible. Though it was asked to consider the entire revenue account, it restricted itself to an assessment of non-Plan revenue account because of practical problems. The transfer scheme recommended by the Commission was guided by the consideration that even if a part of the Plan expenditure was to be financed through borrowings at the State level, there should not be any revenue deficit. The Central grants were tailored accordingly. Like its predecessor, the eleventh Commission recommended debt relief linked to certain performance indicators. It also recommended a Fiscal Reforms Facility linked to performance indicators.

The endeavour of the Twelfth Finance Commission was to recommend a scheme of transfers that could serve the objectives of promoting equity based on normative criteria, efficiency, and predictability. It took the view that larger transfers were necessary to address the fall in the volume of transfers relative to GDP. For this purpose, it suggested an increase in the indicative ceiling of transfers from 37.5 per cent to 38 per cent of the total revenue receipts of the Centre. In addressing the horizontal imbalances, the Commission held that while the deficiency in fiscal capacity should be redressed, deficiency in revenue effort should be discouraged. The Commission took into account needs, cost disabilities, and fiscal efficiency in its scheme of horizontal distribution. On the issue of grants, it felt that for ensuring a minimum level of services in education and health sectors, conditional grants based on normative assessment were necessary. A similar view was taken in respect of maintenance expenditure. In accordance with its mandate, the Commission recommended major restructuring of public finances, including a revised roadmap for fiscal consolidation and termination of on-lending by the Centre to States. It felt that reduction in primary deficit would provide the key to reducing the debt–GDP ratio. The Commission's approach was to strengthen the incentive mechanism that was forward looking. These had been built into the Medium Term Reform Facility and debt relief recommended by the Commission. Its approach towards local bodies was to strengthen them in terms of expanding their fiscal domain, thereby making them effective local self-governance institutions.

The basic approach of the Thirteenth Finance Commission (2009) differed somewhat from the previous Commissions, and it set out to foster 'inclusive and green growth promoting fiscal federalism'. Given this broad approach, the Commission took into account the need for maintaining symmetry between the Centre and the States;

equalization of services and not equity; predictability; and incentivizing better performance while recommending its scheme of transfers. For promoting the objective of inclusive growth, the Commission assigned the highest weight to variables for correcting the disability of States in its tax-devolution formula. The Commission recommended grants in a number of areas, taking the stand that even relatively small ones would show results, provided they were directed properly towards meeting the felt needs. Perhaps no other Commission in the past recommended as many grants as the Thirteenth Finance Commission. Though it preferred forward-looking indicators in its scheme of transfers, such grants were restricted to the environment sector because of practical difficulties. Most of the grants recommended by the Commission were conditional and subject to making available additional resources without fungibility and improving accountability, transparency, and effective monitoring. For recommending grants to local bodies, the Commission followed a platform-based incentive approach.

The Commission took the view that it was necessary to incentivize fiscal consolidation as it was growth promoting. It favoured an expansionary fiscal consolidation with no compression of development expenditure in order to create a proper environment for the promotion of both private and public expenditure. The fiscal roadmap recommended by the Commission was towards the development of physical infrastructure.

The Fourteenth Finance Commission strictly adhered to its ToR while taking a comprehensive view of federal fiscal relations. The Commission tried to maintain symmetry, comprehensiveness, and promotion of trust between the Union and the States while making its recommendations. While it made a detailed assessment of the entire revenue account, the implicit capital outlay was broadly touched upon. On the issue of vertical distribution, the Commission felt that there was limited scope for increasing transfers to States from the current levels. However, the Commission strongly felt the need to alter the composition in favour of untied transfers. With regard to horizontal distribution, the Commission did not make a distinction between general-category and special-category States. It felt that intra-State inequality was more a matter to be addressed by the States. With regard to tax devolution, the Commission considered the need to take into account the change in the population of States since 1971 and to properly compensate those with a higher forest cover.

The Commission desisted from recommending any specific-purpose grants because past experience had proved that these were either insufficient or poorly utilized. While recommending them to local bodies, it enhanced the level of grants with minimum conditionalities and emphasized the need to strengthen the role of State Finance Commissions and trust local bodies. While following the broad principles of fiscal sustainability, the Commission felt the need to provide some flexibility to States in their borrowings based on certain performance indicators.

▼▲▼

There are five issues that every Finance Commission has had to address. The first issue is whether the Commission should restrict itself to assessment and recommendations in regard to revenue resources and revenue expenditure. This position was more or less accepted by most Commissions. In reality, over the years, both the Union and the States had to resort to borrowings to finance not only capital expenditure, but also part of the revenue expenditure. This is evident from the revenue account of the Centre and States (see Annexure 4A.1). The record of the Union relative to States is striking.

The revenue deficit of the Centre in 2009–10 reached alarming proportions, touching 5.2 per cent of the GDP. In recent years, there has been a marginal moderation in the deficit levels. The Union target of eliminating revenue deficit remains elusive. In contrast, deficits in the State revenue accounts surfaced only in 1987–8, and in recent years, States have by and large adhered to the target of eliminating it. The position with regard to fiscal deficits of the Union and the States followed a similar trend (see Annexure 4A.2).

The second issue is regarding the responsibility of the Finance Commission in regard to horizontal balance. The question is whether the goal should be reduction in inequalities in the broadest terms and provision of uniform standards of defined social services, or whether it should be to ensure or enable minimum standards of such services. Finance Commissions have differed in regard to their interpretation of the responsibilities as well as the means by which such responsibilities had to be carried out.

Third, the relative roles of tax devolution and grants partly depend on a view taken in regard to the objectives. There was a general agreement with few exceptions that tax devolution should be the preferred form. Fourth, a view has to be taken about the conditions that have to be imposed while recommending grants-in-aid. Where grants for financing anticipated revenue deficit are concerned, no conditionality has ever been recommended. However, in regard to other grants, there have been contrasting views. This is particularly evident in the approaches of the Thirteenth Finance Commission, which resorted to a significant recourse to grants-in-aid and imposed a range of conditionalities, and the Fourteenth Finance Commission, which took the opposite view. Fifth, the stipulation that the 1971 population be used was not meant to penalize those States that conformed to population policy. This was externally imposed. Finally, rewards for good performance and incentives for better performance were incorporated in the award by a few Commissions.

SELECT REFERENCE

1. Ministry of Finance. Various Years. *Report of the Finance Commission,* I–XIV. New Delhi: Government of India.

ANNEXURE

Table 4A.1   Revenue Deficit of the Centre and States

Year	GSDP	Revenue Deficit, Centre		Revenue Deficit, States	
	Rs in Crore	Rs in Crore	As Per Cent of GDP	Rs in Crore	As Per Cent of GDP
1980–1	149,642	2,037	1.4	–1,486	–1.0
1981–2	175,805	392	0.2	–1,379	–0.8
1982–3	196,644	1,308	0.7	–888	–0.5
1983–4	229,021	2,540	1.1	–210	–0.1
1984–5	256,611	4,225	1.6	923	0.4
1985–6	289,524	5,889	2.0	–654	–0.2
1986–7	323,949	7,777	2.4	–170	–0.1
1987–8	368,211	9,137	2.5	1,088	0.3
1988–9	436,893	10,515	2.4	1,807	0.4
1989–90	501,928	11,914	2.4	3,682	0.7
1990–1	586,212	18,562	3.2	5,309	0.9
1991–2	673,875	16,261	2.4	5,651	0.8
1992–3	774,545	18,574	2.4	5,114	0.7
1993–4	891,355	32,716	3.7	3,872	0.4
1994–5	1,045,590	31,029	3.0	6,706	0.6
1995–6	1,226,725	29,731	2.4	8,620	0.7
1996–7	1,419,277	32,654	2.3	16,878	1.2
1997–8	1,572,394	46,449	3.0	17,492	1.1
1998–9	1,803,378	66,976	3.7	44,462	2.5
1999–2000	2,023,130	67,596	3.3	54,549	2.7
2000–1	2,177,413	85,234	3.9	55,316	2.5
2001–2	2,355,845	100,162	4.3	60,398	2.6
2002–3	2,536,327	107,879	4.3	57,179	2.3
2003–4	2,841,503	98,261	3.5	63,407	2.2
2004–5	3,242,209	78,338	2.4	39,158	1.2
2005–6	3,693,369	92,300	2.5	7,013	0.2
2006–7	4,294,706	80,222	1.9	–24,857	–0.6
2007–8	4,987,090	52,569	1.1	–42,943	–0.9
2008–9	5,630,063	253,539	4.5	–12,672	–0.2
2009–10	6,477,827	338,998	5.2	31,017	0.5

(*Cont'd*)

Table 4A.1   (*Cont'd*)

Year	GSDP	Revenue Deficit, Centre		Revenue Deficit, States	
	Rs in Crore	Rs in Crore	As Per Cent of GDP	Rs in Crore	As Per Cent of GDP
2010–11	7,784,115	252,252	3.2	–3,051	0.0
2011–12	8,736,329	394,348	4.5	–23,960	–0.3
2012–13	9,944,013	364,282	3.7	–20,322	–0.2
2013–14	11,233,522	357,048	3.2	10,563	0.1
2014–15	12,445,128	365,519	2.9	45,704	0.4
2015–16	13,682,035	342,736	2.5	5,380	0.0

Source: For 1980–1 to 2007–8, from *Handbook of Statistics on Indian Economy*, RBI, 2008–9. For 2008–9 to 2015–16, from *Handbook of Statistics on Indian Economy*, RBI, 2016–17.
Note: The sign (–) denotes surplus.

Table 4A.2   Fiscal Deficit of the Centre and States

Year	GSDP	Fiscal Deficit, Centre		Fiscal Deficit, States	
	Rs in Crore	Rs in Crore	As Per Cent of GDP	Rs in Crore	As Per Cent of GDP
1980–1	149,642	8,299	5.5	3,713	2.5
1981–2	175,805	8,666	4.9	4,062	2.3
1982–3	196,644	10,627	5.4	4,986	2.5
1983–4	229,021	13,030	5.7	6,359	2.8
1984–5	256,611	17,416	6.8	8,199	3.2
1985–6	289,524	21,858	7.5	7,521	2.6
1986–7	323,949	26,342	8.1	9,269	2.9
1987–8	368,211	27,044	7.3	11,219	3.0
1988–9	436,893	30,923	7.1	11,672	2.7
1989–90	501,928	35,632	7.1	15,433	3.1
1990–1	586,212	44,632	7.6	18,787	3.2
1991–2	673,875	36,325	5.4	18,900	2.8
1992–3	774,545	40,173	5.2	20,892	2.7

(*Cont'd*)

Table **4A.2** (*Cont'd*)

Year	GSDP	Fiscal Deficit, Centre		Fiscal Deficit, States	
	Rs in Crore	Rs in Crore	As Per Cent of GDP	Rs in Crore	As Per Cent of GDP
1993–4	891,355	60,257	6.8	20,364	2.3
1994–5	1,045,590	57,703	5.5	27,308	2.6
1995–6	1,226,725	60,243	4.9	30,870	2.5
1996–7	1,419,277	66,733	4.7	36,561	2.6
1997–8	1,572,394	88,937	5.7	43,474	2.8
1998–9	1,803,378	113,348	6.3	73,295	4.1
1999–2000	2,023,130	104,716	5.2	90,098	4.5
2000–1	2,177,413	118,816	5.5	87,922	4.0
2001–2	2,355,845	140,955	6.0	94,261	4.0
2002–3	2,536,327	145,072	5.7	99,727	3.9
2003–4	2,841,503	123,273	4.3	120,631	4.2
2004–5	3,242,209	125,794	3.9	107,774	3.3
2005–6	3,693,369	146,435	4.0	90,084	2.4
2006–7	4,294,706	142,573	3.3	77,509	1.8
2007–8	4,987,090	126,912	2.5	75,455	1.5
2008–9	5,630,063	336,992	6.0	134,589	2.4
2009–10	6,477,827	418,482	6.5	188,819	2.9
2010–11	7,784,115	373,591	4.8	161,461	2.1
2011–12	8,736,329	515,990	5.9	168,353	1.9
2012–13	9,944,013	490,190	4.9	195,470	2.0
2013–14	11,233,522	502,858	4.5	247,852	2.2
2014–15	12,445,128	510,817	4.1	327,191	2.6
2015–16	13,682,035	532,791	3.9	420,670	3.1

Source: For 1980–1 to 2007–8, *Handbook of Statistics on Indian Economy*, RBI, 2008–9. For 2008–9 to 2015–16, *Handbook of Statistics on Indian Economy*, RBI, 2016–17.

5

VERTICAL DISTRIBUTION
CHANGING BALANCES

VERTICAL FISCAL IMBALANCES REFER TO the differences in the expenditure responsibilities and revenue-raising avenues assigned to different layers of government in a federation. The assignment of functional responsibilities and sources of revenue based on comparative advantage results in vertical imbalances. Such imbalances are common to most federations, and India is no exception. Central Governments have a comparative advantage in raising taxes with a nationwide base, while States have a comparative advantage in delivering services to people, being closer to them and having the administrative machinery suitable for such service delivery. In the Indian Constitution, while buoyant taxes with a nationwide base are assigned to the Union, more functions touching on the lives of the people are assigned to States. Recognizing this implicit vertical imbalance, the Constitution provides for the institution of the Finance Commission to recommend resource transfers to States.

The Finance Commission has the unenviable task of reconciling the conflicting claims of the Union and the States and distributing the resources in a judicious manner to serve the larger interests of the country. The Union has predictably been putting forth its claim for a larger share of the cake for meeting national priorities. The States have similarly been pitching for an increase in their fiscal space, taking into account the large functional responsibilities assigned to them.

There are broadly two phases of vertical distribution in India. In the first phase, the period covered by the first ten Commissions, only two taxes were shareable with States. Until the year 2000 when the 80th Amendment was passed, the Constitution provided for the mandatory sharing of the net proceeds of income tax and permissible sharing of Union excise duties. In the second phase, starting from the Eleventh Commission, all Union taxes became shareable with the States.

THE FIRST PHASE

At the time of the appointment of the First Finance Commission, 50 per cent of the net proceeds of income tax were assigned to States. The First Finance Commission was initially not given any ToR. It recommended an increase in the share of the States in the net proceeds of income tax from 50 to 55 per cent. This was raised to 60 per cent by the second Commission. The Commission did not accept the demands of the States for the inclusion of corporation tax, the tax on Union emoluments, or the surcharge on income tax in the divisible pool, as this would be against the provisions of the Constitution. The Third Finance Commission recommended an increase in the States' share in income tax from 60 per cent to 66.66 per cent. The Fourth Finance Commission recommended a further increase, to 75 per cent.

The Fifth Finance Commission, taking into account the increase in the tax base, did not recommend any increase in the share of the States in the proceeds of income tax. The Commission was given an additional ToR to recommend the distribution of the proceeds of unadjusted advance tax collections up to 1966–7. It took 75 per cent as the share of the States in the unadjusted advance tax collections.

The Sixth Finance Commission recommended an increase in the share of the States in the proceeds of income tax from 75 to 80 per cent, taking into account the increase in the Union surcharge from 10 to 15 per cent in 1971–2, and because the benefit of arrears of advance tax collections was no longer available. The States' share was further increased to 85 per cent by the Seventh Finance Commission. Thus, every Commission, with the exception of the Fifth, recommended an increase in the share of States in the net proceeds of income tax. The Eighth Finance Commission departed from this practice. While recommending the status quo in the share of the States, it suggested that the Union surcharge should be withdrawn with the commencement of the financial year 1985–6. Furthermore, the Commission recommended the inclusion of penalties and interest recoveries in the net proceeds of income tax. The ninth Commission did not consider it necessary to increase the share of the States in income tax and recommended its retention at 85 per cent.

The Tenth Finance Commission recommended that the share of the States be fixed at 77.5 per cent on the grounds that the Centre should have sufficient incentive to improve income tax collections. Thus, it was the first Commission to have recommended a reduction in the States' share of income tax.

As far as the vertical distribution of Union excise duties was concerned, the First Finance Commission took the stand that it was within its remit to recommend the distribution of the proceeds of Union excise duties. It was of the view that excise duties on tobacco (including cigarettes, cigars, etc.), matches, and vegetable products were the most suitable for distribution and recommended 40 per cent of the proceeds of these duties to be allocated to States. The Second Finance Commission felt that with income tax ceasing to be an expanding source of revenue, substantial devolution would have to come from the proceeds of Union excise duties as the levy of these duties was extended from 13 commodities in 1952–3 to 29 commodities in 1957–8. Therefore, the Commission added excise duties on tea, coffee, sugar, paper, and vegetable non-essential oils in the divisible pool of excise duties and recommended that the States be given 25 per cent of the shareable Union excise duties. The reduction in percentage share was justified by the expanded coverage whereby each State would receive a larger amount as compared with the previous dispensation.

The Third Finance Commission felt the need for a more extensive use of the provision relating to the permissible sharing of Union excise duties on the grounds of shrinkage in the divisible pool of income tax and the inadequacy of the States' resources following the Planning process and increasing expenditure on Plan schemes. The Commission came to the conclusion that the States would require a larger devolution of Union excise duties and recommended that 20 per cent of the proceeds on all commodities (35 in all) be allocated to States. The Commission excluded the proceeds of Union excise duties on motor spirits from the purview of this allocation, taking into account another of its recommendation that 20 per cent of the excise duties on motor spirits should be given as a special-purpose grant for the maintenance and improvement of communications. The Fourth Finance Commission did not recommend any change in regard to sharing the proceeds of duties that might be levied during its award period. The Commission did not agree with the contention of the States on the sharing of the proceeds of regulatory duties that were introduced for the first time in 1961, as no collections were made under the head till 1964–5.

The Fifth Finance Commission recommended that during the first three years of its award period (1969–70 to 1971–2), 20 per cent of the proceeds of all excise duties, excluding special excise duties, regulatory duties, and duties and cesses levied under special Acts and earmarked for special purposes, should be paid to the States. The Commission recommended that in the remaining two years of its award period (1972–3 to 1973–4), special excise duties should be included for sharing in the same ratio.

The Sixth Finance Commission did not recommend any change in the share of States in excise duties during its award period of 1974–5 to 1978–9, on the grounds that any increase in the share would confer disproportionate benefits on revenue-surplus States. The Finance Act 1973 replaced regulatory duties of excise with auxiliary duties of excise on all excisable commodities for the exclusive purpose of the Union. The Commission recommended that 20 per cent of the proceeds from these duties should also be distributed to States in the years 1976–7 to 1978–9.

The Seventh Finance Commission departed from the previous Commissions and recommended doubling the share of the States in the proceeds of Union excise duties on all commodities, excluding additional excise duties in lieu of sales tax, from 20 to 40 per cent. This was the steepest ever recommended increase in the share of States. Though the previous Commissions recognized that tax devolution should be the predominant channel of transfers, the seventh Commission was the first to have put this into practice in a substantive manner and not incrementally. This amount was raised to 45 per cent by the Eighth Finance Commission taking into consideration the increase in the revenue deficits of the States and the amount of surplus with the Centre as reassessed by it. The Tenth Finance Commission recommended a marginal increase in the share of the States in Union excise duties, from 45 to 47.5 per cent.

Thus, the States saw a phased increase in the share of the proceeds of both income tax and Union excise duties on account of pressures building on their finances.

THE SECOND PHASE

There was a fundamental change in the pattern of sharing of Central taxes with the States following the 80th Amendment of the Constitution. Under Article 270, as amended, all taxes included in the Union List (except the duties and taxes referred to in Articles 268, 269, and 269-A, surcharges, and any cess levied for a specific purpose under an Act of Parliament) are shareable with the States. The Amendment came into operation from 9 June 2000. The Eleventh Finance Commission, in its interim recommendations for the year 2000–1, recommended the States' share in income tax and Union excise duties to be maintained at 80 per cent and 52 per cent respectively. On analysing the budgetary requirements of the Centre and the States, the Commission recommended that the States' share in the net proceeds of all Union taxes—except taxes and duties mentioned in Articles 268 and 269, and cesses and surcharges—be fixed at 28 per cent in each of the remaining four years of its award period. A consequence of the Constitutional Amendment was that the proceeds of additional duties of excise could not be passed on to States because of the deletion of Article 272. These proceeds became part of Central revenues. The Commission therefore recommended that an additional 1.5 per cent of net proceeds of all taxes be passed on to States as compensation, taking the States' share in the net proceeds of all Union taxes to 29.5 per cent. As indicated in the previous chapter, the Eleventh Finance Commission suggested an indicative ceiling of overall transfers to States at 37.5 per cent of the gross revenue receipts of the Centre. This was done taking into account past trends. This is the first time that a Finance Commission suggested an indicative ceiling on the overall transfers to States.

The Twelfth Finance Commission took a different view with regard to tax devolution. It noted that if the share of the States was increased, the redistributive content in the inter se distribution would have to be increased significantly by altering the weightage in the distribution criteria so as to be consistent with the objective of equalization. The Commission came to the view that grants would provide a more effective mechanism for this purpose and therefore used grants to a larger extent as an instrument of transfers. It recommended that the share of the States in the divisible pool of Central taxes be raised from 29.5 per cent to 30.5 per cent. The proceeds of additional duties of excise in lieu of sales tax were treated as part of the divisible pool. The indicative ceiling on overall transfers to States was raised by the Twelfth Finance Commission to 38 per cent of the total revenue receipts of the Centre.

For arriving at its recommendations on vertical distribution, the Thirteenth Finance Commission first assessed the vertical gap, defined as the difference between normatively assessed expenditure shares and the revenue capacities of the Union and the States. The States, for the first time, submitted a combined memorandum urging the Commission to increase tax devolution from 30.5 to 50 per cent on the grounds that their share in developmental expenditure was much higher than that of the Centre. As indicated by the Commission, its recommendation on vertical distribution was informed by the revenue-raising capacity of the Centre and the States and the pressure on their expenditure commitments. Taking into account the higher buoyancy of Central taxes vis-à-vis State taxes; the increase in the share of cesses and surcharges in the gross tax revenue of the Centre from 3.51 per cent in 2001–2 to 13.63 per cent in 2009–10 (Budget Estimate, BE); and the significant increase in the non-tax revenues of the Centre from the sale of spectrum, royalties from off-shore hydrocarbon resources, increasing commitments of States on account of implementation of CSS, and entitlement-based legislations of the Union Government, the Commission recommended an increase in the share of the States in shareable Central taxes from 30.5 to 32 per cent. It expressed the view that this increase could easily be accommodated by the Centre by pruning some of its subsidies. With the abolition of additional excise duties and consequent adjustments in the basic rates of excise duties on sugar, textiles, and tobacco from 1 March 2006, the Commission did not earmark any share attributable to them in the recommended 32 per cent.

The Fourteenth Finance Commission brought a path-breaking change in its approach to the vertical distribution of resources between the Centre and the States. For arriving at its recommendations, the Commission examined the spirit of Constitutional provisions; the concerns expressed by the Union and the States about their fiscal space; and the respective functional and expenditure responsibilities of the Union and the States in the interest of sound federal fiscal relations. It also considered the increased share of non-divisible cesses and surcharges in the gross revenue receipts of the Centre (7.53 per cent in 2000–1 to 13.14 per cent in 2013–14). The Commission indicated that while aggregate transfers as percentage of gross revenues of the Union remained around 52 per cent between 2009–10 and 2014–15 (BE), the relative shares of tax devolution and other transfers (Plan grants including CSS, and non-Plan grants) remained at 46.8 per cent and 54 per cent respectively. It further observed that the share of non-Plan grants, including the grants provided by Finance Commissions, in total transfer declined from 11.3 per cent to 8.7 per cent in the same period.

Taking the above developments into consideration, the Fourteenth Finance Commission expressed the view that tax devolution should be the primary channel of resource transfers to States since it was formula based and conducive to sound fiscal federalism. Since aggregate transfers already amounted to 60 per cent of the divisible pool of Central taxes, the Commission strongly recommended a compositional shift from grants to tax devolution, arguing that such a shift would not impose any additional burden on the Union and that it would increase unconditional transfers to States. It recommended increasing the tax devolution from 32 to 42 per cent to serve the twin objectives of increasing unconditional transfers to States without affecting the fiscal space of the Union. It expressed the hope that the Union Government would continue to maintain the prevailing level of aggregate transfers to States at about 49 per cent of its gross revenue receipts.

Following the acceptance of the recommendation to increase tax devolution to 42 per cent of the divisible pool of Union taxes, an impression had gained ground that the fiscal space available to the States had increased significantly. Unlike the previous Commissions, the Fourteenth Finance Commission considered the entire revenue account of States—and therefore normal Plan assistance and other assistance for State Plans was subsumed under tax devolution. Thus, the tax devolution of 42 per cent recommended by the Fourteenth Finance Commission is not comparable with the devolution of 32 per cent recommended by its immediate predecessor. In addition, it did not recommend any sector-specific grants. The tax devolution that the Commission recommended subsumes normal Plan assistance, special Plan assistance, and special Central assistance as also sector-specific grants. Thus, effectively, there is only a marginal increase in the aggregate transfers but a substantial change in the composition of transfers in favour of untied tax devolution.

The vertical distribution of resources had undergone a major change, from sharing the divisible pool of net proceeds of income tax and Union excise duties to sharing the divisible pool of all Union taxes. Despite this major change, there had been a remarkable stability in the relative shares of the Centre and the States in the combined revenue expenditure, with the share of the Centre fluctuating in the narrow range of 43 to 44 per cent since 1984. With the increase in tax devolution recommended by the Fourteenth Finance Commission, there has been a significant qualitative shift towards untied transfers.

The vertical distribution as recommended by all the Commissions so far is summarized in Table 5.1.

One noteworthy feature is that though successive Finance Commissions have attempted to increase the tax devolution to States, there has been remarkable stability in the vertical distribution of resources between the Centre and the States.

Table 5.1 States' Share in the Divisible Pool of Central Taxes Recommended by Finance Commissions

Finance Commissions	States' Share in the Net Proceeds of Income Tax (%)	States' Share in the Net Proceeds of Union Excise Duties (%)	States' Share in All Shareable Union Taxes (%)
First	55.00	40.0 (3 commodities)	
Second	60.00	25.0 (8 commodities)	
Third	66.66	20.0[1] (35 commodities)	
Fourth	75.00	20.0 (all commodities)	
Fifth	75.00	20.0 (all commodities)	
Sixth	80.00	20.0 (all commodities)	
Seventh	85.00	40.0 (all commodities)	
Eighth	85.00	45.0[2] (all commodities)	
Ninth	85.00	45.0 (all commodities)	
Tenth	77.50	47.5[3] (all commodities)	
Eleventh			29.5[4]
Twelfth			30.5
Thirteenth			32.0
Fourteenth			42.0

Source: Compiled from Reports of the Finance Commission, I–XIV.

Notes: [1] 20 per cent of the net proceeds of excise duties on motor spirits earmarked as a special-purpose grant for the maintenance and improvement of communications.

[2] Of this, 5 per cent earmarked for post-devolution deficit States.

[3] 7.5 per cent earmarked for deficit States.

[4] Of this, 1.5 per cent is on account of additional excise duties in lieu of sales tax on sugar, textiles, and tobacco.

A clear picture regarding vertical transfers in aggregate will emerge only if the yield from cesses and surcharges (which are not shareable with States), non-Finance Commission transfers, and growth in the non-tax revenues of the Centre are taken into account. Some of these issues are covered in the chapter on aggregate Central transfers to States.

POLICY SPACE FOR THE UNION AND STATES

The Union government pleads for adequate resources to discharge functions listed in the Union List and also to transfer funds to States for a number of justifiable reasons. The State Governments argue that the Union Government has been given more fiscal space than necessary by the Finance Commission. Over the years, there has been an enlargement of the Concurrent List and the Centre's spending on State Subjects, presumably on the grounds that such expenditure will serve national priorities better.

The State Governments contend that the transfers through CSS impose severe burdens on them: First, there is a sharing pattern, and the State Governments are forced to part with their resources to accommodate the schemes imposed by the Centre. Second, when such schemes were discontinued, the State Governments had to continue them because of the service conditions attached to government employees and from political pressures. It is not easy to start and close institutions or modify them. In a way, therefore, schemes that have been initiated by the Centre become a burden on the State irrespective of support from the Centre. In fact, following the increase in tax devolution, the Centre terminated a number of schemes, such as the scheme of model schools and the Backward Regions' Grant Fund. Third, some of the States have better designed schemes than the Centre, but are forced to modify or roll them back, mainly because of resource constraints as some of their resources are earmarked towards matching the contribution to CSS. Above all, despite using the State administrative machinery and contributing to the schemes while accepting the priorities of the Centre, the credit for the whole programme is taken by the Government of India. These schemes are generally publicized as Government of India schemes or the Prime Minister's schemes either by name or by designation.

▼▲▼

There are large elements of continuity in the approaches of the fourteen Finance Commissions in terms of fundamental principles as well as operating procedures. At the same time, owing to the compulsions of the structural transformation of the economy and the changing roles of the Centre and States, changes were made and nuances expressed. But it is hard to find arbitrariness or avoidable ambiguity in most of the recommendations, and almost all the fundamental issues that arose in fiscal federalism were addressed at some point or the other.

However, there are two important unresolved issues. First, though a number of cesses have been subsumed under GST, new cesses have been levied on custom duties. Second, the continuation of a number of CSS under 28 broad umbrella heads without any substantial reduction in their number points to the excess policy space still available with the Centre.

The most sensitive part of Centre–State fiscal relations is mainly the area of transfers outside the Finance Commission that is implicitly available to the Centre. The States feel that the magnitudes of the transfers are large; their inter-State distribution is discretionary, arbitrary, and regressive; the transfers create multiplier responsibilities on them; that they distort the designs of State schemes even if the latter are better and more advanced; and above all, the entire credit is taken by the Central Government, whereas the schemes are jointly funded and the implementation is done entirely by the States.

SELECT REFERENCE

1. Ministry of Finance. Various Years. *Report of the Finance Commission*, I–XIV. New Delhi: Government of India.

6

HORIZONTAL DISTRIBUTION
CHANGING BALANCES

VERTICAL IMBALANCES IN FISCAL FEDERALISM arise from a mismatch in the functional responsibilities and the sources of revenue between the Union and State Governments in general. However, the magnitudes of imbalance vary among State Governments, depending on several circumstances. Hence, any mechanism of transfers from the Union to a State has to simultaneously achieve a balance between the Central and State Governments on one hand and among the State Governments on the other. The latter constitutes the problem of horizontal distribution of vertical transfers.

The history of horizontal distribution of the divisible pool of Central tax revenue by the Finance Commission so far can be divided into three phases. In the first phase, the first seven Finance Commissions adopted separate criteria for the inter se distribution of States' share of income tax and Union excise duties. In the second phase, the eighth to the tenth Commissions adopted uniform criteria for the distribution of income tax and Union excise duties. In the third phase, starting from the eleventh Commission, the aggregate of all Union taxes became shareable with the States.

THE FIRST PHASE

On the issue of horizontal distribution of States' share in income tax, the First Finance Commission felt that two considerations were important. These were a general measure of needs represented by population and contribution. The Commission recommended that 80 per cent of the divisible pool of income tax should be distributed to States on the basis of their relative shares in population based on the 1951 census, and the remaining 20 per cent on the basis of relative collections. In the early 1950s, the cities of Bombay and Calcutta accounted for three-fourths of income tax collections in the country. Thus, the distribution criteria favoured industrially advanced States. With population being scale neutral, there was no element of equity in the criteria.

The Second Finance Commission felt that the criterion of contribution should be completely done away with. Though the Commission was in favour of distributing the proceeds on the basis of population alone, it felt that such an arrangement would cause a sudden break in continuity. Therefore, it recommended that the distribution of the States' share in income tax be 10 per cent on the basis of contribution and 90 per cent on the basis of population.

The Third Finance Commission was of the view that the criteria for distribution of income tax should be both population and collection. The Commission saw merit in the argument put forth by the industrialized States that larger collections also entailed problems, such as concentration of population and increased demand for social and administrative services. The Commission thought that it would be fair and equitable to restore the formula of the First Finance Commission for distributing income tax. The Fourth Finance Commission felt that there should be stability and certainty as regards the principles of distribution of income tax among States. Therefore, it decided to continue the principles followed by the First and Third Finance Commissions, that is, 80 per cent on the basis of population and 20 per cent on the basis of contribution.

While acknowledging that it would be desirable to continue with the same distribution formula, the Fifth Finance Commission did not go with the observation of the previous Commission that the principles of distribution should not be reviewed every time a new Finance Commission was appointed. It felt that instead of collections, assessments in different States after due adjustments for reductions on account of appellate orders, revisions, etc., would better represent the contribution of a State. The Commission worked out the distribution of income tax among States by assigning a 90 per cent weightage to population and 10 per cent to figures of assessments. The Sixth Finance Commission did not recommend any change in the formula for distribution of income tax as recommended by its predecessor and used the 1971 population figures in the distribution formula. The Seventh Finance Commission retained the formula for the inter se distribution of income tax as recommended by the previous two Commissions.

There was no element of equity in the inter se distribution of the States' share of income tax as recommended by the first seven Finance Commissions. The distribution was largely on the basis of population and partly on the basis of contribution to income tax collections.

The First Finance Commission did not consider consumption as the basis for the distribution of the divisible pool of Union excise duties as no reliable information was available and instead recommended that the States' share might be distributed on the basis of population. It felt that the proportion of Scheduled Castes and Scheduled Tribes in the total population was not relevant for the purpose of distribution of the proceeds of a tax. Thus, there was no element of equity in the horizontal distribution of Union excise duties in its recommendations. The Second Finance Commission was also opposed to giving any weight to consumption for the purpose of distribution of the States' share of Union excise duties, but on different grounds. It felt that such weightage would only benefit urbanized States. Though the Commission was in favour of distributing the proceeds on the basis of population alone, it felt that such an arrangement would place certain States in an advantageous position. Therefore, the Commission recommended that 90 per cent of the States' share in the divisible pool of Union excise duties should be distributed on the basis of population, with the remaining 10 per cent used for adjustment.

For distributing the proceeds of the divisible pool of excise duties among States, the Third Finance Commission considered that while population should be the main factor, other factors such as the relative financial weaknesses of States, disparities in the levels of development, percentage of Scheduled Caste and Scheduled Tribe population in the total population should also be taken into account. The exact method followed in arriving at the inter se shares of States was not specified. Thus, for the first time, an element of equity was introduced in the formula for the distribution of Union excise duties. This element of equity continued to be one of the factors in the formulae adopted by subsequent Commissions.

For the purpose of distributing the States' share in Union excise duties, the Fourth Finance Commission did not consider relative financial weakness as it felt that non-Plan revenue deficits should be covered by grants rather than incorporating such a factor in the distribution formula. The Commission assigned a weightage of 80 per cent to population and 20 per cent to relative economic and social backwardness. Like the Third Finance Commission, this Commission also did not spell out the details of the factors of relative backwardness considered in arriving at the percentage shares of States in the Union excise duties.

Though the recommendation of the Fifth Finance Commission with regard to distribution was broadly similar in terms of weightage assigned to population and backwardness, it differed in respect of the criterion for the latter. Of the 20 per cent to be distributed on the basis of backwardness, the Commission recommended that two-thirds should be distributed to those States with per capita income below the average per capita income of all States in proportion to the shortfall of a State's per capita income from all States' average, multiplied by the population of the State. The remaining one-third was to be distributed according to an integrated index of backwardness worked out from the following six criteria: Scheduled Tribe population; number of factory workers per lakh population; net irrigated area per cultivator; length of railways and surfaced roads per 100 square kilometres; shortfall in the number of schoolgoing children as compared to those of schoolgoing age; and number of hospital beds per 1,000 people. Thus, for the first time, per capita income was used as a factor for determining the shares of States in the formula for the distribution of Union excise duties.

For the purpose of distributing the shares of States in Union excise duties, the Sixth Finance Commission increased the weightage assigned to backwardness from 20 to 25 per cent. The criteria followed by the Commission for determining backwardness differed from those adopted by the previous Commissions. The Commission took the distance of a State's per capita income from that of the State with the highest per capita income, multiplied by the 1971 population of the State concerned, for the purpose of arriving at its relative backwardness. It recommended that the remaining 75 per cent be distributed on the basis of the population as per the 1971 census.

The Seventh Finance Commission felt that since the proportion of net proceeds of excise duties distributed on the basis of equity parameters was not large, the contribution of past Commissions towards the reduction of economic inequalities was modest. Therefore, it felt that a lot more was required to be done in this direction. In a radical departure from the past, it significantly reduced the weightage of population from 75 per cent to 25 per cent in the formula for inter se distribution. Since population was scale neutral, it introduced three factors, viz., the inverse of per capita income, the percentage of poor in each State, and revenue equalization. Each one of these three factors was assigned a weightage of 25 per cent.

Thus, an element of equity crept into the criteria for the distribution of the States' share of Union excises duties.

THE SECOND PHASE

The Eighth Finance Commission agreed with the dissenting note of Dr Raj Krishna in the report of the Seventh Finance Commission that there was no legal or economic basis for allocating the shareable proceeds of income tax and excise revenue on different criteria. The Commission saw no reason as to why excise duties, and not income tax, should be used for addressing backwardness of States. After careful consideration, the Commission came to the conclusion that there was nothing in the Constitution that barred the allocation of income tax on the same criteria as that of excise duties. It recommended uniform criteria for the inter se distribution of 90 per cent of the States' share in income tax and the distribution of 40 per cent of the divisible pool of excise duties. The Commission proposed that this amount be distributed by giving a weightage of 25 per cent to population; 25 per cent to the inverse of per capita income multiplied by population; and 50 per cent to the distance of per capita income. In the case of income tax, the Commission recommended that the remaining 10 per cent of the States' share be distributed on the basis of contribution as represented by assessments. It also recommended that an additional 5 per cent of the net proceeds of excise duties should be distributed to States that had deficits after taking into account their shares in the devolution of all taxes and duties. The distribution would be in proportion to the deficit of each State to the total of the deficits of all States as estimated by it.

The Eighth Finance Commission charted a new path by recommending the same criteria for the distribution of the States' shares in income tax and Union excise duties, introducing progressivity in the distribution of income tax for the first time and addressing the problem of deficits, hitherto addressed entirely through grants, by tax devolution. The Ninth Finance Commission continued with the practice of including equity parameters in the formula for the distribution of the States' share of 85 per cent in the divisible proceeds of income tax as recommended by it. It also held that the States' share in income tax should be distributed in this manner: 10 per cent on the basis of contribution as measured by assessment; 45 per cent on the basis of distance of the per capita income of the State from that of the State with the highest income multiplied by the 1971 population of the State concerned; 22.5 per cent on the basis of the 1971 census of the State concerned; 11.25 per cent on the basis of a composite index of backwardness; and 11.25 per cent on the basis of inverse of per capita income multiplied by the population of the State in 1971. For the distribution of Union excise duties, the Commission took the view that under a normative assessment, it was only equitable that the resultant revenue deficits of States were also considered in the broad scheme of devolution itself. This was, in a way, an extension of the approach adopted by the Eighth Finance Commission in earmarking a portion of the States' share in the divisible pool of Union excise duties for revenue-deficit States. The Commission's formula for the distribution of the proceeds of Union excise duties was 25 per cent on the basis of the 1971 population; 12.5 per cent on the basis of Income Adjusted Total Population; 12.5 per cent on index of backwardness; 33.5 per cent on the basis of distance of per capita income multiplied by 1971 population; and the remaining 16.5 per cent to be distributed to States with revenue deficits, after taking into account their share in income tax, Union excise duties, additional excise duties in lieu of sales tax, and grant in lieu of repealed tax on railway passenger fares. Under the dispensation of the Ninth Finance Commission, deficit States were given a higher share of the net proceeds of excise duties, at 7.5 per cent (16.5 per cent of 45 per cent) as compared with the 5 per cent earmarked by its predecessor. Although the Commission assigned weightage to the poverty ratio in devolution in its first report for 1989–90, it stated that the appropriateness would be discussed with experts before finalizing the second report. In the second report, instead of the poverty ratio, it included the proportion of Scheduled Castes and Scheduled Tribes and agricultural labourers while working out backwardness.

Though the eighth and ninth Commissions had tried to bring about uniformity in the formula for the distribution of the States' share in the proceeds of income tax and Union excise duties, they could not bring about complete uniformity because of the weightage assigned to the factor of contribution in the formula for the distribution of income tax proceeds. The Tenth Finance Commission observed that the country as a whole represented a common economic space and market and that the growing interdependence in economic activities had considerably weakened the case for locally originating non-agricultural income. Accordingly, the Commission dropped the factor of contribution in the formula for the devolution of income tax to States. This paved the way for the Commission to recommend uniform criteria for the devolution of income tax as well as Union excise duties. As the population criterion would result in the same per capita transfers to all States, the Commission reduced the weightage assigned to population from 25 per cent to 20 per cent. It preferred the criterion of distance of per capita income to the inverse income criterion as the latter would result in a higher burden on the middle-income States owing to the implicit convexity in it. The Commission therefore decided to use the distance formula, instead of using both distance and inverse of per capita, for making the transfers more progressive and assigned it a weightage of 60 per cent. While considering area as one of the factors, the Commission observed that the differences in the cost of providing services might increase with the size of a State but only at a decreasing rate. Considering this, it assigned a lower weightage, of 5 per cent, to area, with certain adjustments. These were that no State would get a share higher than 10 per cent at the upper end or less than 2 per cent at the lower end. The Commission was of the view that some corrections were needed for addressing the relative disparities in infrastructure across States and recommended that a committee be appointed to arrive at a set of indices which would reflect inter-State differences in infrastructure development. It assigned a weightage of 5 per cent to the index of infrastructure. The tenth Commission was the first to have recognized the need to incentivize States to do better fiscally. Therefore, it assigned a weightage of 10 per cent to the index of tax effort as measured by the ratio of per capita own tax revenue to the square of per capita income.

THE THIRD PHASE

The eleventh Commission was the first one to be appointed after the 80th Amendment to the Constitution, facilitating sharing of all Union tax revenues with the States. The Commission, while retaining all the five criteria adopted by the tenth Commission for the inter se distribution of the States' share in the divisible pool of taxes, added one more criterion, of fiscal discipline. Given the then fiscal situation of the States and the reference to better fiscal management in the ToR, the Commission considered it necessary to provide further incentives to fiscal discipline and accordingly recommended the use of an index of fiscal discipline as an additional criterion in the tax-devolution formula. This was the first time that that this criterion was added. For working out the index, the Commission adopted the improvement in the ratio of own revenues of a State to its total revenue expenditure relative to a similar ratio for all the States. For determining the inter se shares of States in tax devolution, the Commission assigned a weightage of 10 per cent to population; 62.5 per cent to income distance; 5 per cent to tax effort; and 7.5 per cent each to area, index of infrastructure, and fiscal discipline.

Though the Eleventh Finance Commiussion introduced an additional element of fiscal discipline, its devolution criteria came under severe criticism on the grounds that the middle-income and performing States lost out heavily following the reduction in the weightage assigned to population and marginally higher weightage assigned to the index of infrastructure and distance of per capita income. This was perhaps the first time that the recommendations of a Finance Commission were criticized.

The Twelfth Finance Commission laid emphasis on evolving a formula for horizontal devolution that would balance equity with fiscal efficiency. It expressed the view that in any scheme of federal transfers trying to implement the equalization principle, equity considerations should dominate. It therefore increased the weightage given to population and area to 25 per cent and 10 per cent respectively; reduced the weight to income distance to 50 per cent; and retained the weightage assigned to tax effort and fiscal discipline at 7.5 per cent each. The Commission dropped the index of infrastructure altogether, arguing that its distance was correlated with the distance of per capita income and that the index was better used in an ordinal way.

Like its predecessors, the Thirteenth Finance Commission used a combination of equity and efficiency criteria in its devolution formula because of their wide acceptability. Furthermore, such a combination also addressed the concerns of reforming States. Having decided on the broad principles of devolution, the Commission considered whether such criteria should be forward looking or based on past performance. Though the forward-looking indicators were considered appropriate as the devolutions were linked to future performance, the Commission went by past performance as there was no mechanism in place for arriving at the shares of States based on year-to-year performance. While retaining weightage assigned to population and area at 25 per cent and 10 per cent respectively, the Commission increased the weight assigned to fiscal discipline significantly, from 7.5 per cent to 17.5 per cent. It introduced a new criterion of fiscal capacity distance as an equity parameter and assigned it a weightage of 47.5 per cent. It observed that the equity component by itself would not result in common standards in quality or outcomes in public services; for that to happen, it was necessary that a comparable level of tax effort assumed to hold across States should actually prevail. The Commission further observed that the income distance criteria used by the previous Commission was a proxy for the gap among the States in tax capacity, and when so proxied, it implicitly amounted to a single average tax–GSDP ratio to determine fiscal capacity distance among States. The Commission instead used separate averages for measuring the tax capacity of general- and special-category States. For working out fiscal-capacity distance, the Commission first calculated the three-year average per capita GSDP for individual States for the years 2004–7, and in the next step, the average tax–GSDP ratio was obtained as a weighted mean separately for general- and special-category States. The group-specific averages were then applied to the States in each category to obtain the potential per capita tax revenue of each State. Then the fiscal distance was obtained for each State by the distance of its estimated per capita revenue from the estimated per capita revenue of Haryana, the second highest in per capita income rankings after Goa. These distances, defined as per capita revenue entitlements of each State, were multiplied by the respective 1971 population of each State to arrive at their shares.

The Fourteenth Finance Commission took into account the demographic changes subsequent to 1971 as mandated in the considerations listed out in its ToR, and assigned a weightage of 17.5 per cent to the 1971 population and 10 per cent to the 2011 population figures. The income-distance criterion was assigned a weightage of 50 per cent. Broadly agreeing with the views of the previous Commissions that a State with a larger area would have to incur additional administrative costs, it assigned a weightage of 15 per cent to area with a floor of 2 per cent for smaller States. Taking into account that a large forest cover would provide huge ecological benefits and involved an opportunity cost in terms of area not available for other economic activities, the Commission, for the first time, assigned a weight of 7.5 per cent to forest cover.

CRITERIA USED AND IMPLICATIONS

Over the years, altogether 12 criteria have been used for tax devolution by the Finance Commissions so far. These criteria and their implications are summarized in Annexure 6A.1. The criteria and weightage for the inter se allocation are presented in summary form in Annexure 6A.2.

The criteria adopted by Finance Commissions for horizontal distribution can be broadly classified under five heads: need, represented by population, area, and demographic change; equity, represented by backwardness, per capita income distance, inverse of per capita income, poverty, revenue equalization, infrastructure distance, and fiscal capacity distance; efficiency and performance, represented by contribution, tax effort, and fiscal self-reliance; fiscal disability, represented by forest cover; and non-Plan revenue deficits.

An examination of the weightage assigned to each one of the above criteria reveals that over the years, there has been a shift from need-based parameters to criteria representing equity and efficiency. Figures 6.1 to 6.3 indicate the shifts in the relative weightage assigned to these criteria by different Finance Commissions.

Figure 6.1 Criteria for Distribution of Income Tax Proceeds to States, First to Tenth Finance Commissions (%)

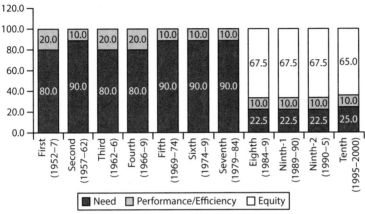

Source: Derived from the weightage assigned by the Finance Commissions as indicated in Annexure 6A.2.

Note: The relative weights to different criteria assigned by the First to Tenth Finance Commissions (see Annexure 6A.2) have been grouped under five broad heads, namely, need, equity, performance/efficiency, fiscal disability, and non-Plan revenue deficits.

Figure 6.2 Criteria for Distribution of Union Excise Duties, First to Tenth Finance Commissions (%)

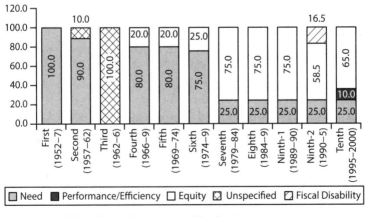

Source: Derived from the weightage assigned by the Finance Commissions as indicated in Annexure 6A.2.

Figure 6.3   Criteria for Distribution of States' Share in All Central Taxes, Eleventh to Fourteenth Finance Commissions (%)

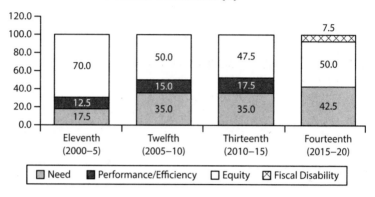

Source: Derived from the weightage assigned by the Finance Commissions as indicated in Annexure 6A.2.

GAINERS AND LOSERS

The simplest and most non-discretionary criterion for tax devolution is the population of the relevant period. The actual shares of States in tax devolution are based on other criteria that have been taken into account in addition to population, as prescribed or allowed in the ToR. An attempt has been made to calculate the percentage shares of States per relevant population and tax devolution as recommended by the Finance Commissions over a period of twenty years. The deviation represents the effect of the use of criteria other than the relevant population. Annexure 6.3 presents the deviation from 2000 to 2020, corresponding to the Eleventh, Twelfth, Thirteenth, and Fourteenth Finance Commissions. Table 6.1 presents the consistent gainers and losers for the entire period of 20 years. States whose share in tax devolution is higher than their share in relevant population have been consistent gainers, while those whose share in devolution is found to be lower than their share in relevant population in the periods covered by the last four Commissions are consistent losers.

Table 6.1 Consistent Gainers and Losers

General-Category States, Consistent Gainers	Bihar; Chhattisgarh; Goa; Madhya Pradesh; Odisha; Uttar Pradesh
General-Category States, Consistent Losers	Gujarat; Haryana; Karnataka; Kerala; Maharashtra; Punjab; Tamil Nadu; West Bengal
Special-Category States, Consistent Gainers	All the special-category States have been consistent gainers, with the exception of Himachal Pradesh, in the period covered by the Twelfth Finance Commission (2005–10)

Source: Derived from the percentage shares of States in tax devolution and their shares in the relevant population of the award periods of Finance Commissions presented in Annexure 6A.3.

By and large, all the States with higher relative per capita incomes have lower shares in tax devolution as compared with their respective shares in relevant population. In contrast, the shares in tax devolution as compared with their respective shares in population are found to be higher in backward and special-category States.

Each State views horizontal distribution incrementally; that is, whether the share given by a Commission is higher or lower than the preceding one. In reality, even if the criteria are exactly the same, some States will lose while others will gain. Further, there cannot be gainers without losers in horizontal distribution. Finance Commissions, in their recommendations on tax devolution, generally moderate the deviation from the prevailing share of each State.

In the initial stages of fiscal federalism, the population and contribution of a State determined its share in income tax. Even in the case of horizontal distribution of Union excise duties, population was a predominant criterion. Over the years, it was felt necessary to promote equity as Finance Commission transfers continued to be predominant in the overall transfer system. Later on, partly on the pleas of States that performance should not be penalized and partly to promote fiscal discipline, performance indicators found a place in the tax devolution formula. The Fourteenth

Finance Commission felt that while a huge forest cover provided ecological benefits, there was an opportunity cost in terms of forest area not being available for other economic activities. The Commission, for the first time, included forest cover in the devolution formula to take care of the disabilities of States. Thus, Finance Commissions have adapted themselves to the changing economic environment and the need to maintain fiscal sustainability both at the Union and State levels.

SELECT REFERENCES

1. Ministry of Finance. Various Years. *Report of the Finance Commission,* I–XIV. New Delhi: Government of India.

2. Rao, Govinda and Tapas Sen. 1996. *Fiscal Federalism in India: Theory and Practice.* New Delhi: Macmillan.

3. Vithal, B.P.R. and M.L. Sastry. 2001. *Fiscal Federalism in India.* New Delhi: Oxford University Press.

ANNEXURE

Table 6A.1 Criteria Used by Different Finance Commissions for Tax Devolution and the Implications Thereof

Criterion	Implications
Population	Population was used by all the Finance Commissions without exception, but with varying weightage. It represents the needs of the people better than other parameters. It is equity neutral, as each State gets the same amount of tax devolution on a per capita basis.
Area	Area had been used as one of the criterion from the Tenth Finance Commission onwards. It also represents the needs of a State, though not as perfectly as the population criterion. Because of the variations in terrain, remote and mountainous areas with low population density, the cost of delivery of services varies widely across States. The tenth Commission felt that the differences in costs of providing services might increase with the size of a State but only at a decreasing rate. At the same time, the Commission pointed out that the costs of providing services in small States with hilly terrain might be higher. Therefore, it adjusted the population of a State to ensure that no State would get a share of lesser than 2 per cent at the lower end and higher than 10 per cent at the upper end. (The share of population of States varies widely across States, with Uttar Pradesh accounting for 16.785 per cent of the total population of States, and Sikkim accounting for a mere 0.051 per cent). From the Twelfth Finance Commission onwards, while the minimum share of a State in population was retained at 2 per cent, the upper limit of 10 per cent was given up.
Contribution	Until the tenth Commission, only two Union taxes, namely income tax and Union excise duties, were included in the divisible pool. The contribution of a State to income tax collections

Table 6A.1 (Cont'd)

Criterion	Implications
	was used as a criterion up to the Tenth Finance Commission. This criterion has an inherent bias towards richer States as their contribution to income tax collections would be higher. This criterion was regressive.
Income Distance	Income distance as a criterion for inter se distribution was used from the fifth Commission onwards. This is progressive, as backward States tend to get a higher per capita tax devolution.
Inverse of Per capita Income	Inverse of per capita income was used in addition to distance of per capita income as a separate criterion from the eighth Commission onwards. These together carried a higher weightage. Though both of them are progressive and use the same database, under the distance criterion, poorer States get higher per capita transfers. In contrast, because of the implicit convexity, middle-income States tend to suffer under the inverse of per capita criterion. Therefore, this criterion was dropped from the tenth Commission onwards.
Backwardness	Backwardness was used by the fourth, fifth, and ninth Commissions. Because of the subjective nature of the criterion, other Commissions did not use this criterion.
Index of Infrastructure	The criterion of index of infrastructure was used by the fifth and ninth Commissions. Because of complexities and subjectivities involved in computing such an index, subsequent Commissions dropped this criterion.
Poverty	Poverty was used as a criterion by the eighth and ninth Commissions.
Tax Effort	Tax effort was given a weightage of 10 per cent for the first time by the tenth Commission. This was continued by the eleventh, twelfth, and thirteenth Commissions. This criterion though not progressive was intended to incentivize States for their tax efforts.

Table 6A.1   (*Cont'd*)

Criterion	Implications
Fiscal Self Reliance/ Discipline	The eleventh Commission introduced the criterion of fiscal self-reliance, measured by the improvement in the ratio of own revenue receipts of a State to its total revenue expenditure related to a similar ratio for all States. This criterion is meant for incentivizing States.
Fiscal Capacity Distance	The thirteenth Commission used fiscal capacity distance as a criterion for the first time. For arriving at such distance, the Commission used separate averages for measuring the tax capacity of general-category and special-category States. For working out the fiscal capacity distance, the Commission first worked out the three-year average per capita GSDP for the individual States for the years 2004–7 and in the next step, the average tax–GSDP ratio had been obtained as a weighted mean separately for general-category and special-category States. The group-specific averages were then applied to the States in each category to obtain the potential per capita tax revenue of each State. Then the fiscal distance was obtained for each State by the distance of its estimated per capita revenue from the estimated per capita revenue of Haryana, the second highest in per capita income rankings after Goa. These distances defined as per capita revenue entitlements of each State were multiplied by the respective 1971 population of each State to arrive at its shares.
Forest Cover	Taking into account that a large forest cover would provide huge ecological benefits and that there was an opportunity cost in terms of area not available for other economic activities, the fourteenth Commission introduced forest cover as a criterion, assigning it a weightage of 7.5 per cent.

Source: Compiled from *Reports of the Finance Commissions*, I–XIV.

Table 6A.2 Criteria and Weights for Inter se Allocation of Tax Devolution

Criterion	First (1952–7)		Second (1957–62)		Third (1962–6)	
	Income Tax	Union Excise	Income Tax	Union Excise	Income Tax	Union Excise
Population	80	100	90	90	80	
Contribution	20		10		20	
Backwardness						
Income Distance						
Inverse Per Capita Income/ Income Adjusted Total Population						
Poverty						
Revenue Equalization						
Non-Plan Deficit						
Area Adjusted						
Infrastructure Distance						
Fiscal Self-reliance						
Tax Effort						
Fiscal Discipline						
Fiscal Capacity						
Forest Cover						
Unspecified				10		100

Fourth (1966–9)		Fifth (1969–74)		Sixth (1974–9)		Seventh (1979–84)	
Income Tax	Union Excise	Income Tax	Union Excise	Income Tax	Union Excise	Income Tax	Union Excise
80	80	90	80	90	75	90	25
20		10		10		10	
	20		6.66				
			13.34		25		
							25
							25
							25

(*Cont'd*)

Table 6A.2   (*Cont'd*)

Criterion	Eighth (1984–9)		Ninth-1 (1989–90)		Ninth-2 (1990–5)	
	Income Tax	Union Excise	Income Tax	Union Excise	Income Tax	Union Excise
Population	22.50	25	22.50	25	22.50	25
Contribution	10		10		10	
Backwardness					11.25	12.50
Income Distance	45	50	45	50	45	33.50
Inverse of Per Capita Income/ Income Adjusted Total Population	22.5	25	11.25	12.50	11.25	12.50
Poverty			11.25	12.50		
Revenue Equalization						
Non-Plan Deficit						16.50
Area Adjusted						
Infrastructure Distance						
Fiscal self-reliance						
Tax Effort						
Fiscal Discipline						
Fiscal Capacity Distance						
Forest Cover						
Unspecified						

Source: Compiled from *Reports of the Finance Commission*, I–XIV.

Tenth (1995–2000)		Eleventh (2000–5)	Twelfth (2005–10)	Thirteenth (2010–15)	Fourteenth (2015–20)
Income Tax	Union Excise	All Taxes	All Taxes	All Taxes	All Taxes
20	20	10	25	25	27.5
60	60	62.50	50		50
5	5	7.50	10	10	15
5	5	7.50			
10	10	5	7.50		
		7.50	7.50	17.50	
				47.50	
					7.5

Table 6A.3   Shares of States in Tax Devolution and Relevant Population of the Award Periods

State	Eleventh Finance Commission (2000–5)		Twelfth Finance Commission (2005–10)	
	Percentage Share in Tax Devolution	Percentage Share in 1991 Population	Percentage Share in Tax Devolution	Percentage Share in 2001 Population
General Category				
1 Andhra Pradesh	7.701	7.966	7.356	7.529
2 Bihar	14.597	10.346	11.028	8.201
3 Chhattisgarh	–	–	2.654	2.055
4 Goa	0.206	0.140	0.259	0.128
5 Gujarat	2.821	4.948	3.569	5.009
6 Haryana	0.944	1.972	1.075	2.085
7 Jharkhand	–	–	3.361	2.658
8 Karnataka	4.930	5.387	4.459	5.227
9 Kerala	3.057	3.485	2.665	3.142
10 Madhya Pradesh	8.838	7.927	6.711	5.958
11 Maharashtra	4.632	9.455	4.997	9.574
12 Odisha	5.056	3.792	5.161	3.636
13 Punjab	1.147	2.429	1.299	2.411
14 Rajasthan	5.473	5.271	5.609	5.582
15 Tamil Nadu	5.385	6.691	5.305	6.165
16 Telangana	–	–	–	–

(Cont'd)

Table 6A.3 (Cont'd)

State	Eleventh Finance Commission (2000–5)		Twelfth Finance Commission (2005–10)	
	Percentage Share in Tax Devolution	Percentage Share in 1991 Population	Percentage Share in Tax Devolution	Percentage Share in 2001 Population
17 Uttar Pradesh	19.798	16.663	19.264	16.421
18 West Bengal	8.116	8.154	7.057	7.924
Total (I)	92.701	94.626	91.829	93.705
Special Category				
1 Arunachal Pradesh	0.244	0.103	0.288	0.109
2 Assam	3.285	2.685	3.235	2.638
3 Himachal Pradesh	0.683	0.619	0.522	0.603
4 Jammu & Kashmir	1.290	0.925	1.297	0.998
5 Manipur	0.366	0.220	0.362	0.227
6 Meghalaya	0.342	0.213	0.371	0.227
7 Mizoram	0.198	0.083	0.239	0.089
8 Nagaland	0.220	0.145	0.263	0.198
9 Sikkim	0.184	0.049	0.227	0.049
10 Tripura	0.487	0.330	0.428	0.316
11 Uttarakhand	–	–	0.939	0.840
Total (II)	7.299	5.372	8.171	6.294
All States	100.00	100.00	100.00	100.00

(Cont'd)

Table 6A.3 *(Cont'd)*

State	Thirteenth Finance Commission (2010–15)		Fourteenth Finance Commission (2015–20)	
	Percentage Share in Tax Devolution	Percentage Share in 2001 Population	Percentage Share in Tax Devolution	Percentage Share in 2011 Population
General Category				
1 Andhra Pradesh	6.937	7.529	4.305	4.149
2 Bihar	10.917	8.201	9.665	8.745
3 Chhattisgarh	2.470	2.055	3.080	2.146
4 Goa	0.266	0.128	0.378	0.123
5 Gujarat	3.041	5.009	3.084	5.077
6 Haryana	1.048	2.085	1.084	2.130
7 Jharkhand	2.802	2.658	3.139	2.771
8 Karnataka	4.328	5.227	4.713	5.132
9 Kerala	2.341	3.142	2.500	2.806
10 Madhya Pradesh	7.120	5.958	7.548	6.101
11 Maharashtra	5.199	9.574	5.521	9.440
12 Odisha	4.779	3.636	4.642	3.526
13 Punjab	1.389	2.411	1.577	2.330
14 Rajasthan	5.853	5.582	5.495	5.758
15 Tamil Nadu	4.969	6.165	4.023	6.061
16 Telangana	–	–	2.437	2.956

(Cont'd)

Table 6A.3 (Cont'd)

	State	Thirteenth Finance Commission (2010–15)		Fourteenth Finance Commission (2015–20)	
		Percentage Share in Tax Devolution	Percentage Share in 2001 Population	Percentage Share in Tax Devolution	Percentage Share in 2011 Population
17	Uttar Pradesh	19.677	16.421	17.959	16.785
18	West Bengal	7.264	7.924	7.324	7.667
	Total (I)	**90.400**	**93.705**	**88.474**	**93.703**
	Special Category				
1	Arunachal Pradesh	0.328	0.109	1.370	0.116
2	Assam	3.628	2.638	3.311	2.621
3	Himachal Pradesh	0.781	0.603	0.713	0.577
4	Jammu & Kashmir	1.551	0.998	1.854	1.053
5	Manipur	0.451	0.227	0.617	0.216
6	Meghalaya	0.408	0.227	0.642	0.249
7	Mizoram	0.269	0.089	0.460	0.092
8	Nagaland	0.314	0.198	0.498	0.166
9	Sikkim	0.239	0.049	0.367	0.051
10	Tripura	0.511	0.316	0.642	0.309
11	Uttarakhand	1.120	0.840	1.052	0.847
	Total (II)	**9.600**	**6.294**	**11.526**	**6.298**
	All States	**100.00**	**100.00**	**100.00**	**100.00**

Source: Compiled from Reports of the Finance Commission, I–XIV, and the Census 2001 and 2011.
Note: As the percentage are rounded off to the third decimal point, they may not add up exactly to 100.

7

GRANTS-IN-AID
MAGNITUDE AND COMPOSITION

FINANCE COMMISSIONS ARE MANDATED TO recommend sharing of taxes and grants-in-aid of revenues to States. The share of taxes due to the States is the net of the collection expenses of the Union, cesses and surcharges, and accrues to the States without being routed through the Consolidated Fund of India. In a way, the devolution of taxes should not, therefore, be treated as a transfer. The grants-in-aid, on the other hand, are routed through the Consolidated Fund of India, but are charged and not subject to voting by Parliament. They are recommended for States in need of assistance and to local bodies as well as for specific purposes such as calamity relief and for specific sectors and schemes in States.

DOMINANT PRINCIPLES

The First Finance Commission laid down budgetary needs as the dominant principle that should govern grants to States. For assessing such needs, the budget of a State was taken as the starting point subject to several adjustments to make all budgets comparable. The

Commission felt that even after such adjustments, five other factors should also be considered. First, the extent of tax effort by a State and the economy in expenditure should determine its eligibility for grant as well as the amount of such help from the Centre. Second, a State should first utilize the existing resources to good effect before making a claim for assistance from the Centre. Third, grants should help in equalizing the standards of basic social services. Fourth, they might be given to help a State to meet special burdens or obligations of national concern, though within the State sphere, if they involved undue strain on its finances. Fifth, they might be given independent of the budgetary criterion to incentivize any reforms or further any beneficent service of primary importance in the national interest.

The First Finance Commission considered the issue of grants-in-aid under a broad perspective of securing an equitable allocation of resources among States. The Commission took the view that the scope of Article 275 should not be limited to completely unconditional grants but should also include broad but well-defined purposes. It held that unconditional grants should reinforce the general resources of State Governments and that grants for broad purposes might be given to stimulate the expansion of specific categories of services rather than specified schemes under those categories.

The Commission recommended grants to a few States for meeting their overall budgetary needs on revenue account; for addressing special problems like the movement of displaced persons from East Pakistan; inadequate social services; and law and order. It also recommended grants to eight States for expanding primary educational facilities.

The succeeding Finance Commissions were in broad agreement with the principles laid down by the first Commission for determining grants to States.

PLAN PRIORITIES

The Second Finance Commission was required under its ToR to take into consideration the requirements of the Second Five-Year Plan while recommending grants to States. The Commission observed that, to the extent possible, normal revenue expenditure should be met by sharing of taxes, and grants should be only a residual form of assistance. A lump sum grant to 11 States out of the then-existing 14 was recommended for meeting the revenue expenditure for developmental needs and addressing special problems. This was the beginning of the overlap between the Finance and Planning Commissions.

As with the Second Finance Commission, the ToR of the third Commission stipulated that it should take into account the requirements of the Five-Year Plan (Third) while making recommendations regarding grants to States. The Third Finance Commission was the first to have pointed out the unsoundness of drawing an arbitrary line between Plan and non-Plan expenditure. It felt that there was considerable advantage in devising machinery for taking an integrated view of Plan and non-Plan expenditure of a State as a whole. The Commission recommended grants to enable States, along with any surplus out of the devolution, to cover 75 per cent of the revenue component of their Plans. For arriving at such amounts, it deducted the total additional revenue to be raised by each State as incorporated in the Plan. The Commission recommended grants accordingly to all States, with the exception of Maharashtra. The Government of India did not accept this recommendation and instead accepted the note of dissent of the Member-Secretary that the Commission should desist from assessing the Plan revenue expenditure requirements and that the entire grant for Plan purposes should be in the domain of the Planning Commission.

In the ToR of the Fourth Finance Commission, there was no consideration with regard to the requirements of the Five-Year Plan. Yet, the Commission was asked to take into account the requirements of those States for meeting the committed expenditure on maintenance and upkeep of Plan schemes completed during the Third Plan. The Commission felt that it was desirable to ensure that the Planning Commission, which was specifically constituted for this purpose, should have unhampered authority in this domain. It arrived at the non-Plan revenue gap based on an assessment of the revenue receipts and non-Plan expenditure of States, including the committed expenditure on completed Plan schemes. For those States which were surplus after taking into account their share in various Central taxes and duties, no grants were recommended under Article 275. They were recommended to 10 States that were estimated to have revenue deficits after tax devolution. Thus, for the first time, a gap-filling approach was introduced explicitly. The Commission did not recommend any grants for special problems.

The ToR of the Fifth Finance Commission with regard to grants precluded it from taking into account the requirements of the Five-Year Plan. The Commission recommended a lump sum grant to each of the 10 States to cover their deficits on non-Plan revenue account on the basis of its assessment.

While recommending the principles for grants, the Sixth Finance Commission was mandated to take into account, among others, the existing practice in regard to the distribution of Central assistance for financing State Plans; adequate maintenance of Plan schemes completed by the end of 1973–4; and the requirements of States which were backward in standards of general administration. The Commission identified certain administrative and social services and proposed that it should enable States whose expenditure in per capita terms was below the all-States' average to come up to such an average by the last year of its award period (1978–9). Accordingly, it recommended grants to 15 States covering general administration and social services, regardless of whether they had a deficit on the non-Plan revenue account. The Sixth Finance Commission did not recommend any grants for meeting the Plan revenue expenditure.

The ToR of the Seventh Finance Commission mandated it to take into account the resources of the Central Government and the demands thereon. This was in addition to the existing practice with regard to the distribution of Central assistance for State Plans, non-Plan commitments, requirements for the maintenance of completed plan schemes, and those for the upgrade of standards of administration. This gave rise to the apprehension that the Centre's intent in including the demands on its own resources and the existing practice for distribution of Central assistance would curtail the freedom of the Commission in recommending grants under Article 275. However, the seventh Commission felt that its freedom was in no way restricted. It observed that the only constraints on it were that it had to operate within the four corners of the Constitutional provisions and that it should leave the area of Plan investment and Central assistance to the Planning Commission. The Commission took the stand that grants-in-aid might be given in the first place to States to enable them to cover fiscal gaps, if any, left after tax devolution, and to correct, as far as possible, disparities in the availability of various administrative and social services.

The Seventh Finance Commission also took the stand that grants could be given to individual States to meet special burdens on account of peculiar circumstances or matters of national concern. Like its predecessor, the Commission did not propose any Plan grants, but recommended non-Plan deficit grants to 8 States and grants for the upgrade of standards of administration to 17 States. It did not recommend any grants for developmental sectors like education and health as it felt that they fell within the domain of the Planning Commission.

The considerations for the Eighth Finance Commission were similar to those of the Seventh Finance Commission. It recommended grants for meeting both capital and revenue requirements and awarded grants to 10 States for special problems. Based on its reassessment of revenue and non-Plan commitments, the Commission also recommended revenue-deficit grants to 11 States.

The Ninth Finance Commission considered revenue expenditure on both Plan and non-Plan accounts and recommended separate gap grants to meet the revenue deficits for each. It felt that it had to deal with the revenue account, since one of the considerations mandated it to keep in view the objective of not only balancing the receipts and expenditure on the revenue accounts of both the States and the Centre, but also generating surpluses for capital investment. The Commission felt that it was very much within its purview to recommend grants for financing the Plan. Thus, even some States that had a surplus on the non-Plan revenue account ended up getting Plan-deficit grants. The Commission did not recommend any Plan-deficit grants to special-category States on the grounds that the Central assistance dispensed to them was in the grant–loan ratio of 90:10, and a part of the grant component was being used for meeting Plan capital expenditure. The Commission did not recommend grants for special problems and for the upgrade of administration as these were not mentioned in its ToR.

The Tenth Finance Commission was asked to keep in view, among others, the objective of reducing the fiscal deficit while making its recommendations on tax devolution and grants-in-aid. This consideration was included for the first time. The Commission did not go into the question of Plan outlays and non-Plan capital account. It took the view that to the extent its recommendations improved the non-Plan revenue account of the Centre and States, it would contribute to a reduction in fiscal deficit. In addition to non-Plan revenue-deficit grants, the Commission also recommended grants for the upgrade of administration; special problems; and, for the first time ever, to local bodies.

The eleventh Commission's ToR remained more or less the same as those of the tenth Commission, except that it was asked explicitly to make recommendations regarding the measures needed to augment the Consolidated Fund of a State to supplement the resources of Panchayats/Municipalities following the 73rd and 74th Amendments to the Constitution. The Commission recommended post-devolution non-Plan revenue-deficit grants, and grants for special problems and to local bodies.

The Twelfth Finance Commission followed a similar normative approach to arrive at post-devolution non-Plan revenue-deficit grants to States. The Commission took into account both Plan and non-Plan revenue expenditure by States in the education and health sectors and followed a two-step normative approach to determine their eligibility for grants under these sectors. In the first step, the low-expenditure preferences of States was corrected by adjusting the actual expenditure to a minimum percentage of their total revenue expenditure, both revenue and capital. In the next step, States whose expenditure fell short of a normative level of per capita expenditure even after spending the required percentage were identified. While eight States were recommended grants under education, seven were recommended grants under the health sector. Some of these States were not assessed to have post-devolution non-Plan revenue deficits.

The Twelfth Finance Commission observed that maintenance of roads and buildings was not being given adequate importance by the States and therefore recommended separate grants for the maintenance of roads and bridges and of buildings for all the 28 States. This was in contrast to the practice followed by the previous Commissions of subsuming maintenance requirements in the overall assessment of non-Plan expenditure of States.

The Commission also recommended a few additional grants to States on the grounds that the formula used for horizontal distribution of shareable taxes could not take care of all the dimensions of the fiscal needs of a State. The previous Commissions, starting from the sixth Commission, had recommended grants for special sectors even when there was no specific reference to such grants in the ToR. Based on the representations received and the impressions gained during its visits to States, the Twelfth Finance Commission recommended grants for the maintenance of forests, heritage conservation, and addressing State-specific needs.

Though the ToR remained more or less the same with regard to grants, the Thirteenth Finance Commission further extended the scope of grants under Article 275. The Commission took the view that grants were an important instrument to make its scheme of transfers more comprehensive and address the issues spelt out in the ToR. It further observed that grants would enable corrections for the cost disabilities that many States faced, and that were addressed only to a limited extent in any devolution formula. It had accordingly recommended several categories of grants, in addition to non-Plan revenue deficit grants.

The thirteenth Commission recommended grants for elementary education and the protection of environment and forests, and incentive grants for grid-connected renewable energy and the water sector. It also recommended grants for improving outcomes by establishing an incentive framework to target public expenditure; promoting innovation to improve outcomes in public policy and District governance; and improving transparency in government accounts to better reflect and measure outputs and outcomes, and thereby improve accountability. Furthermore, the Commission recommended incentive grants for better targeting of subsidies through unique identification, for reducing infant mortality, and improving justice delivery. For promoting innovations, the Commission recommended a grant to set up a Centre for Innovations in Public Systems at the Administrative Staff College of India, Hyderabad, and grants for creating District Innovation Funds. It also recommended grants for improving transparency in government accounts; setting up a database of government employees; maintenance of roads and bridges; and State-specific grants covering several sectors. In addition, it recommended a grant of Rs 50,000 crore to be provided to all States in the aggregate subject to the adoption of the GST framework consistent with the model suggested by it. As GST was not rolled out during the award period of the Commission, the grant did not materialize.

The grants that the Thirteenth Finance Commission recommended were much broader in their range, number, and coverage than those recommended by previous Commissions.

The Fourteenth Finance Commission made a significant departure from the earlier approach with regard to grants under Article 275. It considered the entire revenue expenditure, both Plan and non-Plan, for arriving at the pre-devolution revenue deficit of each State. With regard to sector-specific grants, it observed that there was a certain inconsistency in such grants recommended by the previous Finance Commissions. It cited the example of the eleventh Commission, which had recommended grants for the upgrade of general administration, and the twelfth, which had discontinued them. Similarly, the twelfth Commission had recommended grants for the maintenance of public buildings, while the thirteenth Commission had not. It saw more of a change than continuity in sector-specific grants. Further, it observed that these grants constituted too small a percentage of the total grants going to States in a particular sector to make any impact. The small size was further compounded by poor utilization on account of a number of conditionalities. The limited tenure of the Finance Commission was a constraint in properly designing these grants. There was a minimum time lag of two years between the formulation of State-specific schemes and their implementation.

The Fourteenth Finance Commission, thus, based its approach to grants on four principles: that the devolution of taxes be based on a formula which should, to a large extent, offset revenue and cost disabilities; the assessment of expenditure should build in additional requirements in the case of those States with per capita expenditure significantly below the all-States' average; if the assessed expenditure need of a State exceeded the sum of its revenue capacity and tax devolution, then it should be eligible for a general-purpose grant; and that grants for State-specific projects or schemes would not be considered as these were best identified, prioritized, and financed by the States themselves.

In a major departure from the approach followed by the previous Commissions, the Fourteenth Finance Commission did not recommend any State-specific or sector-specific grants. Instead, it recommended the evolution of a new institutional mechanism, consistent with cooperative fiscal federalism, to identify sectors that should be eligible for grants from the Union, indicating criteria for inter-State distribution, providing flexibility to States with regard to their implementation, and to identify area-specific grants.

FINANCING OF RELIEF EXPENDITURE

The Sixth Finance Commission, for the first time, was asked to review the policy and arrangements in regard to the financing of relief expenditure by States affected by natural calamities, and examine, inter alia, the feasibility of establishing a National Fund to which the Central and State Governments might contribute a percentage of their revenue receipts.

This issue had been considered by the previous Commissions as well, with the exception of the First Finance Commission. The Second Finance Commission had expressed concern over the dislocation caused to State finances by unforeseen expenditure on natural calamities and felt the need to make some regular provision to meet such expenditure. Accordingly, it had included a margin in its estimates of committed expenditure of States. This margin for each State was arrived at based broadly on the average annual expenditure over the last decade. The Commission suggested that the State Governments might set up separate funds by transferring the margin money estimated by it. It also suggested that the balance available in the Funds should be invested in marketable government securities so that it was available when needed, so that the States would not have to curtail other expenditure or approach the Centre for assistance, except in very abnormal circumstances. The Third Finance Commission retained the margin money estimated by the Second Finance Commission without any changes in the forecast of expenditure of States.

The Fourth Finance Commission reworked the margin money for each State based on the average actual expenditure in the last eight years and included them in the forecast of States' expenditure. A number of States had represented to the Commission that though the Government of India had a scheme to finance relief expenditure in excess of the provisions recommended by the second and third Commissions, the conditions governing them were far too stringent. Taking these concerns into account, the fourth Commission recommended that the existing arrangements might be reviewed by the Government of India in consultation with States. The Fifth Finance Commission took note of the severe failure of the monsoons in 1966 and 1967 and the consequent increase in relief expenditure by States. This had amounted to Rs 73.49 crore and Rs 78.89 crore in 1966–7 and 1967–8 respectively, as compared with the provision of Rs 15.69 crore per annum included in the fourth Commission's forecast. The fifth Commission, therefore, reassessed the requirements of States for calamity relief based on the average annual expenditure from 1957–66 and allowed an increase of 25 per cent. It, however, retained the provision allowed by the fourth Commission regarding relief expenditure, where it was higher than that worked out by it in respect of any State. The Government of India formulated a policy on relief measures in September 1966. In terms of this policy, Central teams would visit States affected by natural calamities for an on-the-spot assessment and recommend ceilings of expenditure on relief measures and loans for rehabilitation and repair to damaged public properties. Of these, only expenditure on relief to the extent of 75 per cent in excess of the margin provided by the Finance Commission was shareable by the Centre in the form of 50 per cent loan and 25 per cent grant. The remaining 25 per cent was to be borne by the State Government.

The Sixth Finance Commission observed that the prevailing arrangements for providing assistance for relief expenditure suffered from two main defects. First, States had no incentive to economize on expenditure and would make efforts to get as much assistance from the Centre as possible, as such assistance was discretionary in the absence of any guidelines. Second, the schemes on which relief expenditure was incurred were not integrated with the overall plans for the development of areas prone to droughts or floods. The Commission recommended that an alternative scheme be formulated for the development of drought- and flood-prone areas to address these defects and their integration into the Plan, and that the establishment of a National Fund was neither feasible nor desirable. The Commission arrived at the annual provisions needed by States for gratuitous and other relief based on the average expenditure on calamity relief over the period 1956–7 to 1971–2.

The Government of India accepted the recommendation of the Sixth Finance Commission and put in place a new scheme for relief expenditure. Under this scheme, on the occurrence of a natural calamity, a Central team would visit the affected areas and present a report assessing the expenditure requirements. After considering the report, a High Level Committee headed by a Member of the Planning Commission would recommend the amount to be given to the concerned State as advance Plan assistance for meeting the relief expenditure. This assistance would be adjusted within the ceiling of Central assistance for the State Plan.

Based on the review of a new scheme put in place by the Central Government, the Seventh Finance Commission suggested a separate arrangement with regard to expenditure on relief and restoration of public works following floods, cyclones, and other calamities. The Commission suggested that in the event of a calamity of rare severity, it might be necessary for the Central Government to extend assistance to a State beyond that recommended under the scheme.

The Eighth Finance Commission recommended the continuation of distinct arrangements for meeting expenditure on droughts and other calamities recommended by its immediate predecessor. It recommended that the Centre contribute 50 per cent of the margin money. The Commission further recommended that on the occurrence of a natural calamity, a State should be entitled to draw on the Centre's share after it exhausted its own share of margin money. If the Centre's contribution was not released in any year, the Commission recommended that it should be carried forward to the next year.

The ToR of the Ninth Finance Commission included a review of the arrangements with regard to financing relief expenditure and of the feasibility of establishing a national insurance fund to which the State Governments might contribute a percentage of their revenue receipts. The Commission came to the conclusion that a calamity, by its very nature and magnitude, would pose problems which no agency outside the government could tackle in full measure. The Commission recommended the replacement of the present scheme of providing margin money with one that would place generous funds at the disposal of States. It recommended the setting up of a CRF for each State with 75 per cent contribution by the Centre and 25 per cent by the State. The size of the Fund was arrived at based on the actual ceiling of expenditure approved during the ten-year period ending 1988–9. The Fund would be kept separate from the general revenues of the State. The Commission observed that following the creation of the Fund, it would be the responsibility of a State to meet all its expenditure on relief without any assistance from the Centre. This recommendation was accepted, and the Ministry of Finance laid down the investment pattern of accretions to the Fund.

The Tenth Finance Commission recommended the continuation of the scheme of CRF and suggested a few modifications: that the Fund should be held outside the public account of a State; and that the investment guidelines issued by the Ministry of Finance should be modified to provide flexibility to States in the choice of investment avenues. The Commission also recommended the setting up of a committee by the Ministry of Agriculture to draw up a list of items which would be charged only to the CRF. It considered the issue of dealing with calamities of rare severity and observed that once a calamity was deemed to be of a severe nature requiring support beyond what was envisaged in the CRF scheme, it should be dealt with as a national calamity and addressed with additional funding from the Central Government.

The Eleventh Finance Commission, while recommending the continuation of CRF with the same funding pattern, suggested that the Fund should be used for providing immediate relief and that expenditure on restoration of infrastructure should be met from the Plan funds on a priority basis. It recommended the establishment of a Centre for Calamity Management to make recommendations to the Central Government as to the severity of a natural calamity and the level of assistance needed by a State, and that such assistance by the Centre should be recouped by the levy of a special surcharge on Central taxes. The Commission recommended that collections from such surcharge should be kept in a separate Fund called the National Calamity Contingency Fund (NCCF) to be created in the Public Account with an initial contribution of Rs 500 crore by the Government of India. The Twelfth Finance Commission recommended the continuation of the scheme of CRF and NCCF.

A major development in the area of disaster relief was the enactment of the Disaster Management Act by the Union in 2005. The Act provides for the setting up of a National Disaster Management Authority (NDMA) to act as a coordinating and monitoring body for disaster management and to prepare a national plan for disaster management as well as a State Disaster Management Authority in each State to lay down the State disaster management policy and to coordinate the implementation of the national and State plans. The Act also envisages a District Disaster Management Authority for each district of a State. Under the Act, the Central Government is mandated to set up a National Disaster Response Fund (NDRF) for meeting any disaster situation and a National Disaster Mitigation Fund (NDMF) exclusively for the purpose of mitigation. In addition, the Act also mandates the setting up of a State Disaster Response Fund (SDRF), District Disaster Response Funds, and District Disaster Mitigation Funds. Though the Act provides the modalities for sourcing the funds for the NDRF through the Central Government, there are no provisions with regard to the size of the State- and District-level funds and their funding.

The Thirteenth Finance Commission recommended merging NCCF with NDRF from 1 April 2010 and that appropriations should be made based on the past trends of outflows from NCCF. On similar lines, the Commission recommended the merger of CRFs into SDRFs. It recommended that 75 per cent of the SDRF requirement for general-category States and 90 per cent for special-category States be met by the Centre through a grant to the States. This recommendation was accepted by the Government of India effective from 1 April 2010.

In the absence of an index of hazard vulnerability, the Fourteenth Finance Commission took the past expenditure for arriving at the size of SDRFs in line with the previous Commissions. It took into account expenditure on disaster relief for the period 2006–7 to 2012–13 to determine the size of the SDRF for each State. With regard to the differential contribution by the special- and general-category States, the Commission felt that an additional burden was cast on States by the Disaster Management Act and the frequency and magnitude of restoration of works undertaken by them. It, therefore, recommended a uniform contribution of 90 per cent by the Centre to the corpus of the annual SDRF. This recommendation was not accepted by the Government of India and the contribution of the Centre to the SDRF of general category States was retained at 75 per cent.

MAGNITUDE OF GRANTS

Tax devolution was the predominant channel of fiscal transfers recommended by the Finance Commission. Though the scope of the grants increased over successive Commissions, their share in total transfers recommended remained in the range of 7.7 per cent (the seventh Commission) to 26.1 per cent (the sixth Commission). The lower percentage share of grants in the award of the seventh Commission was on account of substantial increase in the share of the States in the net proceeds of Union excise duties, from 20 per cent to 40 per cent. The higher share of grants in the dispensation of the Sixth Finance Commission was on account of the provision of Rs 838.43 crore allowed for the upgrade of standards of administration and their inclusion in the post-devolution non-Plan revenue-deficit grants. This procedure adopted by the Commission resulted in a quantum jump in non-Plan revenue-deficit grants. Though the eighth Commission recommended a number of grants, the amounts were not significant enough to increase the share of grants in total transfers. The fourteenth Commission set a benchmark by devoting over 50 per cent of grants to support local bodies while marginally increasing allocations to calamity relief.

The composition of tax devolution and grants in the awards of Finance Commissions is presented in Table 7.1. While the magnitudes of grants relative to tax devolution are important, it is necessary to analyse the changing composition of grants in terms of deficit grants; mandated grants for relief and local bodies; sector-specific and scheme-specific grants; and other grants over the years. A detailed account on grants to local bodies is presented in a separate chapter.

Until the Eighth Finance Commission, non-Plan revenue-deficit grants constituted a predominant share of total grants recommended by Finance Commissions. In fact, the Third to Fifth Finance Commissions recommended only revenue-deficit grants. There was a spike in the share of revenue-deficit grants in the award of the Eleventh Finance Commission. Thereafter, there has been a gradual decline in the share of deficit grants and a corresponding increase in the share of grants to local bodies. The composition of the grants recommended by Finance Commissions is presented in Annexure 7A.1, while percentage shares of each grant in total grants are presented in Annexure 7A.2.

Table 7.1 Relative Shares of Tax Devolution and Grants in Total Transfers Recommended by Finance Commissions

Commission	Recommended Amounts (Rs Crore)			Share in Total Transfers Recommended (Per Cent)		
	Tax Devolution	Grants	Total	Tax Devolution	Grants	Total
First	335	50	385	87.0	13.0	100.0
Second	852	197	1,049	81.2	18.8	100.0
Third	1,067	244	1,311	81.4	18.6	100.0
Fourth	2,183	703	2,886	75.6	24.4	100.0

Commission	Recommended Amounts (Rs Crore)			Share in Total Transfers Recommended (Per Cent)		
	Tax Devolution	Grants	Total	Tax Devolution	Grants	Total
Fifth	3,628	638	4,266	85.0	15.0	100.0
Sixth	7,099	2,510	9,609	73.9	26.1	100.0
Seventh	19,233	1,610	20,843	92.3	7.7	100.0
Eighth	35,683	3,768	39,451	90.4	9.6	100.0
Ninth (1)	11,786	1,878	13,664	86.3	13.7	100.0
Ninth (2)	87,882	18,154	106,036	82.9	17.1	100.0
Tenth	206,343	20,301	226,644	91.0	9.0	100.0
Eleventh	376,318	58,588	434,906	86.5	13.5	100.0
Twelfth	613,112	142,640	755,752	81.1	18.9	100.0
Thirteenth	1,448,096	258,581	1,706,677	84.8	15.2	100.0
Fourteenth	3,948,187	537,353	4,485,540	88.0	12.0	100.0

Source: Compiled from Reports of the Finance Commission, I–XIV.
Note: Grants do not include, among others, grants in respect of additional duties of excise in lieu of sales tax on textiles, tobacco, and sugar (the Second to the Eleventh Finance Commissions), grants in lieu of tax on railway passenger fares (the Second to the Eleventh Finance Commissions), grants in lieu of estate duty (the Second to the Eighth Finance Commissions) and grants in lieu of wealth tax proceeds (the Sixth to the Seventh Finance Commissions). These have not been discussed in this chapter as their magnitude was insignificant.

ISSUES

The most important task for a Finance Commission is to assess the budgetary needs of the States and the Union Government. The major instrument of meeting these needs is undoubtedly the sharing of taxes. The dominant task is, therefore, determining the vertical and horizontal balance on the basis of some criteria.

Having determined the budgetary needs and identifying appropriate formulae, it is likely that some States will not be able to meet the needs as assessed by the Finance Commission with the resources available from estimated own resources and the tax devolution as per the Commission's assessment. In such a case, the first charge of grants-in-aid has to be the gap in resources to meet the needs as estimated by the Finance Commission. If it fails to fill the gap in funding, it can be construed as failing in its task of maintaining vertical and horizontal balance.

In recent years, the Government of India has been mandating recommendations in matters relating to relief and natural calamities. This is squarely a matter relating to burden sharing in a federation in the event of calamities. The Finance Commission has an obligation to apply its mind and make recommendations in this regard. The question, however, arises as to the extent of detail to which the Finance Commission should go into while giving its award. The establishment of a Fund has, in some ways, made the task of the Finance Commission less onerous.

Finance to local bodies has also been added as a mandatory ToR to the Finance Commission. The allocation to local bodies is meant to supplement the resources available to the States. In a way, therefore, the Finance Commission has introduced conditional transfers from Centre to States through this route. It is a complex task. In any case, the considerations that should govern the grants-in-aid on this account are difficult to define. In substance, this amounts to the Finance Commission recommending conditional transfers from Union to States to be passed on to sub-State bodies. However, the fourteenth Commission recommended unconditional transfers to States to support local bodies. With that, for the first time ever, 53 per cent of the total grants recommended were earmarked to local bodies.

Grant-in-aids for sectors like health and education had been considered by several Commissions. But it is not clear whether the Finance Commission is the ideal instrument to achieve sectoral objectives in view of their ad hoc nature and expertise.

Some Commissions had recommended allocation for individual schemes, some of which were on the basis of 'impressions gained'. To avoid the accusation of being arbitrary, Finance Commissions attempt to make adequate justification for recommending grants to individual schemes.

Finance Commissions have not had consistent policies in regard to grants-in-aid for capital expenditure in addition to revenue expenditure.

Similarly, there have been mixed signals towards grants-in-aid for financing developmental expenditure and administrative services. Above all, separate grants for maintenance had been considered, though the maintenance requirements could technically be taken into account in the assessment of the needs of the State concerned.

There have been contradictory positions by Finance Commissions on the overall scope of grants-in-aid. For instance, while the Thirteenth Finance Commission expanded the scope, the Fourteenth Finance Commission restricted it, consistent with the approach of the First Finance Commission.

Grants-in-aid have to be financed out of the Centre's share of the revenue. In other words, some calibration is required to ensure that the magnitude of grants-in-aid recommended can be accommodated in the Centre's budget with a given share in taxes. Above all, there is a potential overlap or duplication between activities recommended for grants-in-aid by the Finance Commission and those funded by other Central transfers to States.

ANNEXURE

Table 7A.1 Composition of Grants Recommended by Finance Commissions

	First	Second	Third	Fourth	Fifth	Sixth	Seventh	Eighth
Deficit	25	185	244	703	638	2,510	1,173	2,200
Performance Incentive								601
Margin Money								
Local Bodies								
Disaster Relief								
Education								
Improving Outcomes #								
Environment related @								
Maintenance of Roads and Bridges								
Maintenance of Buildings								
Maintenance of Forests								
Health Sector								
Plan Deficit								
Special Problems	9							53
Upgradation							437	914
State Specific	16	12						
Heritage Conservation								
Total	50	197	244	703	638	2,510	1,610	3,768

	Ninth (1)	Ninth (2)	Tenth	Eleventh	Twelfth	Thirteenth	Fourteenth
Deficit	984	6,016	7,583	35,359	56,856	51,800	1,94,821
Performance Incentive						1,500	
Margin Money	170						
Local Bodies			5,381	10,000	25,000	87,519	2,87,436
Disaster Relief		3,015	4,728	8,256	16,000	26,373	55,096
Education					10,172	24,068	
Improving Outcomes #						9,446	
Environment related @						10,000	
Maintenance of Roads and Bridges					15,000	19,930	
Maintenance of Buildings					5,000		
Maintenance of Forests					1,000		
Health Sector					5,887		
Plan Deficit		9,001					
Special Problems	552	122	1,246	875			
Upgradation	172		1,363	4,098			
State Specific					7,100	27,945	
Heritage Conservation					625		
Total	1,878	18,154	20,301	58,588	142,640	258,581	537,353

Source: Compiled from Reports of the Finance Commission, I–XIV.

Notes:

1. # Improving Outcomes includes grants for improving justice delivery, incentives for issuing UIDs, District Innovation Fund, improvement of Statistical Systems at State and District Levels, Employee and Pension Database.

2. @ Environment-related grants include forests and water sector management.

Table 7A.2 Percentage Composition of Grants Recommended by Finance Commissions

	First	Second	Third	Fourth	Fifth	Sixth	Seventh	Eighth
Deficit Grants	50.0	93.9	100.0	100.0	100.0	100.0	72.9	58.4
Performance Incentive								
Margin Money								16.0
Local Bodies								
Disaster Relief								
Education								
Improving Outcome #								
Environment related @								
Maintenance of Roads and Bridges								
Maintenance of Buildings								
Maintenance of Forests								
Health Sector								
Plan Deficit								
Special Problems	18.0							1.4
Upgradation grants							27.1	24.3
State Specific	32.0	6.1						
Heritage Conservation								
Total	100.0	100.0	100.0	100.0	100.0	100.0	100.0	100.0

	Ninth (1)	Ninth (2)	Tenth	Eleventh	Twelfth	Thirteenth	Fourteenth
Deficit Grants	52.4	33.1	37.4	60.4	39.9	20.0	36.3
Performance Incentive						0.6	
Margin Money	9.1						
Local Bodies			26.5	17.1	17.5	33.8	53.5
Disaster Relief		16.6	23.3	14.1	11.2	10.2	10.3
Education					7.1	9.3	
Improving Outcome #						3.7	
Environment related @						3.9	
Maintenance of Roads and Bridges					10.5	7.7	
Maintenance of Buildings					3.5		
Maintenance of Forests					0.7		
Health Sector					4.1		
Plan Deficit		49.6					
Special Problems	29.4	0.7	6.1	1.5			
Upgradation grants	9.2		6.7	7.0			
State Specific					5.0	10.8	
Heritage Conservation					0.4		
Total	100.0	100.0	100.0	100.0	100.0	100.0	100.0

Source: Compiled from Reports of the Finance Commission, I–XIV.

Notes:

1. Because of the rounding off, the total may not exactly add up to 100.

2. # Improving Outcomes includes grants for improving justice delivery, incentives for issuing UIDs, District Innovation Fund, improvement of Statistical Systems at State and District Levels, Employee and Pension Database.

3. @ Environment-related grants include forests and water sector management.

8

THE DETAIL MATTERS

FINANCE COMMISSIONS ARE A CRITICAL element of Union–State relations. Their awards are intensely analysed and debated, but invariably accepted. The awards require assumptions, judgments, and forecasts. In particular, the awards are based on forecasts of the needs of the Union and States. These needs are assessed with reference to inputs received from the Union and States, and adjusted for comparability and consistency. Naturally, recommendations are based on the forecasts. Forecasting is itself a complex exercise and the devil is in the detail. Of particular significance is the material received from the Union and the State Governments. While they are, no doubt, governed by common accounting standards, the reliability and timeliness varies. The Union and States are tempted to dress up data to suit the occasion, and the Finance Commission has to go through reams of material to separate the wheat from the chaff. This is a detailed and cumbersome exercise which affects the credibility of its work.

EVOLUTION OF THE CRITERIA FOR ASSESSMENT

It is by now an established practice for all Finance Commissions to obtain forecasts of revenue and expenditure on revenue accounts of the Union and each State for their award periods. The First Finance Commission laid out the principles for assessing the needs of the States, while the Seventh Finance Commission initiated a formal reassessment of the estimates furnished by the Union. The reassessments beginning with the Ninth Finance Commission incorporated assumptions about macroeconomic prospects within which fiscal forecasts had to be made.

The First Finance Commission set out its own approach to make adjustments for the purpose of comparability between the Central and State revenues. The Commission (1952) observed:

> As budgetary needs are an important criterion for determining the eligibility of a State for grants-in-aid as well as the assessment of the amount of the grants-in-aid, the budget has necessarily to be the starting point of an examination of fiscal need. In using the budget as a basis for this purpose, several adjustments are, however, necessary in the State budgets. These adjustments should, in the first place, reduce all the budgets to a comparable basis. Adjustments are called for in respect of any abnormal or unusual and non-recurrent items of expenditure which may vitiate comparisons unless these are excluded.

Besides such adjustments, the First Finance Commission observed that allowances for certain other factors such as tax effort, economy of expenditure, etc., had to be made for the purpose of arriving at what might broadly be termed as normal budget. The budget referred to by the First Commission was the one available to it, which was normally the budget of the year preceding the first year of its award period. This came to be known as the base year in the periods covered by the first three Commissions.

The sound principles laid down by the First Commission for assessing the revenue and expenditure of States were followed by all the successor Finance Commissions, with a few modifications. The report of the First Finance Commission refers to the memoranda and other material received from the States. Though the first to the sixth Commissions received forecasts of revenue and expenditure from the States, the Commissions did not give detailed accounts of their reassessment. The practice of obtaining forecasts from the Union and explicitly reassessing them started from the seventh Commission onwards.

In the ToR of the first three Finance Commissions, there was no mention with regard to the assessment of the resources of the Union or the States. The ToR of the Fourth Finance Commission specifically mandated the Commission to take into account the revenue resources of States for five years ending with the financial year 1970–1 on the basis of the levels of taxation likely to be reached in the financial year 1965–6. This was required for recommendations with regard to grants-in-aid to States which were in need of assistance under Article 275. From the fourth Commission onwards, a base year was specified in the ToR of all Commissions with the exception of the recently constituted fifteenth Commission.

It was during the Seventh Finance Commission that, for the first time, the ToR mandated it to take into account the resources of the Central Government and the demands thereon on account of expenditure on civil administration, defence, and border security, debt servicing, and other committed expenditure or liabilities. However, no base year had been prescribed for assessing the revenues.

It was not until the eighth Commission that a separate chapter on the reassessment of the forecast of the Centre started appearing in the reports of the Finance Commissions. This position with regard to the assessment of the Centre's fiscal position continued till the Eleventh Finance Commission. In the case of the Twelfth Finance Commission, there was a specific reference to the base year for assessing the resources of the Central Government. It was asked to take into account the resources of the Central Government for five years commencing on 1 April 2005, on the basis of the levels of taxation and non-tax revenues likely to be reached at the end of 2003–4. This position continued till the fourteenth Commission.

The Fifteenth Finance Commission has been mandated to take into consideration the resources of the Central Government and the State Governments for the five years commencing on 1 April 2020 on the basis of the levels of tax and the non-tax revenues likely to be reached by 2024–5, the terminal year of its award period. In addition, the Commission has been asked to take into account the potential to raise tax and non-tax revenues and fiscal capacity. Thus, there has been a reversal of the definition of base year. Instead of the year immediately preceding the first year of the award period, the base period has been shifted to the terminal year of the award period.

To bring more rigour to the reassessment of the forecasts, the sixth Commission had adjusted the revenue receipts of the base year based on the preliminary accounts of the year preceding the base year (1972–3) and based its assessment of expenditure on the actuals of 1971–2. Other succeeding Commissions made adjustments to the base year figures to arrive at a realistic assessment of the forecast of revenues and expenditure. Further refining the process, the fourteenth Commission took into account the fiscal data of States for the period 2004–5 to 2012–13, the revised estimates for 2013–14, and the budget estimates for 2014–15 for arriving at its forecast of States' revenue and expenditure for the period 2015–16 to 2019–20 after suitable adjustments.

There were other refinements in the methodology used for arriving at the forecasts for the award periods. The Sixth Finance Commission felt that fixing high growth rates based solely on the performance of recent years would amount to penalizing the States for such efficiency. The Commission felt that broad considerations of the relative economic position of States, efficiency in collection of taxes, and past growth of taxes after elimination of the distortions caused by the rise in prices should be taken into account. Broadly, the Finance Commissions discounted unusual and one-off items of revenue and expenditures in their reassessments. The Eighth Finance Commission assumed price stability and a 5 per cent annual increase in income to arrive at the growth rates of income tax and corporation tax during its award period.

Recent Finance Commissions, including the Fourteenth, tried to make the State finances data comparable by making certain adjustments by deducting non-comparable sector receipts (and expenditures). For example, receipts from power, transport, and dairy were removed from the data series (the same was done for expenditure under these heads). The Thirteenth Finance Commission had also adjusted own tax revenue data by deducting VAT compensation.

ASSUMPTIONS

The Ninth Finance Commission, for the first time, made clear macroeconomic assumptions. It adopted the GDP growth of 6 per cent as had been forecast in the Eighth Five-Year Plan and allowed for a price rise of 5 per cent per annum. The Commission felt that revenues of the Union should be made to grow at a rate faster than the GDP growth rate and postulated an increase in the tax revenues of the Centre at 12.8 per cent per annum and that of the States as a whole at 11.5 per cent per annum in nominal terms. The Commission regressed the revenue from each major State tax on relevant tax bases or their proxies to determine the regression average effective rates. By applying these averages on actual base of each State, taxable capacity was derived. The taxable capacity estimated for the initial year was applied to the base year and then for the period of the forecast. The Tenth Finance Commission worked out buoyancy-based growth rates for different taxes. The Eleventh Finance Commission assumed a nominal GDP growth of 7 to 7.5 per cent per annum and inflation in the range of 5 to 5.5 per cent of GDP, and derived the growth rates of Central revenues based on past buoyancies. For estimating the State tax revenues, the Commission used trend growth rates and applied them to the actuals of 1998–9. After deriving the base year figures, the States were divided into two groups, general category and special category. Where the average tax ratio in a given State fell short of the group average, the Commission made upward adjustments to reduce the gap.

The Twelfth Finance Commission assumed a nominal GDP growth at 12 per cent per annum. The buoyancy of each Central tax had been worked out on the basis of growth rates from 1999–2000 to 2003–4 and these had been used for the forecast period. The Commission explicitly assumed State-specific nominal GSDP growth rates for the first time. For realizing an increase in the State tax–GSDP ratio, prescriptive buoyancy levels were assigned to individual States. The Thirteenth Finance Commission took into account the exogenous shocks faced by the economy in the year 2007–8, necessitating significant incremental counter-recessionary public expenditure. Keeping in view the possibility of another setback in the global financial system, the Commission did not assume a constant GDP growth over its award period. It adopted a nominal growth rate of 12.5 per cent in 2010–11, 13 per cent in 2011–12, and 13.5 per cent for 2012–13 to 2014–15.

As was the case with the previous Commissions, the thirteenth Commission, too, adopted a two-step approach comprising adjustments to the base year figures and projections for the award period. Though the buoyancy of Union taxes based on the trend for the period 1999–2000 to 2007–8 worked out to 1.43, it moderated the buoyancy to 1.33 during the award period, considering the fact that the period 2004–8 witnessed a significant growth in the direct and service tax bases. Using the comparable estimates of GSDP from 1999–2000 to 2006–7, the Commission derived the GSDP estimates for 2007–8 to 2009–10 sectorally for each State. Following this, a target rate of incremental growth was fixed for each State depending on the projected growth rate for the Eleventh Five-Year Plan. Growth rates, consistent with the GDP growth projected for the award period, were fixed for each year to reach the targeted growth rate by the terminal year.

The approach followed by the Fourteenth Finance Commission to arrive at the base year figures and to make projections for revenue and expenditure was similar to that of the previous Commissions. The Commission assumed a nominal GDP growth of 13.5 per cent for the assessment period and assessed the tax revenues of the Union based on tax-specific buoyancies from 2001–2 to 2012–13. It made a downward adjustment for corporation and service taxes, as the revenue from these taxes had grown at 19.08 per cent and 39.28 per cent respectively, between 2001–2 and 2012–13. The Commission arrived at the base-year estimates of GSDP for all States based on the trend growth rates of comparable GSDP for the period 2004–5 to 2012–13 to project rates for the award period. The Commission adopted a tax buoyancy of 1.05 for those States with above average tax–GSDP ratio of 8.26 and a higher buoyancy of 1.5 for those States with below average tax–GSDP ratio.

Starting from the ninth Commission, a normative approach was followed in assessing non-tax revenues and revenue expenditure more explicitly. Some of the previous Commissions too used norms to assess returns from irrigation, transport, and public enterprises. For assessing receipts from irrigation projections, while some Commissions assumed returns to be at least equivalent to operations and maintenance expenditure, others assumed a positive rate of return. Going by past trends, growth in revenue expenditure was assumed in the forecasts. In the case of the Union, while a few Commissions allowed an annual increase in the subsidies for food, fertilizer, and other commodities, other Commissions moderated and even reduced the rates of growth of these subsidies. Maintenance expenditure on roads, buildings, etc., were assessed based on norms.

FORECASTS

The Finance Commissions, without exception, attempted to make their forecasts as realistic as possible. Forecasting the future for an emerging economy like India, which is becoming globalized and is hence not immune to global developments, is not an easy task. There are bound to be differences between the forecasts and the actual outcomes. This prompted the Tenth Finance Commission (1994) to observe that '[i]f in actual practice, the picture that emerges turns to be worse than what is being projected, even our conservative assessment of what can realistically be done would have been proved wrong. It is a perpetual battle between hope and experience'.

What makes the job of a Finance Commission more difficult is the tendency on the part of both the Centre and the States to understate their revenue and overstate their expenditure commitments. The States as a whole projected their pre-devolution revenue deficit at Rs 59.39 lakh crore for the period 2015–20, which was 56 per cent of the gross tax revenue of the Centre for the same period as reassessed by the Fourteenth Finance Commission (Rs 106.04 lakh crore). If the Commission had gone by the forecast of the States, 56 per cent of the gross tax revenue of the Centre would have gone as tax devolution and revenue deficit grants. In the case of the Eighth Finance Commission, all the States, with the exception of Haryana, projected pre-devolution deficits in their non-Plan revenue accounts.

The reassessment of revenues and expenditure and their accuracy is important, as the needs of the States and the Centre are based on this. This issue is of particular importance to the States as the grants to meet the non-Plan/revenue deficits are based on the reassessment done by the Finance Commission. In addition, the States had been nursing a feeling that the Finance Commission adopted more stringent norms while assessing their revenues and expenditure vis-à-vis those of the Centre. These apprehensions were also due to the fact that the forecasts of the States were reassessed in greater detail as compared with those of the Union and due to the absence of any reference to the assessment of revenues and expenditure of the Centre until the seventh Commission.

The practice of devoting a separate chapter to the reassessment of the forecasts of the States and presenting the forecasts and reassessments started only from the sixth Commission, while that for the forecasts and reassessments of the Centre started from the seventh Commission.

Over the years, the reassessment of the Centre's forecast had become almost as elaborate as that of the States. But the difference in the presentation of the reassessments in the annexes of the Reports of the Finance Commissions still persists. While in the case of States, the forecasts by the States and reassessments by the Commissions are presented, in respect of the Centre, only the reassessments are presented in most cases.

Overall, the apprehensions of States were allayed by most Finance Commissions. The ninth Commission (1989) observed that '[t]he normative approach should be applied as much to the assessment of centre's receipts and expenditure as to that of states' receipts and expenditures. Whatever norms are chosen must be applied with the same degree of rigidity in both cases. But the norms themselves cannot be uniform or identical.'

OUTCOMES

The underlying macroeconomic assumptions are critical for realistic forecasting. They are not available in all the Reports, though more recently the relevant technical papers are published on the Finance Commission website. Broadly speaking, the macro assumptions about normal growth rate in GDP and tax-revenue elasticities were disturbed by shocks such as droughts, oil price hikes, global developments, or political uncertainties. They had an impact on the outcomes relative to reassessments made by the Finance Commission. Reassessments were, in fact, based on forecasts presented to the Commission by the Union and States.

In the reports of the Finance Commission, there is no uniformity in the presentation of forecasts submitted by the Centre and the States. While some reports detailed the original forecasts submitted, most have only presented the forecasts based on the Commission's reassessment.

It is difficult to gauge whether reassessment by the Finance Commission was closer to the outcomes in all the cases. In any case, part of reassessment is for comparability, and hence the complexity in analysis. However, it is possible to compare the reassessments made by the Finance Commission with the actual outcomes with regard to the Centre's gross tax revenue; tax devolutions to States as recommended; Centre's non-Plan expenditure; tax revenues of the States; and the non-Plan revenue deficits of the States. The positive and negative deviation of outcomes as a percentage of reassessments would capture the direction and magnitudes over a period.

From the projections made by the five Finance Commissions starting from the ninth (second report) to the thirteenth, the actuals in four out of five cases are lower than the projections of gross tax revenues of the Centre (see Table 8.1). It is only in the case of the Twelfth Finance Commission that the actuals are higher than the projected, primarily because during the period covered by it (2005–10), the growth of the economy was buoyant and there was significant growth in revenue from income tax because of the introduction of the Tax Information Network. With the increase in the base of service tax, there was also an increase in its buoyancy.

Table 8.1   Gross Tax Revenue of the Centre

(Rs in Crore)

	Finance Commission	Finance Commission Projection	Actual	Variation (Actual Over Projection)	Percentage Variation
1	Ninth-1 (1989–90)	49,000	51,636	2,636	5.4
2	Ninth-2 (1990–5)	370,014	367,613	–2,401	–0.6
3	Tenth (1995–2000)	707,411	694,756	–12,655	–1.8
4	Eleventh (2000–5)	1,378,207	1,151,235	–226,972	–16.5
5	Twelfth (2005–10)	2,300,411	2,662,637	362,226	15.7
6	Thirteenth (2010–15)	5,318,246	5,102,103	–216,143	–4.1

Source: Compiled from Reports of the Finance Commission and Union Budgets of various years.

TAX DEVOLUTION

The tax devolution to States broadly reflects the outcomes in gross tax revenue of the Centre (see Table 8.2). However, this was not what happened in the case of actual tax devolutions during the award period of the ninth Commission (1990–95). Though the gross tax revenue fell short of the projections, tax devolution to States was higher than the assessment. This could be due to the fact that whereas tax devolution was related to only two Central taxes, gross tax revenue was the total revenue derived from all taxes. In fact, during the period covered by the ninth Commission, revenue from income tax was very buoyant. Since the States' share in income tax was much higher than that in Union excise duties, actual tax devolution to States exceeded the projections made by the Finance Commission. When all the Union

Table 8.2 Tax Devolution

(Rs in Crore)

Finance Commission	Special-Category States				General-Category States			
	Finance Commission Projection	Actual	Variation (Actual Over Projection)	Percentage Variation	Finance Commission Projection	Actual	Variation (Actual Over Projection)	Percentage Variation
1 Eighth (1984–9)	3,809	4,424	615	16.1	31,873	37,478	5,605	17.6
2 Ninth-1 (1989–90)	1,161	1,344	183	15.8	10,624	11,755	1,131	10.6
3 Ninth-2 (1990–5)	10,781	11,435	654	6.1	77,101	87,517	10,416	13.5
4 Tenth (1995–2000)	27,781	23,852	–3,929	–14.1	178,562	164,198	–14,364	–8.0
5 Eleventh (2000–5)	27,467	23,417	–4,050	–14.7	348,851	281,822	–67,029	–19.2
6 Twelfth (2005–10)	49,622	55,901	6,279	12.7	563,490	635,886	72,396	12.8
7 Thirteenth (2010–15)	136,924	133,915	–3,009	–2.2	1,311,173	1,282,074	–29,099	–2.2

Source: Compiled from Reports of the Finance Commission and Union Budgets of various years.

taxes became shareable with the States starting from the award period of the Eleventh Finance Commission, close correspondence was noticed in the trends in gross tax revenue and tax devolution.

NON-PLAN EXPENDITURE OF THE CENTRE

The Centre's non-Plan revenue expenditure projections are found to be lower than the actual expenditure incurred in three out of four award periods of Finance Commissions (see Table 8.3). The Centre's non-Plan revenue expenditure exceeded by as much as 38.6 per cent and 40.9 per cent in the periods covered by the twelfth and thirteenth Commissions respectively.

Table 8.3   Non-Plan Revenue Expenditure of the Centre

(Rs in Crore)

Finance Commission	Finance Commission Projection	Actual	Variation (Actual Over Projection)	Percentage Variation
1 Tenth (1995–2000)	656,640	762,522	105,882	16.1
2 Eleventh (2000–5)	1,364,024	1,315,169	–48,855	–3.6
3 Twelfth (2005–10)	1,687,400	2,337,904	650,504	38.6
4 Thirteenth (2010–15)	3,252,026	4,581,280	1,329,254	40.9

Sources: Compiled from Reports of the Finance Commission and Union Budgets of various years.

STATES' OWN TAX REVENUE

The actual realization of own tax revenue of general-category States had been higher than the projections, except in the period covered by the Eleventh Finance Commission (see Table 8.4). This clearly indicates that norms adopted by the Finance Commissions in assessing the tax revenues of the States had not been unrealistic and that there had been no bias in favour of the Centre. While the projections of the Centre's revenue had been higher than the realization in the case

Table 8.4 Own Tax Revenue

(Rs in Crore)

Finance Commission	Special-Category States				General-Category States			
	Finance Commission Projection	Actual	Variation (Actual Over Projection)	Percentage Variation	Finance Commission Projections	Actual	Variation (Actual Over Projection)	Percentage Variation
1 Eighth (1984–9)	1,463	2,525	1,062	72.6	61,756	82,731	20,975	34.0
2 Ninth-1 (1989–90)	779	701	–78	–10.0	22,729	25,295	2,566	11.3
3 Ninth-2 (1990–5)	5,287	5,510	223	4.2	164,402	200,286	35,884	21.8
4 Tenth (1995–2000)	10,689	10,247	–442	–4.1	374,789	383,429	8,640	2.3
5 Eleventh (2000–5)	20,143	27,625	7,482	37.1	824,049	682,043	–142,006	–17.2
6 Twelfth (2005–10)	58,674	61,408	2,734	4.7	1,364,828	1,374,985	10,157	0.7
7 Thirteenth (2010–15)	119,695	139,621	19,926	16.6	2,875,110	3,024,802	149,691	5.2

Source: Compiled from Reports of the Finance Commission of various years, and various issues of *Study of State Budgets*.

of four out of five Finance Commissions, the projections of States' tax revenue made by five out of six Commissions had been lower than the actual outcomes. This is indicative of even-handedness by the Finance Commission while assessing the revenue of the Centre and the States.

In the case of special-category States, the revenue growth was higher than the projections, except in the case of the tenth Commission. Most of the general-category States too registered higher growth than projected in own tax revenues. The exceptions are the States of Bihar, Haryana, Kerala, Uttar Pradesh, and West Bengal in the periods covered by the recent Finance Commissions (see Annexure 8A.1).

NON-TAX REVENUE OF STATES

While reassessing non-tax revenues of States, each Commission made its own assumptions and excluded certain items of revenue. Therefore, adjustments were required to be made in actual non-tax receipts to make them comparable. Therefore, no attempt has been made to compare the actuals with the forecasts arrived at by the Finance Commissions.

REVENUE EXPENDITURE (NON-PLAN AND PLAN)

A comparison of non-Plan revenue and total revenue expenditure as assessed by the Finance Commission with the actual expenditures presents a contrasting picture. Both the general-category States and the special-category States as a whole had run up higher expenditure on non-Plan revenue account than the expenditures as assessed by the Finance Commission (see Table 8.5).

States in both the general and special categories recorded higher non-Plan revenue expenditure as compared with the assessments based by the recent Finance Commissions (see Annexure 8A.2). A few States, like Punjab, West Bengal, and Bihar, had consistently under-performed in revenue in the periods covered by the recent Finance Commissions, resulting in revenue deficits.

Table 8.5 Non-Plan Revenue Expenditure

(Rs in Crore)

Finance Commission	Special-Category States			General-Category States		
	Finance Commission Projection	Actual	Variation (Actual Over Projection)	Finance Commission Projection	Actual	Variation (Actual Over Projection)
1 Ninth-1 (1989–90)	3,444	4,125	681	34,137	44,350	10,213
2 Tenth (1995–2000)	47,174	67,416	20,242	520,269	747,025	226,756
3 Eleventh (2000–5)	87,590	132,997	45,407	1,077,552	1,328,942	251,390
4 Twelfth (2005–10)	174,278	242,412	68,134	1,704,912	2,179,984	475,072
5 Thirteenth (2010–15)	330,081	481,501	151,420	3,161,495	4,319,387	1,157,892

Source: Compiled from Reports of the Finance Commission, various years.

Total Revenue Expenditure

(Rs in Crore)

Finance Commission	Special-Category States			General-Category States		
	Finance Commission Projection	Actual	Variation (Actual Over Projection)	Finance Commission Projection	Actual	Variation (Actual Over Projection)
1 Eighth (1984–9)	10,608	17,934	7,326	121,601	178,558	56,957
2 Ninth-2 (1990–5)	23,539	41,956	18,417	247,391	448,088	200,697

Source: Compiled from Reports of the Eighth and Ninth Finance Commissions, and issues of *State Finances: A Study of Budgets.*
Note: The Eighth and Ninth Finance Commissions assessed the entire expenditure on revenue account.

NON-PLAN REVENUE-DEFICIT GRANTS

A comparison of the revenue-deficit grants recommended by the Finance Commission with the outcomes has been attempted.

In the periods covered by the Ninth to Thirteenth Finance Commissions, aggregate non-Plan revenue deficits of those States identified by the Commissions as post devolution non-Plan revenue-deficit States far exceeded the assessment made by the Finance Commission. The excess non-Plan revenue deficit as compared with the assessments made by the Finance Commissions was in the range of 67.7 per cent to 715.4 per cent (see Table 8.6). State-wise deficits on the non-Plan revenue account are presented in Annexure 8A.3.

The broad conclusion that emerges from this analysis is that, by and large, the assessments of tax revenue made by the Finance Commission had been higher than the actual realization by the Centre, but lower than the realization by the general-category States. This could be because of a combination of global developments impacting revenue growth; lack of efforts to widen the tax base; and the higher buoyancy assumed by the Finance Commission. In fact, the

Table 8.6   Non-Plan Revenue Deficits, Projections, and Actuals

(Rs in Crore)

	Finance Commission	Finance Commission Projection	Actual	Variation (Actual Over Projection)	Percentage Variation
1	Eighth (1984–9)	2,201	−3,039	−5,240	−238.1
2	Ninth-1 (1989–90)	986	1,650	664	67.3
3	Ninth-2 (1990–5)	6,017	20,317	14,300	237.7
4	Tenth (1995–2000)	7,582	61,831	54,249	715.5
5	Eleventh (2000–5)	35,359	183,997	148,638	420.4
6	Twelfth (2005–10)	56,857	164,964	108,107	190.1
7	Thirteenth (2010–15)	51,799	139,689	87,890	169.7

Source: Compiled from Report of the Finance Commissions, VIII–XIII, and various issues of *State Finances: A Study of Budgets*.

Ninth Finance Commission observed that the Centre should set an example to the States and that the tax-revenue yield should rise with better efficiency in taxation policy and administration. In contrast, the expenditure incurred by the States as well as the Centre exceeded the projections of the Finance Commission by a wide margin in a few cases. This could be on account of the failure of the States and the Centre to regulate their expenditure growth and the underestimation of the expenditure liabilities by successive Finance Commissions. It is difficult, however, to pass judgment as to which of these two factors contributed more to the variation.

▼▲▼

The methodology of analysing quantitative inputs was built on the solid foundation laid by the First and Second Finance Commissions, and successive Finance Commissions worked to refine it further. The growing importance attached to this work is evident from the fact that many States are progressively using outside expertise and consultancies to assist them in preparing their memoranda to Finance Commissions. Finance Commissions have also been drawing upon expertise from several sources and making the technical documents underscoring their work available in public domain.

Finance Commissions face the dilemma of how to deal with legacy issues while assessing expenditures. First there is the question of what items of expenditures should be excluded and what should not be. Often, Commissions in the past have excluded items like Mid-Day Meals and Two-Rupee Rice Schemes, but subsequently, the Centre has considered these as national programmes. More importantly, States like Punjab, Kerala, and particularly West Bengal have gone about borrowing profusely, often violating the Constitutional provisions (borrowing from Peerless insurance) and often through their enterprises, leaving a huge interest burden. In contrast, States like Odisha have been austere, and that does not help them to gain more from the transfers.

Assessments of the Centre and States have different effects. It is difficult to punish the Centre for its poor tax effort and profligacy in spending whereas the States can be taken to task even when uniform yardsticks are adopted.

SELECT REFERENCES

1. Ministry of Finance. Various Years. Budget Documents. New Delhi: Government of India.

2. Ministry of Finance. Various Years. *Report of the Finance Commission*, I–XIV. New Delhi: Government of India.

3. RBI. *State Finances: A Study of Budgets*, Various Issues. Mumbai: RBI.

4. Srivastava, D.K. and B. Bhujanga Rao. 2000. 'Review of Trends in Fiscal Federalism in India', Madras School of Economics, Study sponsored by the Thirteenth Finance Commission.

5. Vithal, B.P.R. and M.L. Sastry. 2001. *Fiscal Federalism in India*. New Delhi: Oxford University Press.

ANNEXURE

Table 8A.1   States' Own Tax Revenue

(Rs in Crore) (*Cont'd*)

	State	Eighth		Ninth-1		Ninth-2	
		Projection	Actual	Projection	Actual	Projection	Actual
	General Category						
1	Andhra Pradesh	5,813	8,113	2,290	2,384	16,470	17,151
2	Bihar	2,589	3,291	1,100	925	6,557	7,600
3	Chhattisgarh	0	0	0	0	0	0
4	Goa	0	175	88	70	548	757
5	Gujarat	4,640	6,716	1,785	2,160	13,091	17,435
6	Haryana	2,467	2,933	779	910	6,152	7,294
7	Jharkhand	0	0	0	0	0	0
8	Karnataka	4,637	6,305	1,939	1,932	13,031	16,431
9	Kerala	2,854	4,158	1,162	1,233	8,341	10,045
10	Madhya Pradesh	3,365	4,971	1,080	1,578	8,482	11,754
11	Maharashtra	11,457	14,177	4,041	4,401	28,418	34,786
12	Odisha	1,302	1,682	458	525	2,910	3,888
13	Punjab	3,506	3,997	1,097	1,228	8,291	9,342
14	Rajasthan	2,651	3,375	810	1,073	6,500	8,757
15	Tamil Nadu	6,551	8,359	2,156	2,489	17,875	21,655
16	Telangana	0	0	0	0	0	0
17	Uttar Pradesh	5,367	8,015	2,170	2,449	16,082	19,555
18	West Bengal	4,555	6,464	1,775	1,938	11,654	13,836
	Total (I)	**61,754**	**82,731**	**22,730**	**25,295**	**164,402**	**200,286**
	Special Category						
19	Arunachal Pradesh	0	6	2	2	13	21
20	Assam	642	1,197	367	333	2,516	2,695
21	Himachal Pradesh	274	448	139	142	1,026	1,131
22	Jammu & Kashmir	388	562	168	133	1,140	1,004
23	Manipur	29	46	14	13	78	89
24	Meghalaya	36	93	26	31	172	227
25	Mizoram	0	8	6	3	16	21
26	Nagaland	40	63	24	12	128	90
27	Sikkim	23	40	16	11	78	62
28	Tripura	31	62	16	21	120	170
29	Uttarakhand	0	0	0	0	0	0
	Total (II)	**1,463**	**2,525**	**778**	**701**	**5,287**	**5,510**
	All States	**63,217**	**85,256**	**23,508**	**25,996**	**169,689**	**205,796**

Source: Compiled from *Report of the Finance Commission*, VIII–XIII, and Union Budget documents of various years.

Tenth		Eleventh		Twelfth		Thirteenth	
Projection	Actual	Projection	Actual	Projection	Actual	Projection	Actual
27,479	33,086	80,308	65,794	127,147	140,461	306,347	265,040
13,366	12,924	24,520	14,845	32,648	26,943	53,526	79,446
0	0	0	10,886	22,419	28,433	57,392	62,802
1,263	1,756	3,516	3,253	7,404	7,202	15,004	15,109
33,352	33,758	76,332	51,945	96,785	106,345	243,284	252,200
14,430	13,319	31,621	28,622	57,029	56,499	118,023	113,950
0	0	0	9,034	19,480	20,211	48,871	40,875
34,508	32,141	65,752	57,978	121,505	126,144	274,057	271,487
20,259	21,627	44,436	36,149	73,975	69,005	144,490	144,744
22,241	23,090	48,824	31,074	60,192	62,493	111,292	149,094
64,527	67,835	144,787	119,591	224,168	232,304	472,621	489,815
8,021	7,082	13,407	15,002	28,355	34,901	69,182	76,390
17,046	15,641	32,401	28,517	54,902	51,095	116,027	107,906
17,568	17,936	40,351	32,885	64,675	66,121	128,020	148,788
36,916	44,365	92,157	74,936	141,812	150,947	300,714	330,929
0	0	0	0	0	0	0	29,288
38,396	36,084	75,913	63,371	130,537	129,352	238,771	292,822
25,417	22,785	49,724	38,161	101,796	66,528	177,491	154,118
374,789	383,429	824,049	682,043	1,364,829	1,374,984	2,875,112	3,024,803

52	52	142	184	702	548	996	1,746
5,072	4,559	8,260	9,697	20,334	19,212	33,931	40,263
2,111	2,422	5,263	4,768	9,667	9,929	20,812	23,438
2,138	1,956	3,817	5,134	10,878	11,659	24,433	26,667
161	149	378	316	963	730	1,460	1,958
471	408	797	786	1,583	1,691	3,254	4,005
45	41	114	135	450	402	855	1,028
158	164	344	317	1,006	693	1,273	1,593
121	130	240	477	798	926	1,290	2,061
360	366	789	929	2,556	1,978	3,699	4,733
0	0	0	4,882	9,736	13,641	27,690	32,129
10,689	10,247	20,144	27,625	58,673	61,409	119,693	139,621
385,478	393,676	844,193	709,668	1,423,502	1,436,393	2,994,805	3,164,424

Table 8A.2 Non-Plan Revenue Expenditure of States

(Rs in Crore)

State	Ninth-1		Tenth		Eleventh		Twelfth		Thirteenth	
	Projection	Actual	Projection	Actual	Projection	Actual	Projection	Actual	Projection	Actual
I. General Category										
1 Andhra Pradesh	3,319	3,887	46,047	62,632	84,380	106,187	157,901	191,304	290,837	384,351
2 Bihar	2,626	3,277	40,226	45,422	72,292	62,800	84,642	96,895	152,625	189,520
3 Chhattisgarh	0	0	0	0	0	20,019	31,283	37,727	60,771	76,196
4 Goa	148	188	1,975	4,924	4,399	8,328	7,379	12,236	14,308	23,773
5 Gujarat	2,281	3,111	35,289	55,682	72,221	97,915	103,499	134,871	198,350	251,458
6 Haryana	925	1,335	11,821	29,009	28,851	40,889	47,430	75,044	99,564	142,990
7 Jharkhand	0	0	0	0	0	19,690	32,237	43,991	71,142	78,091
8 Karnataka	2,146	2,835	33,721	45,038	65,950	80,975	106,426	144,010	220,118	272,479
9 Kerala	1,730	1,980	25,636	33,547	53,979	58,696	94,024	108,239	172,395	232,739
10 Madhya Pradesh	2,518	2,860	36,983	50,656	75,481	66,006	80,878	100,008	155,156	219,699
11 Maharashtra	3,867	6,498	59,405	99,190	128,052	192,555	218,212	296,112	422,718	580,208
12 Odisha	1,341	1,340	19,779	22,924	37,986	43,148	65,257	73,730	110,669	136,430
13 Punjab	1,357	1,762	20,519	35,889	40,186	68,695	74,891	105,838	135,183	178,576
14 Rajasthan	1,702	2,216	26,982	43,576	67,338	75,438	98,359	125,886	163,917	251,828
15 Tamil Nadu	2,861	3,726	46,603	66,238	103,884	106,895	146,815	182,270	271,145	376,548
16 Telangana	0	0	0	0	0	0	0	0	0	36,610

(Cont'd)

Table 8A.2 (Cont'd)

State	Ninth-1		Tenth		Eleventh		Twelfth		Thirteenth	
	Projection	Actual	Projection	Actual	Projection	Actual	Projection	Actual	Projection	Actual
17 Uttar Pradesh	4,198	6,125	74,512	97,046	153,279	171,383	206,115	272,002	370,799	567,005
18 West Bengal	3,118	3,210	40,771	55,252	89,274	109,323	149,564	179,821	251,798	320,886
Total (I)	34,137	44,350	520,269	747,025	1,077,552	1,328,942	1,704,912	2,179,984	3,161,495	4,319,387
II. Special Category										
19 Arunachal Pradesh	169	184	1,982	2,133	2,828	3,567	4,359	7,630	10,159	16,678
20 Assam	1,159	1,245	15,132	16,490	23,670	31,522	45,399	57,059	89,309	114,205
21 Himachal Pradesh	442	572	6,911	9,789	14,401	19,831	25,615	37,193	47,247	69,435
22 Jammu & Kashmir	701	861	9,528	17,177	23,309	29,443	32,515	55,403	62,775	114,227
23 Manipur	167	236	2,285	3,315	3,801	6,037	7,825	9,871	14,887	20,740
24 Meghalaya	154	190	2,434	2,744	4,187	4,766	6,663	7,870	13,564	16,470
25 Mizoram	178	163	1,879	2,461	2,873	4,237	5,205	6,801	9,443	13,923
26 Nagaland	199	309	2,860	3,788	4,919	6,457	8,409	10,500	14,459	22,358
27 Sikkim	60	75	880	5,610	2,101	6,134	2,869	8,895	6,095	11,912
28 Tripura	215	290	3,283	3,909	5,501	8,098	11,371	12,081	16,349	21,237
29 Uttarakhand	0	0	0	0	0	12,905	24,048	29,109	45,794	60,316
Total (II)	3,444	4,125	47,174	67,416	87,590	132,997	174,278	242,412	330,081	481,501
All States	37,581	48,475	567,443	814,441	1,165,142	1,461,939	1,879,190	2,422,396	3,491,576	4,800,888

Source: Compiled from Report of the Finance Commission, IX–XIII, and *State Finances: A Study of Budgets*, various years.

Table 8A.3   Post-Devolution Non-Plan Revenue Deficits of States

	State	Eighth		Ninth–1		Ninth–2	
		Projection	Actual	Projection	Actual	Projection	Actual
	General Category						
1	Andhra Pradesh						
2	Bihar						
3	Chhattisgarh						
4	Goa			17	31	167	–57
5	Gujarat						
6	Haryana						
7	Jharkhand						
8	Karnataka						
9	Kerala						
10	Madhya Pradesh						
11	Maharashtra						
12	Odisha	208	132	57	43	528	808
13	Punjab						
14	Rajasthan	43	490	39	30	486	1,522
15	Tamil Nadu						
16	Telangana						
17	Uttar Pradesh					349	7,600
18	West Bengal	444	425				
	Total (I)	**695**	**1,047**	**113**	**104**	**1,530**	**9,873**
	Special Category						
19	Arunachal Pradesh			70	95	303	299
20	Assam	274	–866	140	246	560	1,815
21	Himachal Pradesh	223	–568	99	193	523	1,344
22	Jammu & Kashmir	329	–1,191	192	384	1,083	3,472
23	Manipur	147	–336	67	120	372	564
24	Meghalaya	119	–178	48	74	256	557
25	Mizoram			81	65	380	333

(Rs in Crore)

Tenth		Eleventh		Twelfth		Thirteenth	
Projection	Actual	Projection	Actual	Projection	Actual	Projection	Actual
686	4,974						
333	6,049						
77	101						
772	2,625						
				470	14,282		
372	5,057	674	8,001	488	−10,075		
		284	16,587	3,133	20,548		
33	8,525	1,245	16,879				
982	20,994	1,027	38,970				
		3,246	41,696	3,045	53,274		
3,255	**48,325**	**6,476**	**122,133**	**7,136**	**78,029**		
308	590	1,228	2,229	1,358	2,647	2,516	8,221
712	3,632	111	8,119	306	4,966		
1,184	2,480	4,549	11,620	10,202	16,260	7,889	26,013
		11,211	18,484	12,353	30,766	15,936	58,405
351	1,516	1,745	4,455	4,392	5,720	6,057	11,107
316	748	1,572	2,445	1,797	2,580	2,811	4,552
331	1,046	1,676	3,317	2,978	4,075	3,991	7,958

(Cont'd)

Table 8A.3   (*Cont'd*)

Sl. No.	State	Eighth		Ninth–1		Ninth–2	
		Projection	Actual	Projection	Actual	Projection	Actual
	Special Category						
26	Nagaland	191	–575	80	198	459	1,084
27	Sikkim	36	–69	14	21	85	218
28	Tripura	187	–303	82	150	466	758
29	Uttarakhand						
	Total (II)	**1,506**	**–4,086**	**873**	**1,546**	**4,487**	**10,444**
	All States	**2,201**	**–3,039**	**986**	**1,650**	**6,017**	**20,317**

Source: Compiled from Report of the Finance Commission, IX–XIII, and *State Finances: A Study of Budgets*, various years.

Note: For the States for which the Finance Commissions had not assessed any post-devolution non-Plan revenue deficits, the relevant columns have been left blank.

Tenth		Eleventh		Twelfth		Thirteenth	
Projection	Actual	Projection	Actual	Projection	Actual	Projection	Actual
530	1,572	3,536	5,144	5,537	7,371	8,146	15,180
106	579	841	942	189	414		
489	1,343	2,414	5,109	5,494	6,591	4,453	8,253
				5,115	5,545		
4,327	13,506	28,883	61,864	49,721	86,935	51,799	139,689
7,582	61,831	35,359	183,997	56,857	164,964	51,799	139,689

9

LOCAL SELF-GOVERNMENTS
AND FINANCE COMMISSIONS

THE CONCEPT OF LOCAL SELF-GOVERNMENTS in India arguably goes back to around 600 BCE. During this period, the territory north of the river Ganga comprising modern Bihar and eastern Uttar Pradesh was under the governance of small republics called *Janapadas*. The affairs of the State were conducted in Janapadas by an assembly consisting of local chieftains. In the Chola kingdom of south India, village councils or Panchayats played an important role in administration, arbitration of disputes, and management of social affairs. The word 'panchayat' denotes an assembly of people presided over by five members. Some Panchayats were caste based and their decisions were binding on the members of the community. These ancient institutions were not necessarily territorial and rarely democratic, but successive rulers allowed them to continue. Under British rule, however, the local bodies and their dispute settlement mechanisms were replaced with British laws and courts of justice.

The origin of the present structure of local bodies can be traced to 1687, when the East India Company, acting on the authority delegated to it by King James II of Great Britain, established a Municipal

Corporation in Madras, composed of British and Indian members for the purpose of local taxation. Similar corporations were set up in Bombay and Calcutta in 1726. But it was only in 1793 that these corporations were constituted on a statutory basis by a Charter Act of that year. The Act empowered the Governor General to appoint Justices of the Peace for the three corporations of Madras, Bombay, and Calcutta, with powers to levy taxes on houses and lands to meet the cost of scavenging, maintaining law and order, and upkeep of roads.

The creation of municipalities in small towns began with the Bengal Act of 1843, followed by a new Act in 1850, which was applicable to all of British India. Along with the formation of municipalities, the development of local institutions in rural areas also began taking place with the establishment of Local Funds in 1865.

Local self-governments took shape following Lord Mayo's Resolution of 1870, introducing elected representation to the municipalities and handing over to Provincial Governments certain subjects like education, medical services, and roads. The Provincial Governments were asked to review provincial, local, and municipal accounts and apply the same principles to local bodies as those made applicable to the Provinces. The functions assigned to rural local bodies were more or less the same as those assigned to municipalities. The main source of income was cess on land, which was collected by a Government agency, but proceeds were adjusted to Local Funds.

The Royal Commission on Decentralisation reviewed the subject of local self-government in 1907–8. The Commission recommended that the functions of Panchayats should be largely determined by local circumstances and that they should receive 25 per cent of the land cess and grants for specific purposes. It also suggested that Municipalities should have full powers with regard to the functions assigned to them. The Commission did not recommend any subvention from the Government but suggested that they should receive assistance for executing large projects. It also proposed that Municipalities be vested with full powers to impose or alter taxation within the limits of municipal laws, a liberty which the Municipalities did not have till then.

The next major development in the evolution of local bodies was the Montagu-Chelmsford Report on Indian Constitutional Reforms, 1918.

The report suggested that the evolution of rural local bodies should depend on local conditions and the functions and powers allocated to them should vary accordingly. Municipalities could have the liberty to impose or alter taxes. This was followed by the Government of India Act, 1919, which resulted in the division of subjects into Central and Provincial. Provincial subjects were subdivided into 'Transferred' and 'Reserved'. Under this division, local governments became a Transferred subject, and the taxes which could be imposed by local bodies were separated from those imposed for Provincial purposes.

The next development was the enactment of the Government of India Act, 1935, following the report of the Indian Statutory Commission, 1930 (better known as the Simon Commission). Local self-government was not a part of the Constitution Act of 1935, as this subject was assigned to the Provinces and it was for them to make laws relating to local bodies and their constitution. The Legislative Lists appended to the Act provided that Provincial Governments should make laws regarding local governments.

With this, almost every Province passed legislations to widen the powers and functions of local bodies. However, while taxes levied by the local bodies remained more or less the same even after the Government of India Act, 1935 came into force, their functions were widened. Hence, the finances of local bodies came under stress. The 1935 Act introduced a ceiling on the levy of profession tax at Rs 50 per annum per assessee. Any fresh proposal for taxation by local bodies continued to be subject to the prior approval of Provincial Governments. Consequently, local bodies came to depend on grants-in-aid, which resulted in greater scrutiny of income and expenditure by Provincial Governments.

The form of local self-government that was in place by the time of Independence was essentially a legacy of British rule. It was first introduced in regard to Municipalities, and later to rural local bodies, at the discretion of Provincial Governments. It is interesting that substantive provisions relating to taxation, discretion in expenditure, and dependence on transferred funds that prevailed at the time of Independence remain even now.

LOCAL SELF-GOVERNMENTS AND THE CONSTITUTION

Presenting the draft Constitution to the Constituent Assembly, B.R. Ambedkar (Constituent Assembly of India Debates (Proceedings) 1948) had stated:

> Another criticism against the Draft Constitution is that no part of it represents the ancient polity of India. It is said that the new Constitution should have been drafted on the ancient Hindu model of a State and that instead of incorporating Western theories the new Constitution should have been raised and built upon village Panchayats and District Panchayats. There are others who have taken a more extreme view. They do not want any Central or Provincial Governments. They just want India to contain so many village Governments. The love of the intellectual Indians for the village community is of course infinite if not pathetic. It is largely due to the fulsome praise bestowed upon it by Metcalfe who described them as little republics having nearly everything that they want within themselves, and almost independent of any foreign relations.... I hold that these village republics have been the ruination of India. I am therefore surprised that those who condemn provincialism and communalism should come forward as champions of the village. What is the village but a sink of localism, a den of ignorance, narrow-mindedness and communalism? I am glad that the Draft Constitution has discarded the village and adopted the individual as its unit.

Ambedkar was apprehensive that in the hierarchical society of India, with its highly skewed nature of asset and power distribution, vesting more powers at the village level would only perpetuate exploitation of the dispossessed.

This should be viewed in light of Gandhiji's beliefs. Writing in the 26 July 1942 issue of *Harijan*, Mahatma Gandhi had said:

> My idea of village swaraj is that it is a complete republic, independent of its neighbours for its vital wants, and yet independent for many others in which dependence is a necessity.... The panchayat of five persons annually elected by the adult villagers, male and female, possessing minimum prescribed qualifications will conduct the government of the village. These will have the authority and jurisdiction required. Since there will be no system of punishments in the accepted sense, this Panchayat will be the legislature, judiciary, and executive combined to operate for its year in office.

It is no surprise then that K. Santhanam and many others participating in the debate disagreed with the stand taken by Ambedkar. Monomohan Das supported Ambedkar's statement on the grounds that there was nothing in the draft Constitution which would prevent the Provinces from empowering the Panchayats if it was felt that the Panchayat system would benefit the country.

As a compromise, K. Santhanam moved an amendment to the draft dealing with the Directive Principles of State Policy: 'The State shall take steps to organize village panchayats and endow them with such powers and authority as may be necessary to enable them to function as units of self-government (Constituent Assembly of India Debates (Proceedings) 1948).' This was approved by the Constituent Assembly and included in the Constitution. Thus, the issue of the status of rural local bodies was resolved by leaving it open-ended.

In the debates of the Constituent Assembly, there was hardly any reference to urban local bodies. But the general view was that local government institutions would be the creatures of State Legislatures and that there was nothing preventing the States from empowering them. Local self-government, as a system, was to be considered entirely at the discretion of States in the Union. The Directive Principles, which are in the nature of exhortation to both Union and States equally, suggest the promotion of Panchayats. Obviously, they are not synonymous with local self-government, though they are a part of self-government.

COMMUNITY DEVELOPMENT TRIGGERS PANCHAYATI RAJ

The establishment of the Planning Commission in 1950 and the adoption of development planning as a countrywide goal led to several programmes. Local self-governments across the country had to adopt relevant national policies, which included local self-governing institutions.

The Community Development Programme was launched in 1952 as an important component of national planning. The main thrust of the programme was transformation of village life through community participation. Under the programme, 100 to 150 villages constituted a Community Development Block. The Second Five-Year Plan recommended organic linkage of Panchayats with organizations at higher levels. To operationalize this, the Balwant Rai Mehta Committee was appointed in 1957. The Committee recommended that Community Development Blocks be designed as democratic units with an elected Panchayat Samiti. To ensure coordination, the Committee recommended the formation of Zilla Parishads at the district level consisting of the Presidents of Panchayat Samitis, Members of Legislative Assemblies, and Members of Parliament. Many of the States passed legislation to give effect to these recommendations.

The Panchayati Raj set-up is thus an off-shoot of the Community Development Programme, in the sense that democratic decentralization followed administrative decentralization of developmental activity. The structure was three-tiered, but there were vast differences among the States on the details. Some, like Rajasthan and Andhra Pradesh, took the lead while others, like Tamil Nadu, refrained from adopting the system. Further, the association of Members of Parliament and Legislature with local self-government in an ex-officio capacity complicated the accountability to the electorate. However, the Government of India was committed to encourage the States to adopt decentralization.

The K. Santhanam Committee appointed by the Government of India in 1963 recommended that powers should be conferred on Panchayats to levy special tax on land revenue, house tax, etc., and that all grants should be untied. The Asoka Mehta Committee appointed in 1977 recommended Districts as the first point of decentralization, and that Zilla Parishads should take up planning for the entire District and coordinate programmes with the lower tiers. The formation of Mandal Panchayats for villages with a population of around 10,000 to 15,000 constituted the lower tier. The Committee commented that unless there was a Constitutional mandate, the empowerment of local bodies would remain elusive. Based on the recommendations of the Asoka Mehta Committee, some States passed Amendments to their Panchayati Raj Acts.

CHANGES IN THE CONSTITUTION

While advocating democratic decentralization, the Government of India initiated several programmes at the District level in the 1970s, taking advantage of the presence of nationalized banks in all parts of the country. Agencies were created at sub-State level under the Societies Act or Trusts Act, and funds were made available to them bypassing the State Government's budget and local bodies.

With no financial decentralization and a number of programmes like Small Farmers' Development Agency, Drought Prone Area Programme, and Intensive Tribal Development Programme being implemented without the involvement of Panchayats, and with the postponement of elections to Panchayati Raj Institutions (PRIs) in several States, there was considerable dilution of the role of rural local self-governing bodies. Incidentally, the role of State Governments was also diluted.

The 73rd and 74th Amendments to the Constitution of India, with new Parts-IX and IX-A relating to Panchayats and Municipalities respectively, were passed by Parliament in 1992 and came into force in 1993. They mandate the constitution of Panchayats at Village, Intermediate, and District levels in every State and contain provisions with regard to the composition of Panchayats, reservation of seats to Scheduled Castes and Scheduled Tribes, and five-year terms for PRIs. State Legislatures are also mandated to authorize Panchayats to levy, collect, and appropriate certain taxes; assign to Panchayats certain taxes, duties, tolls collected by the State Government; and provide grants-in-aid to Panchayats, as may be specified in the law. Elections to Panchayats/Municipalities by the State Election Commission are also mandated.

The amendments provide for the constitution of a State Finance Commission in each State within one year of the commencement of the Act and thereafter at the expiration of every fifth year to review the financial position of Panchayats. Under this Article, the Commission's mandate is to make recommendations regarding the principles which should govern the distribution between the State and the Panchayats of the net proceeds of taxes and duties which may be divided between them, and the allocation among the Panchayats of their respective shares of such proceeds; the determination of taxes, duties, tolls, and fees which may be assigned to, or appropriated by, the Panchayats; grants-in-aid to Panchayats from the Consolidated Fund of the State; the measures needed to improve the financial position of Panchayats; and any other matter referred to the Commission in the interest of sound finance. There are similar provisions with regard to Municipalities.

The Constitution mandates the State Legislatures, by law, to endow the Panchayats/Municipalities with such powers and authority as may be necessary to enable them to function as institutions of self-government, and devolve powers and responsibilities on them with respect to the preparation of plans for economic development and the implementation of schemes for economic development and social justice. The Eleventh Schedule of the Constitution lists out the responsibilities that could be entrusted to rural local bodies. These include agriculture and allied activities, rural housing, drinking water, rural roads, poverty alleviation programmes, primary and secondary education, markets and fairs, primary health centres, women and child development, and maintenance of community assets. In respect of urban areas (Twelfth Schedule), these are urban planning, planning for social and economic development, urban water supply, fire services, slum improvement, urban poverty alleviation, provision of urban amenities, and regulation of slaughter houses.

There is considerable overlap between the subjects in the State List of the Constitution and those listed for local bodies. In any case, the operationalization of the Constitutional provisions was left to individual States. Naturally, the designs of local self-governments had both commonalities and differences with States. In any case, the initial conditions of local self-government in States differed vastly, and hence the progress in nature and pace of compliance with the Constitutional provisions vary considerably across States and over time.

ROLE OF CENTRAL FINANCE COMMISSIONS

The Central Finance Commission was designed to deal with Union–State fiscal relations. So, its award had to deal only with them, and not local bodies, which had to be the creatures of the States concerned. Therefore, an innovative approach was adopted to enable financial support to local bodies by casting an additional responsibility on the Central Finance Commission through the expansion of the core ToR. This required the Central Finance Commissions to make recommendations on the measures needed to augment the Consolidated Fund of a State to supplement the resources of its Panchayats/Municipalities based on the recommendations of the Finance Commission of the State. The Tenth Finance Commission acted on the Amendment even without a formal ToR.

This Commission was constituted on 15 June 1992 and was not given any additional ToR following the Constitutional Amendments. It took the stand that it was not precluded from making recommendations regarding grants-in-aid to local bodies. It concluded that ad hoc augmentation of the Consolidated Funds of States would be in keeping with the spirit of the Constitution since the recommendations of the State Finance Commissions were not available to it. The Commission approached the issue as one of making ad hoc provision of specific grants, and stipulated that these grants should not be used for meeting establishment expenditure and that local bodies would provide suitable matching contributions by raising resources.

The ToR of subsequent Commissions had a specific item requiring them to make recommendations to augment the Consolidated Funds of States to supplement the resources of local bodies.

The Eleventh Finance Commission expressed a number of concerns with regard to State Finance Commission Reports. These were: non-synchronization of the periods covered by State Finance Commissions with those of the Central Finance Commission; failure by many State Finance Commissions to indicate the responsibilities actually entrusted to local bodies and the principles of sharing or assignment of State taxes; delay in placing the Action Taken Reports on the recommendations of State Finance Commissions in State Legislatures in the absence of a time limit prescribed either in the Constitution or in the State legislations; lack of uniformity in the approach of State Finance Commissions; and deficiencies in their composition, such as serving bureaucrats being appointed by a few States as chairpersons and members. These concerns were expressed by almost all subsequent Commissions as progress had been painfully slow.

The Eleventh Finance Commission recommended an amount of Rs 1,600 crore for Panchayats and Rs 400 crore for Municipalities for each of the five years starting from 2000–1. All the subsequent Commissions followed this lead; the amounts were augmented significantly over the years. The Commissions stipulated that these grants should be utilized for the operation and maintenance of core civic services of primary education, health, drinking water, and sanitation.

For the inter se distribution of these provisions among States, the Eleventh Finance Commission assigned a weightage of 40 per cent to population, 20 per cent to the index of decentralization, 20 per cent to distance from the highest per capita income, and 10 per cent each to area and revenue effort. For the purpose of working out the index of decentralization, the Commission took into account a number of parameters, such as the enactment of legislation, assignment of functions, actual transfer of functions, assignment of powers to local bodies, the extent of action taken on the reports of the State Finance Commissions, elections to local bodies, and constitution of District Planning Committees. The Twelfth Finance Commission dropped the index of decentralization as a criterion.

The Thirteenth Finance Commission reintroduced the index of decentralization to encourage States to empower local bodies. For the first time, the Commission introduced the criterion of the local body grant utilization index. The fourteenth Commission took the stand that the distribution of grants among the Panchayats and the Municipalities should best be left to State Governments, provided that it was based on the recommendations of the State Finance Commission. In case that formula was not available, a default option was provided whereby the distribution was on the basis of the 2011 population with a weightage of 90 per cent for population and 10 per cent for area.

The background to this innovation was best described by Y.V. Reddy (2017), the Chairman of the Commission:

We applied the idea of default option in public policy advocated in the book *The Nudge* by Richard H. Thaler and Cass R. Sunstein. The default option meant that, if you do not decide or till you decide, what we proposed will amount to your decision. We intensively debated whether the state governments should be free to evolve criteria for distribution among the local bodies in each state, or it should be on the basis of the criteria prescribed by the FFC [Fourteenth Finance Commission]. Ultimately, we gave a formula for distribution of funds among local bodies by a state, which could be replaced once a state finance commission gave its recommendations. We faced complex issues in regard to local bodies because of several incongruities in the constitutional arrangements, precedents and experience gained so far. We were unanimous in supporting the local bodies, and we had to find a simple and defensible way of doing it.

Incidentally, Professor Thaler won the Nobel Prize in 2017.

MAGNITUDE OF TRANSFERS TO LOCAL BODIES BY CENTRAL FINANCE COMMISSIONS

There has been a significant increase in the share of grants to local bodies in the total grants recommended by the Fourteenth Finance Commission. The percentage share of grants to local bodies it recommended amounted to 53.49 per cent of the total grants. Thus, it effected a paradigm shift in the dispensation of grants to local bodies (see Table 9.1).

Table 9.1 Grants Recommended by Finance Commissions and Share of Local Bodies

Commission	Total Grants Recommended	Grants to Local Bodies Total	Percentage Share of Grants to Local Bodies
Tenth	20,300	5,381	26.50
Eleventh	58,587	10,000	17.07
Twelfth	142,640	25,000	17.53
Thirteenth	258,581	87,519	33.85
Fourteenth	537,353	287,436	53.49

Source: Compiled from Reports of the Finance Commission, X–XIV.

AN ASSESSMENT

The 73rd and 74th Amendments are more in the nature of advisories to States than mandatory in nature, insofar as the transfer of powers, functions, and finances to local bodies are concerned. Articles 243-G and 243-W provide that the Legislature of a State may, by law, endow the Panchayats/Municipalities with powers and authority as may be necessary to enable them to function as institutions of self-government and such law may contain provisions for the devolution of powers and responsibilities upon them. Thus, taking forward the process of decentralization rests solely on the States. What has been their record of performance?

The record of the States has been dismal even with regard to the mandatory provisions in the Constitution such as setting up a State Finance Commission at the expiry of every fifth year. There are numerous instances of States having failed to constitute Finance Commissions at five-year intervals, a clear breach of the Constitutional provision. Most States have also not complied with the Constitutional provisions with regard to the setting up of Gram Sabhas, ward committees, District planning committees, and metropolitan planning committees. Even where the functions are notionally transferred to local bodies, the staff remains accountable to the State Government, thus adversely impacting the efficacy of carrying out the functions.

In a study sponsored by the Union Ministry of Panchayati Raj, the Indian Institute of Public Administration had constructed six indices of devolution separately for institutional framework, functions, finances, functionaries, capacity building, and accountability. Based on these sub-indices a composite index of devolution had been worked out for the year 2012–13. This study revealed that the composite index exceeded 50 only in five States, namely Maharashtra (64.04), Karnataka (62.22), Kerala (55.41), Rajasthan (52.10), and Tamil Nadu (52.05). The national average composite index was placed at 38.52.

The States have their reasons for the present state of affairs. They point out that the Union Government has been gradually and systematically encroaching into the fiscal space of States. Increased devolution will enfeeble the authority of the States. Second, the

States have varying challenges in the design of local self-governments and a uniform pattern prescribed by the Union does not serve any purpose except as a guideline. Third, many of the functions are local services, especially education and health. In any case, their design is determined as part of centrally sponsored schemes, and neither local bodies nor State Governments have much discretion. Fourth, services rendered by local bodies are manned by staff whose services are already part of State services. The courts do not permit their transfer to local bodies.

ISSUES WITH TRANSFER OF RESOURCES TO LOCAL BODIES

The transfer and allocation of resources by the Finance Commission to local bodies is beset with several complications. The recommendations are meant only to indicate measures to supplement the resources available to the States to support the local bodies. They are to be made on the basis of the recommendations made by State Finance Commissions. In fact, many States have failed to constitute Finance Commissions in a timely manner, or their recommendations are not up to date. Also, the amounts that each State sets apart from its own resources for transfer to Local Governments from the Consolidated Funds are unclear.

There are certain areas (Scheduled areas covered under the proviso to Article 275(1)) which are explicitly excluded from the jurisdiction of the Finance Commission. The local bodies come under the primary responsibility of States, both in the spirit of the Constitution and in the wording of the ToR.

It may be necessary to significantly enhance the resources available to local bodies to discharge the responsibilities assigned to them under the respective legislations of State Governments. Such an approach will be consistent with the ToR that stipulate resources to be made available to States for supporting local bodies. Ideally, such grants should be on an assured basis and without the imposition of conditions by the Union or States. In brief, the role of the Central Finance Commission in creating awareness in Local Governments appears somewhat limited.

SELECT REFERENCES

1. Alok, V.N. 2013. *Strengthening of Panchayats in India: Comparing Devolution across States.* New Delhi: Indian Institute of Public Administration.

2. Constituent Assembly of India Debates (Proceedings), Volume VII, 4 November 1948, http://164.100.47.194/loksabha/writereaddata/cadebatefiles/C04111948.pdf, viewed on 25 October 2018.

3. Department of Administrative Reforms and Public Grievances, Ministry of Personnel, Public Grievances and Pensions. *Report of the Second Administrative Reforms Commission.* New Delhi: Government of India.

4. Department of Rural Development, Ministry of Agriculture. 1978. *Report of the Committee on Panchayati Raj Institutions (Asoka Mehta Committee).* New Delhi: Government of India.

5. Government of India. 1957. *Team for the Study of Community Projects and National Extension Service (Report of the Balwant Rai Mehta Committee).* New Delhi: Government of India.

6. Ministry of Finance. Various Years. *Report of the Finance Commission,* I-XIV. New Delhi: Government of India.

7. Prasad, Bisheshwar. 1941. *The Origins of Provincial Autonomy.* Allahabad: Kitabistan.

8. Rao, B.N. 1960. *India's Constitution in the Making.* Bombay: Allied Publishers.

9. Reddy, Y.V. 2017. *Advice and Dissent: My Life in Public Service.* New Delhi: HarperCollins.

10. Roberts, P.E. 1921. *History of British India under the Company and the Crown.* London: Oxford University Press.

GOODS AND SERVICES TAX COUNCIL
A NEW INSTITUTION IN INDIAN FISCAL FEDERALISM

THE SYSTEM OF INDIRECT TAXATION at both the Union and State levels was plagued by a number of inefficiencies. These had to be overcome through a series of steps involving political bargaining and professional inputs. The journey had been characterized by participation of leaders from all political parties in the country. The inefficiencies at the Union level were addressed partially by the introduction of the Modified Value Added Tax (MODVAT) in 1986, its replacement by Central Value Added Tax (CENVAT) in 2000–1, and the introduction tax on services in 1994.

The first step towards the transition from sales tax to the Value Added Tax (VAT) regime at the State level was taken at a meeting of the Chief Ministers convened by the Union Finance Minister in 1995. After a lull, a Standing Committee of State Finance Ministers was constituted in 1999 to deliberate on the design of VAT. The Standing Committee was rechristened as the Empowered Committee (EC) of Finance Ministers in 2000. (The precursor to the Goods and Services Tax Council, a Constitutional body, the EC was initially set up with the Union Finance Minister and Chief Ministers of select States to monitor the implementation of floor rates of sales tax and to decide the modalities for the switchover to VAT. This was reconstituted with all the Finance Ministers of State Governments and Union Territories with Legislatures and registered as a society in 2014.) By 2005, most of the States implemented VAT following the consensus arrived at by the EC.

GST, THE NEXT STEP

The first move towards the introduction of the Goods and Services Tax (GST) was made with the announcement by the Union Finance Minister in his budget speech for 2007–8 that GST would be introduced from 1 April 2010, and that the EC in association with the Union Finance Ministry would prepare a roadmap for the introduction of GST. After discussions with the States and the Union, the EC came out with its First Discussion Paper on GST in November 2009.

In the paper, the EC suggested a dual GST model, with the Union and the States having concurrent powers to tax goods and services by separate statutes. For inter-State transactions, the EC suggested the levy of an Integrated GST (IGST) by the Union consisting of Central GST (CGST) and State GST (SGST), with the complete phasing out of Central Sales Tax (CST).

The EC suggested a two-rate structure, with a low rate for goods of basic importance and a standard rate for goods in general. For precious metals, the EC suggested a special rate. While it suggested zero-rating exports, GST on imports was proposed with a full set-off. As it would be difficult to estimate gains from the service tax and revenue loss from input tax credit (ITC), the EC felt that it was essential to provide adequately for the likely loss of revenue by the States in the first five years of the rollout of GST.

The GST Bill was introduced in the Lok Sabha by the UPA government on 22 March 2011. The Bill was referred to the Standing Committee on Finance on 29 March 2011. The Union Cabinet approved the Constitutional Amendment Bill for the introduction of GST on 18 December 2014. The Bill was introduced in Lok Sabha the next day and passed on 6 May 2015. The Bill was passed by a majority of two-thirds in the Rajya Sabha on 3 August 2016. By 2 September 2016, it was ratified by the requisite number of States and received the assent of the President of India in the same month. The Constitution (101st Amendment) Act was notified on 8 September 2016. The enactment of GST legislation is the culmination of nearly 17 years of continuous effort in building consensus and marks a milestone in the reforms of indirect taxation system in the country.

The GST Act confers powers on the Parliament and State Legislatures to make laws relating to GST. The powers of the State Legislatures are subject to certain limitations. Only Parliament is vested with powers to make laws relating to inter-State supply of goods and services and levy tax on such transactions, with the proceeds of such a tax being apportioned between the Union and the States in a manner as may be provided by Parliament. The GST, to be collected by the Union, is made shareable between the Union and the States. Under the Act, the Union is not empowered to levy any surcharge on GST for meeting its purposes. Alcohol for human consumption and entertainment tax levied by the local bodies are kept out of the purview of GST. The powers to tax these will remain exclusively with the States.

THE GST COUNCIL

As per the GST Act, the Union is mandated to constitute a GST Council within 60 days of its commencement. The Council should consist of the Union Finance Minister as Chairperson, and the Union Minister of State in charge of Revenue or Finance, and either the Minister in charge of Finance, Taxation, or any other Minister nominated by each State. The functions of the GST Council are to make recommendations on the taxes, cesses, and surcharges levied by the Union, States and the local bodies that may be subsumed in GST; the goods and services that may be subjected to, or exempted from GST; model GST laws, principles of levy, apportionment of GST levied on supplies in the course of inter-State trade or commerce, and the principles that govern place of supply; the threshold limit of turnover below which goods and services may be exempted from GST; the rates, including floor rates with bands of GST; any special rate or rates for a specified period to raise additional resources during any natural calamity or disaster; a special provision with respect to Arunachal Pradesh, Assam, Jammu & Kashmir, Manipur, Meghalaya, Mizoram, Nagaland, Sikkim, Tripura, Himachal Pradesh, and Uttarakhand; and any other matter relating to GST. It is also required under the Act to recommend the date from which the GST be levied on petroleum crude, high-speed diesel, motor spirit, natural gas, and aviation turbine fuel.

The quorum for the meetings of the GST Council is prescribed as half of the total members, and every decision shall be taken by a majority of not less than three-fourths of the weighted votes of the members present and voting. The Act lays down that the vote of the Central Government shall have a weight of one-third of the total votes and the vote of all the States taken together shall have a weightage of two-thirds. Based on the weightage assigned to the votes cast, a majority decision would require the vote of the Centre and 19 States on the assumption that the Centre and all the States have cast their votes. The Council is also vested with the responsibility of establishing a mechanism to adjudicate any dispute between the Union and one or more States, or between the Union and any State or States on one side, and one or more States on the other side, or between two or more States.

The GST Council is a permanent body representing the Union and all the States with powers to decide on almost all matters relating to GST administration in the country.

PREPARATORY WORK BY THE GST COUNCIL

The GST Council constituted on 12 September 2016 recommended the enactment of five laws. These were Central GST law (CGST), Union Territories GST law (UTGST), Integrated GST law (IGST), State GST law (SGST), and Compensation law. Even before the constitution of the GSTC, the EC had been working on the formulation of the model GST laws. These model laws as recommended by the GSTC were enacted by the Parliament and all the State Legislatures, paving the way for the introduction of a nationwide GST.

As recommended by the GSTC, the following taxes levied by the Centre in the pre-GST era are subsumed in GST: Central excise duty, duties of excise on medicinal and toilet preparations, additional duties of excise (goods of special importance), additional duties of excise on textile and textile products, additional duties of customs (commonly known as countervailing duty), special additional duty of customs, service tax, and cesses and surcharges insofar as they relate to the supply of goods or services. The State taxes subsumed in GST are: State VAT, CSTC, purchase tax, luxury tax, all forms of entry tax, entertainment tax except those levied by local bodies, taxes on advertisements, taxes on lotteries, betting, and gambling, and State cesses and surcharges insofar as they relate to supply of goods or services.

The threshold exemption limit for GST was also fixed by the GSTC, which considered important matters relating to tax administration. To minimize the interface of tax payers with multiple agencies, the administrative control over 90 per cent of taxpayers with turnover below Rs 1.5 crore vests with the States, and 10 per cent with the Union. The control over taxpayers with turnover exceeding Rs 1.5 crore per annum vests equally with the States and the Union. The government also set up a Goods and Services Tax Network (GSTN) to provide front-end services to taxpayers, such as registration, payment of taxes, and filing returns.

After completion of the above preparatory work, a special midnight session of Parliament was held on 30 June 2017 to formally launch GST from 1 July 2017 across the country. Thus, the journey for the introduction of GST, a major game-changing reform in the system of indirect taxation in the country reached the finishing line, overcoming many challenges and hurdles along the way.

THE CHALLENGES

Any major change will invariably face teething problems, and a landmark tax reform like the introduction of GST is no exception. A number of apprehensions have been expressed about the design of the GST structure. First, the four-rate structure that has been put in place has been perceived to deprive the tax of its simplicity and result in classification disputes. In most of the countries where GST has been implemented, there is a dual or flat rate, and the redistributive issues are addressed through direct taxes. But given the apprehensions of the States about the loss of revenue, and the need to maintain revenue neutrality and bring the States on board, this seems to have been a practical solution.

Second, as petroleum products, alcohol for human consumption, and electricity are currently out of the purview of GST, there are concerns that the full benefits of the tax will not be realized. For instance, transporters cannot avail the benefit of ITC on petroleum products. One way out that has been suggested is that instead of exclusions, States should be empowered to levy supplementary charges on these products. This is not a perfect solution, as it will defeat the purpose of making the indirect tax system in the country simpler.

Apart from design-related issues, a number of concerns related to the implementation of the provisions of the GST Act and rules have arisen since the tax's implementation. These issues came about because of the differences in the rate structure for similar categories of goods and services, exempted categories, and demands for reduction of rates on a number of goods and services. There were problems with regard to the availment of ITC in respect of stocks lying with dealers as of 1 July 2017. Delays in getting the ITC resulted in blockage of working capital for many exporters. In addition, the GSTN, the technology backbone of GST, developed a few glitches, presumably because of lack of time for testing before launch.

Responding to these teething problems, a number of corrective measures were taken. The rates of a number of goods and services were tweaked at frequent intervals to address the concerns expressed by the stakeholders. Following the decisions taken at the GST Council at its meeting on 6 October 2017, the threshold limit for availing the benefit of composition was raised from Rs 75 lakh to

Rs 1 crore, and the time for exercising the option for composition was extended. Under the composition scheme, only a quarterly report is required to be submitted, as against the requirement of filing three returns by other taxpayers. A number of changes were announced to ease the burden on exporters following the delays in getting ITC.

MULTIPLE PERSPECTIVES AND ISSUES

Since the rollout of GST, there has been a feeling among the States that they have ceded more ground to the Union, and the freedom that they enjoyed with regard to changing the rates of VAT, the main source of their own tax revenue, has been entirely lost. The Union has buoyant sources of revenue, such as income tax, corporation tax, and customs duties, which are outside the GST purview. Such buoyant sources of revenue are not available to States. However, the higher realization of revenue under IGST being passed on to States on the principle of destination is likely to offset the disadvantage of the States in ceding more ground to the Union. Just as the States lost their freedom to change the rates of VAT, the Union too lost the freedom to change the rates of Union excise and service taxes, and more importantly, to levy cesses and surcharges on these taxes, the proceeds of which were outside the divisible pool.

As GST is a destination-based tax, there is an apprehension that the manufacturing States will suffer loss of revenue. Another concern of the States is the likely revenue loss following the introduction of GST. (The Constitutional Amendment provides for compensation only for a period of five years. Strictly, this cannot be termed full compensation as it is capped at the difference between the actual revenue and the revenue based on 14 per cent annual growth over the base year 2015–16. As the compensation is available only for a period of five years, those States with a lower consumption may suffer revenue loss after the expiry of the compensation period.)

Third, the decision-making power of the GST Council seems to be loaded in favour of the Union, as it can veto any proposal before the GST Council. (This is based on the weightage of one-third of the total votes cast assigned to it.) Also, it only needs the support of 19 States to introduce any change.

Fourth, the Union's decision to restrict area-based excise concessions to 58 per cent in the post-GST regime on the plea that the States' share in the tax collections is 42 per cent is not in the spirit of cooperative fiscal federalism. In the pre-GST regime, the Union had been extending excise duty exemptions to the northeastern States, Jammu & Kashmir, and Uttarakhand without taking into account the States' share in tax devolution. Logically, the same dispensation should have continued in the post-GST regime.

Fifth, and importantly, the Centre is keen to bring petroleum products under the purview of GST sooner than later. As VAT on petroleum products is a major source of revenue, States are justifiably concerned about the Centre's intent. As the GST regime is just stabilizing, this decision should not be rushed through.

The Union, too, has a few concerns. One of these is the exclusion of petroleum products from GST until the GST Council takes a decision. The contention is that with the exclusion of petroleum products, the oil industry and the transport sector will not be able to avail of the ITC. In the current dispensation, 90 per cent of the taxpayers below the turnover limit of Rs 1.5 crore per annum will be under the control of State Governments. The Centre is in favour of cross empowerment, but such a policy will result in taxpayers interfacing with multiple agencies.

There have been some disruptions in the economy following the implementation of GST affecting the informal sector more than the formal sector. The formal sector is reported to be back on track with the problem of destocking getting sorted out.

Any major systemic change will involve a few teething problems. This is a small price to pay for the enduring benefits that GST offers. Unlike in other countries, there has been no spike in inflation in the months immediately following its introduction. The revenue loss in the initial months was moderate and did not result in any major financial crunch either for the Union or the States. As the 1991 economic crisis proved, crisis compels immediate policy changes and responses.

With a veto power, it is the responsibility of the Centre to build consensus on important decisions and bridge the trust deficit. The Centre's failure to pay full Central Sales Tax compensation to States has dented their trust. This will be an important step in cooperative federalism and strengthen the concept of Team India.

Hopefully, the concerns of the States will be addressed once the system stabilizes. Despite the initial problems, the introduction of GST is a major milestone in the history of fiscal federalism in India. GST paved the way for cooperative fiscal federalism, and the GST Council has emerged as a fully federal and functional institution. The erstwhile National Development Council (NDC) and even a Constitutionally mandated body like the Inter-State Council remained dysfunctional and acted as agents of the Union rather than take independent decisions. It is to the credit of the GST Council that all the decisions taken so far have been arrived at by consensus. As the States have ceded more ground, the Union should accommodate the States' concerns and restrain itself from exercising the veto.

▼▲▼

The GST Council—and its constitution—is unique in that it helps reduce the transaction cost of bargaining and conflict resolution. This is the result of the trade-off between fiscal autonomy of States and trade harmonization. Like GST, there are many areas where there is a need for an institutional mechanism for bargaining and dispute resolution to promote cooperative fiscal federalism. One may expect cooperative federalism to be extended to other areas with the active involvement of the States.

To sum up, the GST Council is a shining example of cooperative fiscal federalism at its best. For the first time, despite having differences, the Union and the States have voluntarily come together to share a common tax base. This was a step that not even the founding fathers of the Indian Constitution envisaged. No doubt, the process of hammering out a consensus and its operating framework has brought to the fore a number of issues. While the arrangement is yet to stand the test of time, the functioning so far gives rise to hope that it will be a pillar of strength on the indirect revenue side, just as the Finance Commission is on the revenue expenditure side of the Centre–State fiscal relations.

SELECT REFERENCES

1. Department of Revenue. 2018. *Goods and Services Tax-Concept & Status* (As on 1 August 2018). New Delhi: Government of India.

2. Empowered Committee of State Finance Ministers. 2009. First Discussion Paper on Goods and Services Tax in India.

3. Ministry of Finance and Company Affairs. 2002. *Report of the Task Force on Indirect Taxes (Vijay Kelkar Committee)*. New Delhi: Government of India.

4. Kelkar, Vijay, Satya Poddar, and V. Bhaskar. 2016. 'GST—Make Haste Slowly', *Live Mint*, 19 October.

5. Kelkar, Vijay, and V. Bhaskar. 2018. 'Amending the GST Law: Let the Numbers Speak', *Live Mint*, 30 July.

6. National Institute of Public Finance and Policy. 1994. *Reform of Domestic Trade Taxes in India: Issues and Options*. New Delhi: National Institute of Public Finance and Policy.

7. Rao, M. Govinda. 2017. 'Entering the Age of GST', *The Hindu*, 1 July.

8. Rao, M. Govinda. 2017. 'GST—A Work in Progress', *The Hindu*, 22 December.

9. Rao, M. Govinda. 2018. 'A Year from Roll Out, GST's Roots get Firmer', *Financial Express*, 7 August.

10. Sarma, J.V.M, and V. Bhaskar. 2012. 'A Road Map for Implementing the Goods and Services Tax', *Economic and Political Weekly*, XLVII (20), 4 August.

11

ASYMMETRIC FEDERALISM

WHEN INDIA BECAME A REPUBLIC, the Constitution directed a fourfold classification of the States of the Indian Union, into Parts A, B, C, and D. In all, they numbered 29. Part-A States comprised nine erstwhile Governor's Provinces of British India. Part-B States consisted of nine erstwhile Princely States with legislatures. Part-C States consisted of erstwhile Chief Commissioner's Provinces of British India and some of the erstwhile Princely States. These Part-C States (in all 10 in number) were administered by the Centre. The Andaman and Nicobar Islands were kept as the solitary Part-D State.

The creation of Andhra in 1953 intensified the demand from other regions for the creation of States on a linguistic basis. In December of that year, the Government of India appointed a three-member States Reorganisation Commission under the chairmanship of Fazal Ali to re-examine the whole question. It submitted its report in September 1955 and broadly accepted language as the basis of the reorganization of States. But it rejected the theory of 'one language one State'. Its view was that the unity of India should be regarded as the primary consideration in any redrawing of the country's political units. It identified four major factors that could be taken into account: preservation and strengthening of the unity and security of the country; linguistic and cultural homogeneity; financial, economic, and administrative considerations; and planning and promotion of the welfare of the people in each State as well as of the nation as a whole. The Commission suggested the abolition of the fourfold classification of States under the original Constitution and the creation of 16 States and 3 Centrally Administered Territories. The Government of India accepted these recommendations with certain minor modifications. By the States Reorganisation Act (1956) and the 7th Constitutional Amendment Act (1956), the distinction between Part-A and Part-B States was done away with, and Part-C States were abolished. Some of them were merged with adjacent States and some others were designated as Union Territories. As a result, 14 States and 6 Union Territories were created on 1 November 1956. Over the years, these States were bifurcated or reorganized, and currently we have 29 States and 7 Union Territories. However, there are asymmetries in our federal system.

KINDS OF ASYMMETRY

Asymmetric federalism, also known as asymmetrical federalism, is found in a federation when different constituent units are accorded different powers. In other words, some States may have more autonomy than others. Asymmetric federalism may be accorded through Constitutional provisions, or differential treatment may be given in the policies by the federal government. The differential treatment in national policy may be for specific units, and it may be ad hoc or longer term. In other words, there can be de jure asymmetry or de facto asymmetry.

The Union Territories are administered by the President. However, by an Act of Parliament, Legislative Assemblies were created for Union Territories. Delhi and Pondicherry (now Puducherry) belong to this category.

Under Part XXI of the Constitution titled 'Temporary, Transitional and Special Provisions', Article 370 accords special dispensation to the State of Jammu & Kashmir. Under this special dispensation, the power of the Parliament to make laws is limited to those matters in the Union List and the Concurrent List which, in consultation with the

State, are found to correspond to matters specified in the Instrument of Accession of the State.

Special dispensation, in some form or the other, is accorded from time to time through various provisions in Part XXI of the Constitution to Nagaland, Assam, Manipur, Mizoram, Arunachal Pradesh, Sikkim, and Goa.

This part of the Constitution contains special provisions for other States also. These include separate development boards for Vidarbha and Marathwada regions in Maharashtra; for the then Hyderabad–Karnataka region in present-day Karnataka State; and for Saurashtra and Kutch regions in Gujarat. More recently, following the reorganization of Andhra Pradesh, a special provision was inserted under Article 371-D for the provision of equitable opportunities and facilities for people belonging to different parts of the successor States of Andhra Pradesh and Telangana in matters of public employment and education.

The Sixth Schedule contains provisions with regard to the administration of tribal areas (as notified) in the States of Assam, Meghalaya, Tripura, and Mizoram; the establishment of autonomous Districts and Regional Councils; and enabling special responsibility for the Union Government for these areas. These extraordinary provisions for special dispensation and safeguards to certain States had no or minimum impact on other States.

It is relevant to note that Delhi or Puducherry are not in the category of States and hence they are not treated as such by the Finance Commission. They are Union Territories, but the Parliament, by law, created Legislatures for them as enabled by an Amendment to the Constitution.

In addition to all this, special-category status has been accorded to some States, though not envisaged in the Constitution. This can be described as de facto asymmetry and has become controversial in the recent past.

THE GENESIS OF THE SPECIAL CATEGORY

As noted, special-category States do not find a place in the Constitution. This is a status that was originally accorded by the Union Government in connection with the transfer of resources to States under Five-Year and Annual Plans. This was done with the approval of the National Development Council (NDC), in which all Chief Ministers were members, with the Prime Minister as the Chairperson. The primary purpose of the special-category status was to accord privileged treatment to some States in the size and grant component of Plan assistance from the Centre to States. How did this come about?

During the first three Five-Year Plans, the pattern of central assistance for State Plans was different for different schemes, and was decided based on the schemes approved for each State and the gap in the resources available to finance the approved Plans of individual States. The plethora of schemes, with varying conditions, resulted in an unplanned aggregate transfer of funds from the Union to the States. The Finance Commission was not brought into the picture in these cases, presumably because such transfers were over and above those recommended by it.

The pitfalls in the system gave rise to demands for the adoption of objective criteria for the flow of funds from the Union to the States. The matter was therefore taken up by the NDC, and a formula was adopted and implemented by the Union Government during the Fourth Five-Year Plan (1969–74). The main features of this formula, which came to be known as the Gadgil formula, were that the requirements of the States of Assam, Jammu & Kashmir, and Nagaland should first be met out of the total pool of central assistance. The balance was then distributed on the basis of approved criteria.

Subsequently, it was decided to extend the special dispensation to Himachal Pradesh, along with other northeastern States. This was because these became States after the adoption of the Gadgil formula. Thus, during the Fifth Five-Year Plan, these States were categorized as special-category States for the first time. And though the Gadgil formula was modified in 1980, the benefits to the States continued as before.

The Sixth Five-Year Plan also made a reference to the special status. It stated that '[t]he hill areas which are self-contained politico-administrative units are being treated as Special-Category States whose outlays are met, substantially out of Central assistance. These are the States and Union Territories of the North-Eastern Region, Jammu and Kashmir and Himachal Pradesh.'

The Seventh Five-Year Plan was explicit on the subject. It observed that:

… areas which are co-extensive with the boundaries of the State or Union Territory, i.e., Hill States/Union Territories, namely, Jammu & Kashmir, Himachal Pradesh, Sikkim, Manipur, Meghalaya, Nagaland, Tripura, Arunachal Pradesh and Mizoram, are *called* 'Special Category States'. The amount required for giving Central assistance for their development plan was pre-empted from the divisible pool before making allocations from it to other States categorised as 'Non-Special Category States'.

Uttarakhand was accorded special-category status in 2001–2 and it was ratified by a subsequent meeting of the NDC. In his budget speech (2013–14), P. Chidambaram, then the Union Finance Minister, stated:

The present criteria for determining backwardness are based on terrain, density of population and length of international borders. It may be more relevant to use a measure like the distance of the State from the national average under criteria such as per capita income, literacy and other human development indicators. I propose to evolve new criteria and reflect them in future planning and devolution of funds.

Rao Inderjit Singh, the Union Minister for Planning, in a reply to a Parliament question on 24 April 2015 indicated that special-category status had been granted in the past to some States that were characterized by a number of features necessitating special consideration. These features included hilly terrain, low population density and/or sizeable share of tribal population, strategic location along borders with neighbouring countries, economic and infrastructural backwardness, and non-viable nature of State finances. The words used by the Minister were 'in the past', and the reply was after the bifurcation of Andhra Pradesh.

CONFUSION ABOUT SPECIAL-CATEGORY STATES

The Union Government in a press release dated 8 September 2014, titled 'Central Assistance to Andhra Pradesh', announced that the class of special-category States 'ceases to exist'. In view of the policy significance of the announcement, paragraphs 10 and 11 of the concluding section of the press release are reproduced here.

[Para 10] The statement of the then Prime Minister, Dr. Manmohan Singh on 20.2.2014 contains six paragraphs. There are no issues with regard to five out of the six paragraphs. With regard to the first point i.e. the grant of special status, an apparent conflict has set in, between the statement and the recommendations of the Fourteenth Finance Commission which came subsequently. On page 17 (para 2.29 & 2.30) of the Report, the Commission has stated (inter alia):

'We did not make a distinction between special and general category states in determining our norms and recommendations.... In our assessment of State resources, we have taken into account the disabilities arising from constraints unique to each State to arrive at the expenditure requirements. In this regard, we have observed that the north-eastern and hill States have several unique features that have a bearing on their fiscal resources and expenditure needs, such as low level of economic activity, remoteness and international borders. Our objective has been to fill the resource gaps of each State to the extent possible through tax devolution. However, we have provided post-devolution revenue deficit grants for States where devolution alone could not cover the assessed gap.... We are of the view that intra-state inequality is within the policy jurisdiction of the States and provisioning of adequate resources through tax devolution should enable them to address intra-state inequalities in an effective manner.

Thus following the recommendations of the 14th Finance Commission, the class of special category states ceases to exist. However, the Central Government has agreed to give a special assistance measure for Government of Andhra Pradesh for five years, which would make up for the additional Central share the State might have received during these years, i.e. 2015–16 to 2019–20, as envisaged in the then Prime Minister's statement dated 20.2.2014. This will be in the form of Central Government funding for externally aided projects for the state for Andhra Pradesh signed and disbursed during these years.'

[Para 11:] Thus the Government of India has effectively addressed all commitments made to the State of Andhra Pradesh in the Andhra Pradesh Reorganisation Act, the Fourteenth Finance Commission and the statement of the then Prime Minister on 20.2.2014.

M. Govinda Rao (2018), a member of the Commission, clarified the position of the Fourteenth Finance Commission:

A careful reading of the report shows that it came nowhere near making any recommendation relating to special categorization. The principal task of the Finance Commission is to assess the revenue and cost disabilities of the States and make recommendations to offset these disabilities through tax devolution and grants so that all the States are enabled to provide comparable levels of service at comparable revenue effort. The only reference to categorization was where the report stated, 'We did not make a distinction between special and general category states in determining our norms and recommendations.... In our assessment of State resources, we have taken into account the disabilities arising from constraints unique to each State to arrive at the expenditure requirements....' Therefore, the Statement in the notification on special package that '... following the recommendations of the 14th Finance Commission, the class of special category states ceases to exist' is misleading....

With regard to the bifurcation of Andhra Pradesh, the ToR simply stated, 'The Commission shall also take into account the resources available to the successor or reorganised States in accordance with the Andhra Pradesh Reorganisation Act, 2014 (6 of 2014) and the Ministry of Home Affairs notification number S.O. 655 (E) dated 4th March, 2014 and make recommendations, for successor or reorganized States, on matters under reference in this notification'.

Thus, the additional terms of reference too did not require the FFC [Fourteenth Finance Commission] to dwell on the issue, nor did the Fourteenth Finance Commission do so.

Rao further clarified that the Commission had not made any recommendation with regard to any criteria for the admission of any State to special-category status.

The quote from the Report of the Finance Commission in the press release is drawn from paragraphs 2.29 and 2.30. The former refers to methodology of estimating needs and the latter to intra-State equity. A link between the quotes and categorization of States is difficult to establish.

BENEFITS TO SPECIAL-CATEGORY STATES

What are the benefits that accrue to special-category States? As mentioned, the categorization was made in the context of the transfer of funds under Five-Year Plans. Such transfers took place in three forms, namely, earmarked normal Plan assistance; assistance for specific programmes; and those related to Externally Aided Projects

(EAPs). The benefits accrue to special-category States in terms of the magnitude of the transfers and the extent of the grant element relative to loans. The matching contributions needed from State Governments for centrally sponsored schemes (CSS) are lower in respect of special-category States.

Until 2014–15, 30 per cent of the normal Plan assistance was earmarked for special-category States in the grant–loan ratio of 90:10; for general-category States, this was in the ratio of 30:70. Similarly, assistance for EAPs is dispensed to special-category States in the grant–loan ratio of 90:10, whereas such assistance is on back–to-back basis for other States. Other benefits include provision of 90 per cent of the cost as grants for projects covered under the Accelerated Irrigation Benefit Programme (AIBP). For general-category States, such grants are restricted to 25 per cent of the project cost. Special Plan assistance for projects (90 per cent grant) and untied special central assistance (100 per cent grant) was dispensed only to special-category States.

Several changes over the years have resulted in considerable dilution of benefits to special-category States. The normal Plan assistance and special assistance programmes which were given only to special-category States were dispensed with in 2015–16. Further, allocations under AIBP have been drastically cut down. Though the practice of dispensing assistance for EAPs as 90 per cent grant to special-category States has been continued, the benefit is very limited as there are very few externally aided projects in these States. Also, since 2015–16, the allocations under CSS have come down drastically. This has diluted the benefits to special-category States further. The Union Government, however, retains the freedom to grant additional benefits in the future.

Thus, the special category of States still exists, although with diluted benefits. Therefore, the statement that the special category ceases to exist is not correct.

INCENTIVES FOR THE DEVELOPMENT OF SPECIAL-CATEGORY STATES

All the special-category States have been provided tax concessions and other incentives for development. However, there is no automaticity between the category and the set of incentives. Further, there is no uniform pattern of incentives across these States. Though initially announced for a specified period, these incentives have been extended from time to time.

The North Eastern Region (NER) comprising the States of Arunachal Pradesh, Assam, Manipur, Meghalaya, Mizoram, Nagaland, Sikkim, and Tripura is covered under the North East Industrial Development Scheme (NEIDS), 2017. The incentives under NEIDS include, among others, a Central capital investment incentive for access to credit at 30 per cent of the investment in plant and machinery, with an upper limit of Rs 5 crore; interest incentive at 3 per cent on working capital credit advanced by scheduled banks/State financial institutions for five years from the date of commencement of commercial production/ operation; reimbursement of 100 per cent insurance premium on insurance of building and plant and machinery for a maximum period of five years; reimbursement of GST paid on finished products manufactured in NER up to the extent of central share of CGST and IGST for a period of five years from the date commercial production; and reimbursement of the Centre's share of income tax for the first five years of commercial production.

There are separate Union schemes for industrial promotion in the special-category States of Jammu & Kashmir, Himachal Pradesh, and Uttarakhand. The incentives provided to Jammu & Kashmir are: capital investment subsidy of 30 per cent on investment; interest subsidy of 3 per cent; insurance subsidy for all new units; etc. For Himachal Pradesh and Uttarakhand, capital investment subsidy has been provided for all new units, and, to the existing units, on substantial expansion.

Thus, though Central industrial incentives are provided to all the special-category States, they are not uniform across these States. As evident, the most favoured treatment is accorded to Jammu & Kashmir, followed by NER, and then to Himachal Pradesh and Uttarakhand. Substantively, the States concerned are still eligible for incentives irrespective of their being accorded special category. It is possible that the GST will dilute, if not eliminate, the advantage of location-specific incentives made available to special-category States, irrespective of the diverse tax concessions.

It is pertinent to note that the Prime Minister's assurance in Rajya Sabha on Andhra Pradesh is silent on this issue of incentives. The press release given on the occasion (Prime Minister's Office) noted:

First, for purposes of Central assistance, Special Category Status will be extended to the successor State of Andhra Pradesh comprising 13 districts, including the four districts of Rayalaseema and the three districts of north coastal Andhra for a period of five years. This will put the state's finances on a firmer footing.

INCLUSION OF MORE STATES IN THE SPECIAL CATEGORY

There have been several demands for the inclusion of more States in the special category for decades. Bihar, by virtue of its backwardness in social and economic indicators, has been a strong and persistent contender, but had no success. However, there has been vehement and determined opposition from most Chief Ministers to the inclusion of new States. There was a stalemate on this for decades, but a revival of interest in the subject was seen in 2013, on the eve of electoral battle of 2014. In May 2013, Finance Minister P. Chidambaram mentioned while in Patna that a Committee was being appointed which would consider the claim of Bihar for special category.

The Government of India appointed a committee with Raghuram G. Rajan, then Chief Economic Adviser, Government of India, as Chairman, to evolve a Composite Development Index of States. The committee favoured need-based allocation of funds, and the need was based on a simple index of underdevelopment. It recommended allocations based on the index, but increasing more than lineally to the most underdeveloped States. The committee categorized States that scored 0.6 and above on the development index as 'least developed'; those that scored below 0.6 and above 0.4 as 'less developed'; and those that scored below 0.4 as 'relatively developed' and recommended additional assistance to 10 least-developed States.

The committee felt that States that had raised a claim for inclusion in the special category would find their needs for funds and special attention more than met by the twin recommendations of the basic allocation of 0.3 per cent of overall funds to each State, and the categorization of States as per the index. The committee felt that these recommendations along with the allocation methodology would effectively subsume the 'special category'.

The Government of India has not taken any decision on these recommendations made in September 2013.

THE ANDHRA PRADESH EPISODE

A number of States have staked their claim for special-category status from time to time; Bihar, Odisha, Rajasthan, Madhya Pradesh, Jharkhand, and Uttar Pradesh are among the prominent ones. The new entrant to the list of claimants is Andhra Pradesh. While no positive response was forthcoming in regard to the long-standing claims, the claim of Andhra Pradesh was initially acted upon by the Union Government owing to unusual circumstances.

On 1 March 2014, the Union Cabinet decided to accord special-category Status to the successor State of Andhra Pradesh for a period of five years. The decision was taken to allay the apprehension of the then Andhra region about the possible loss of revenue-generating avenues following the decision to bifurcate it into Telangana and residuary Andhra Pradesh. The decision on special-category Status was in fulfilment of the assurance given by the Prime Minister on the floor of the Parliament and the explicit support of the Opposition. The decision has not been implemented either by the government in position then or by the National Democratic Alliance (NDA) government formed in May 2014.

A decision in favour of a 'special package' instead of special-category status to compensate for the adverse impact of bifurcation on Andhra Pradesh was announced by the Union Government on 8 September 2016. This was in response to the proposals for a special package submitted in October 2014 and January 2015 by the Andhra Pradesh Government led by the Telugu Desam Party (TDP), a partner of the ruling NDA at the Centre. Many thought that the issue was settled. However, an agitation by some of the Opposition parties in Andhra Pradesh in favour of according special-category status rather than special package gained momentum. In mid-2018, TDP walked out of the NDA alliance citing breach of promise in according special-category status to Andhra Pradesh as the main cause.

With the issue of special-category status revived in Andhra Pradesh, many States who have been clamouring for such a status are keenly following the developments.

There are several puzzles surrounding the controversy with regard to according special-category status to Andhra Pradesh. First, why was the dormant issue of special-category States revived? When Finance Minister P. Chidambaram announced the intention to appoint the Raghuram Rajan Committee, he added that 'Bihar will certainly qualify for special category status under the new criteria' (*Deccan Herald*). Bihar's Chief Minister, Nitish Kumar, had earlier met Prime Minister Manmohan Singh and Planning Commission Deputy Chairman Montek Singh Ahluwalia to discuss the issue of granting special status to Bihar. As it turned out, the recommendation of the committee virtually suggested a methodology to abandon the concept of special-category States. The Union Government, however, did not take a decision on the recommendations of the Raghuram Rajan Committee. Further, there is no mention of the existence of such a recommendation in official policy statements, political debates, or in the media while the Cabinet decided to accord special-category status to Andhra Pradesh.

Why was the Cabinet decision to accord special-category status to Andhra Pradesh not implemented? The assurance was given on an emergency basis and the decision of the Cabinet was taken in an equally emergent manner.

The Prime Minister made the statement on according the status in Rajya Sabha on 20 February 2014. On 1 March 2014, the Planning Commission requested the Cabinet to approve the proposal to extend special-category status to Andhra Pradesh. The proposal was approved, and the Cabinet directed the Planning Commission to grant special-category status to the State for a period of five years. Despite this, the formal notification was not issued immediately after the decision.

Why was there no demand for the implementation of a Cabinet decision in which Members of Parliament from Andhra Pradesh were involved? Why did neither the political leaders nor the parties demand implementation before, or soon after, the Parliamentary elections? The fact that the Cabinet had already approved the decision to accord special status was explained in detail by Jairam Ramesh in his book *Old History, New Geography* in 2016.

What was the response of the Fourteenth Finance Commission to the additional ToR relating to Andhra Pradesh? The stand of the Commission as given in paragraph 1.4 of the Report submitted in December 2014 was: 'The bifurcation of Andhra Pradesh and the additional ToR require the Commission to examine again various comparable estimates for financial projections.' In other words, the needs of the States post bifurcation had to be reassessed. Such reassessment encompasses all the States, since the horizontal balance has to be considered in totality on a comparable basis with other States. There was no reference to the list of special-category States, their inclusion or deletion from the list, and the benefits that accrue to them in the report of the Commission.

Was the Government of Andhra Pradesh a silent or willing party to the idea of a special package in lieu of special-category status initially? As indicated by Rao Inderjit Singh, the Minister of State for Planning, in a written reply to a question in Rajya Sabha on 7 December 2015, the Government of Andhra Pradesh submitted a proposal for a special development package vide letter dated 10 October 2014. Thereafter, it sent a revised proposal on 1 January 2015. The Ministry of Finance announced a Special Central Assistance Package on 8 September 2016.

The question then remains as to when and how the special category of States cease to exist. The notification that the category no longer exists was issued through a press release by the Union Government in connection with the special package for Andhra Pradesh. This calls for a number of probing questions: Can a policy decided by the Union Government cease to exist without a conscious decision? How is the decision linked to according the status to Andhra Pradesh? What explains the long periods of silence despite the urgency warranted by the need for immediate relief? The benefit of special-category status assured was for five years, and it was most needed soon after bifurcation.

The puzzle could, perhaps, be explained by recognizing some basic truths. First, all major States in the country, irrespective of the party to which they belong, have been consistently opposing the expansion of the list of States eligible for special category. This is well known to all concerned. Hence, the assurance sought and given in the case of Andhra Pradesh stemmed from the determination to serve the immediate purpose of bifurcation of Andhra Pradesh—and a universal silence on follow-up actions was required to avoid embarrassment. Second, consistent with the ToR, the Fourteenth Finance Commission had taken into consideration the fiscal needs of Andhra Pradesh. This was evident by the revenue deficit grant of Rs 22,113 crore recommended by the Commission. Kerala (Rs 9,519 crore) and West Bengal (Rs 11,716 crore) were the other general-category States that got such grants. Third, the offer of special package and its acceptance by the Government of Andhra Pradesh represented a pragmatic solution. The subsequent retreat from this position by the Government of Andhra Pradesh could be either for political compulsions or on the grounds that the package was not adequate. Fourth, the tax incentives that are associated with a special-category status are currently tailored to meet the strategic and other disadvantages of individual States. These incentives have not seriously affected the interests of neighbouring States. Even so, they protested the idea of extending such concessions to Andhra Pradesh. The Union Government, therefore, had constraints in ignoring the protests of other States. Fifth, the manner in which the announcement (that the special category ceases to exist) was made, in the context of announcing a special package for Andhra Pradesh, by invoking the recommendations of the Fourteenth Finance Commission suggests it was perhaps expedient.

▼▲▼

The Constitution provides for special dispensation to certain States. These provisions are basically intended to address the likely destabilizing tendencies that are inherent in a diverse country like India. Without the special dispensation, some of these States could have felt alienated from the mainstream. While these dispensations under the Constitution reflect de jure asymmetric federalism, the special category to select States reflects de facto asymmetric federalism. Such special dispensations are not unique to India. There are other federations in the world where there are special constitutional provisions protecting the interests of certain regions. Canada is an example where both de jure and de facto asymmetries exist.

SELECT REFERENCES

1. *Deccan Herald.* 2013. 'Bihar Will Get Spl Status under New Criteria: Chidambaram', 11 May. Available at www.deccanherald.com/content/331889/bihar-get-spl-status-criteria.html, viewed on 24 October 2018.

2. Prime Minister's Office. 2014. 'PM's Statement on the Telangana Bill and a Special Package for the Successor State of Andhra Pradesh', Government of India, 20 February.

3. Ramesh, Jairam. 2016. *Old History New Geography—Bifurcating Andhra Pradesh.* New Delhi: Rupa.

4. Rao, M. Govinda, and Nirvikar Singh. 2006. *Political Economy of Federalism in India.* New Delhi: Oxford University Press.

5. Rao, M. Govinda. 2016. 'No Hyderabad Blues', *The Hindu,* 15 September.

6. Rao, M. Govinda. 2018. 'Bifurcation and Blame: On Granting Special Category Status to States', *The Hindu,* 12 March.

7. Reddy, G. R. 2015. 'Hollow Promise of "Special Status"', *The Hindu,* 26 August.

12

THE PLANNING COMMISSION
ITS RISE, FALL, AND REBIRTH

THERE WAS A VIRTUAL UNANIMITY, especially before Independence and in the early decades thereafter, that a planned approach to economic and social development was the most appropriate for Indian conditions. However, the intellectual and political classes had differences on the relative emphasis between the role of markets and the government in planned development.

In regard to the Planning Commission, however, there were substantial differences about the need for such an institution outside the Ministry of Finance. There were two sets of fears expressed: that it would undermine the role of Ministries in the Government of India, in particular, the Finance Ministry. There was also discomfort that it might undermine the role of State Governments, though this was not a dominant concern in the initial years. In view of the differences of opinion, the idea of establishing the Planning Commission by law was given up and it was established through a Cabinet Resolution essentially as an advisory body.

The Finance Commission, on the other hand, was part of the Constitutional design. Its core function has been to deal with sharing of taxes collected by the Union. The Constitution mandated the establishment of the Finance Commission within two years of its own commencement, and then within every five years thereafter, and an enabling legislation was also passed for it to be set up. The composition of the Finance Commission is also indicated in the relevant legislation. It therefore drew its legitimacy and independence from the Constitution as well as a legal framework under the Constitution.

The government's intention of constituting a Planning Commission was announced in the Finance Minister's budget speech in February 1950. The Commission was established on 15 March 1950 through a Cabinet Resolution. There was significant opposition to the establishment of the Planning Commission, even from within the Cabinet. John Mathai, then the Finance Minister, resigned, stating that his objection was not merely to the idea of Planning Commission, but also to the method of its working. Following the Finance Minister's resignation, a number of Ministers expressed their opposition to the Commission. Although there was general consensus in favour of planning as an approach for the reconstruction and development of the economy, there was disagreement about the need for an institution like the Planning Commission.

The Planning Commission has always had the Prime Minister as its ex-officio Chairman, with a Deputy Chairman in the rank of a full Cabinet Minister that he or she has nominated. Some select Cabinet Ministers have also acted as ex-officio members of the Commission. Most of the full-time members nominated by the Prime Minister were subject experts. Membership to the Planning Commission was virtually coterminous with that of the Prime Minister's term. It is very clear that the Planning Commission had been a body of the Union Government and its composition coincided with the political cycles.

There were 25 Deputy Chairmen, of whom three were economists, one was a diplomat, and the rest were political leaders with national stature. (Of these, M.S. Ahluwalia, who officiated from 4 June 2004 to 5 May 2014, had the longest tenure.) Membership was more or less equally divided between economists and other subject-matter specialists.

THE NATIONAL DEVELOPMENT COUNCIL
AND THE INTER-STATE COUNCIL

The National Development Council (NDC) was established in 1952, also by a resolution of the Cabinet on the basis of a recommendation in the draft outline of the First Five-Year Plan. It was composed of the Deputy Chairman and Members of the Planning Commission, the Cabinet Ministers of the Union Government, Chief Ministers of all the States, and representatives of Union Territories and was chaired by the Prime Minister. As the number of members exceeded 50, a Standing Committee was established in November 1954 with only nine Chief Ministers and fewer Union Ministers to improve its effectiveness. The functions of the NDC relate to formulation of the national Plan, reviewing its work, and considering important questions of social and economic policy affecting national development. In a way, therefore, the Planning Commission was to be guided by the NDC, but convening of the NDC, its remit, and its effectiveness was largely determined by the Prime Minister. Table 12.1 shows the frequency of the meetings of the NDC. It was replaced with a Governing Council when the Planning Commission was replaced with NITI Aayog.

No action was taken until 1990 to act upon Article 263 for the establishment of the Inter-State Council (ISC). This is a recommendatory body placed in the Ministry of Home Affairs and has the mandate of investigating and discussing Subjects in which

Table 12.1   Meetings of the National Development Council

Period	Number of Meetings Held
1952–9	13
1960–9	13
1970–9	7
1980–9	7
1990–9	8
2000–14	9

Source: Summary Records of Discussions of National Development Council Meetings, Planning Commission.

some or all of the States or the Union and one or more of the States have a common interest, as may be brought up before it; making recommendations upon any Subject, and, in particular, recommendations for better coordination of policy and action with respect to that Subject; and deliberating upon such other matters of general interest to the States as may be referred by the Chairman to the Council.

The ISC met only eleven times since its establishment and failed to provide an effective forum to States to give expression to their grievances and seek suitable relief from the Centre. There was also no effective follow-up on the decisions arrived at these meetings so far. It was no better than the NDC in terms of the frequency of its meetings (see Table 12.2).

Table 12.2   Meetings of the Inter-State Council

Meeting	Dates Convened
1st	10 October 1990
2nd	15 October 1996
3rd	17 July 1997
4th	28 November 1997
5th	22 January 1999
6th	20 May 2000
7th	16 November 2001
8th	27 and 28 August 2003
9th	28 July 2005
10th	9 December 2006
11th	16 July 2016

Source: Inter-State Council Secretariat.

EVOLUTION OF THE PLANNING COMMISSION

The Planning Commission was meant to be an advisory body, though it evolved into what has been often described as an extra-Constitutional authority. It was expected to function under the overall guidance of the NDC, a body in which both the Union and the States were represented at the highest level. In a way, therefore, the Planning Commission was a Central Government institution serving the interests of the Union and States.

As the Planning Commission evolved, it performed different functions. First, it provided a perspective and a medium-term Plan for the economy as a whole for important sectors. Second, it gave advice on the allocation of investments, particularly capital expenditures, among the ministries of the Union Government. Third, it advised the Union on the transfer of funds to State Governments and, in addition, accorded approval to State Plans. The process also involved approval of the borrowing programme of State Governments. Fourth, on occasion, it represented the interests of the States in the Union Government, though this role was very dependent on the existing political configuration and the personalities involved in the shaping of Union–State relations.

Some landmark developments in regard to the functioning of the Planning Commission should be recognized. A function that contributed to its importance was dispensing Plan assistance to States. The matter became clear when the Government of India accepted the note of dissent of the Member-Secretary of the Third Finance Commission that it should confine itself only to the non-Plan revenue expenditure requirements of the States. From the Fourth Finance Commission onwards, the ToR in the Presidential Order appointing it excluded the consideration of the Plan requirements of the States. The Planning Commission thus became an important parallel channel of transfers. Initially, the Plan assistance—its volume as well as grant-loan components to the States—was decided on the basis of the projects approved. In 1969, a formula for distribution of Central assistance to State Plans was adopted by the NDC (called the Gadgil formula after the then Deputy Chairman of the Planning Commission, D.R. Gadgil). According to the formula, special-category States were to receive 90 per cent of the assistance by way of grants and the remaining 10 per cent as loans, whereas the pattern of assistance to general-category States was 30 per cent grant and 70 per cent loan. Box 12.1 gives information on the Gadgil formula and the modified Gadgil–Mukherjee formula.

Box 12.1   Gadgil Formula

The NDC at its meeting held in April 1969 approved a formula for the distribution of normal central assistance (NCA) for State Plans. This formula came to be known as the Gadgil formula after the Deputy Chairman of the Planning Commission. Under the formula, the requirements of the States of Assam, Jammu & Kashmir, and Nagaland were to be met first out of the total pool of Central assistance, and the balance of the Central assistance was to be distributed 60 per cent on the basis of population, 10 per cent on basis of per capita income (only to those States whose per capita income was below the national average), 10 per cent on the basis tax effort (with the per capita tax receipt as percentage of States' per capita income), 10 per cent on the basis of spillover outlay into the Fourth Five-Year Plan of major irrigation and power schemes, and 10 per cent based on special problems of individual States.

The formula underwent three revisions before it was further revised by the NDC in 1991, when Pranab Mukherjee was the Deputy Chairman. This formula, known as the Gadgil-Mukherjee formula, was in operation till 2014–15, and is as follows:

Criteria	Weightage
Population (1971)	60%
Per capita GSDP	25%
	• 20% for States below the national average (deviation method)
	• 5% for all States (distance method)
Performance	7.5%
	• 2.5% for tax policy
	• 2% for fiscal management,
	• 3% for national objectives (1% each for population control and elimination of poverty, 0.5% each for timely completion of externally aided projects and land reforms)
Special Problems	7.5%

The formula helped to minimize discretionary elements in the transfer of funds to States by the Union, and for a few years remained the predominant channel of Central Plan assistance to States. However, over the years, the proliferation of CSS had resulted in a significant reduction in the formula-based normal Plan assistance. At the time of the formulation of the Fourth Five-Year Plan, the NDC took a decision that Plan transfers to States outside the Gadgil formula should not exceed one-sixth of the total Central assistance for State Plans. This decision was never observed, and transfers outside the formula continued unabated. The reduction in formula-based transfers had been an important source of dissatisfaction to the State governments. Table 12.3 gives the comparative picture of trends in formula-based and discretionary Central assistance for State Plans.

A second important development related to the nationalization of banks, which provided a window for the Union to utilize the resources in the financial sector for policy purposes. In fact, over time, the budget speeches of Finance Ministers contained increasing references to the use of resources available within the banking system or the insurance sector for pursuing public policies. The Planning

Table 12.3 Composition of Central Assistance for State Plans

Years	NCA as Percentage of Total Central Assistance	Discretionary Grants as Percentage of Total Central Assistance
Tenth Plan	34.61	65.39
Eleventh Plan	24.90	75.10
2008–9	21.67	78.33
2009–10	22.03	77.97
2010–11	22.29	77.71
2011–12	20.89	79.11
2012–13	23.09	76.91
2013–14	23.83	76.17
2014–15	9.63	90.37

Sources: For the Tenth and Eleventh Plan periods, *Report of the Working Group on States' Financial Resources for the Twelfth Plan*, 2012, Planning Commission. For other years, Ministry of Finance, *Expenditure Budget*, Volume I, Various Years.

Commission had not been in a position to effectively guide the allocation of such resources.

The third development, which took place mainly because of the Planning Commission, was the recourse to autonomous agencies for implementing government schemes. These autonomous bodies were essentially created as a result of the need to utilize institutional finances for developmental purposes at the local level, at the instance of the Union. For this, agencies such as District Rural Development Agencies were created at the District level. Over a period, these agencies started receiving funds directly from the Union Government, thus bypassing the State Governments in several ways. This practice was discontinued in 2014–15, but the agencies continue and they receive funds through State budgets.

The fourth development relates to the increasing market orientation of public policy. In this context, the Planning Commission took initiatives in regard to implementation of projects through public–private partnership. In a way, therefore, this initiative amounted to the Planning Commission stretching its mandate to operational matters.

The Planning Commission persuaded the States to establish Planning Boards at the State level; the experience with these Boards varied across States and over time. However, they were generally less crucial to the process of policy than the Planning Commission. The Annual Plan was expected to be prepared by States within the framework of the Five-Year Plan, and the Annual Plans of States had to be approved by the Planning Commission and operationalized through Plan components of their respective budgets.

In the initial years, particularly the 1960s, and to some extent the 1970s, State Governments had the benefit of understanding the planning techniques and the associated processes from the Planning Commission. Thus, the Planning Commission exercised soft power over the States, and the States often viewed it as a body representing their interests in the Union Government. From the 1970s, perceptions started changing. The States started to feel that the Planning Commission was becoming a political instrument of the party in power at the Centre. They also felt more confident about their capacity to do their own planning. Further, the meetings of the NDC became less frequent, and it functioned less as a discussion forum and more as what may be called a posture forum. In recent years, State Governments have expressed resentment about the role of the Planning Commission in the transfer of funds from the Union Government to the State Governments outside the awards of the Finance Commissions, particularly through several CSS. They also expressed discomfort with the process of approval of State Plans by the Planning Commission.

There was also a perception among analysts that the Planning Commission was encouraging fiscal profligacy in both Union and State Governments through the advocacy of new investments, Plans, and schemes, and an ever-increasing Plan size. They also believed that non-Plan expenditure, in particular relating to general services such as police and judiciary, had not received the attention it deserved. Additionally, there was considerable resentment among the Union Ministries about the growing importance of the Planning Commission in public investments, including projects involving public-private partnerships.

Whether the Planning Commission's advice contributed to accelerated growth or not is a matter on which there have been genuine differences of opinion. However, the actual outcomes of most Five-Year Plans and Annual Plans generally fell short of the physical targets indicated. The implementation agencies blamed the Planning Commission for wrong design, while the Planning Commission blamed the implementation agencies. Both blamed the political leadership, which in turn pointed to the role of bureaucracy. In 2009, the then Prime Minister Manmohan Singh suggested that the Planning Commission be reformed, but apparently no serious measures were really taken.

Throughout the life of the Planning Commission, there had been some dissatisfaction within the public sector about its functioning: the States resented the tied nature of funds it made available; the Ministry of Finance felt that the Planning Commission had been demanding a larger and larger share of resources in the form of Gross Budgetary Support (GBS), thus, eroding its fiscal management capacity;

Union Ministries, as well as public enterprises, generally resented its involvement in their functioning; finally, there was the perception that the Planning Commission's excessive emphasis on developmental programmes and larger Plan outlays for economic and social services had adversely affected allocations for the maintenance of assets, as well as allocations towards basic functions of the government in the general-services category.

The broad functions of the Planning Commission in practice remained the same since its inception. These were: formulating medium- to long-term Plans; advising on the allocation of funds to Ministries in the Union Government through the annual budget; approving the Plan of each State and allocating transfers of funds from Union to States, both untied and tied to activities or schemes under the Plan; monitoring, evaluation, etc., incidental to planning; and assisting the NDC on these matters. While the Five-Year Plan had a medium-term outlook and strategy, Annual Plans focused on the allocation of funds. The Planning Commission virtually determined the distribution of Plan funds between the Union Government and the States, and among the States. Plan outlays were generally equated with public investments and capital outlays of budgets. The Annual Plans of the Union were operationalized mainly through the Plan components of the budget.

LINKAGES AND OVERLAP WITH THE FINANCE COMMISSION

The remit of the Finance Commission has been determined by Constitutional provisions. These provisions, however, enable the President to refer any matter to the Commission in the interests of sound finance. For the Planning Commission, however, the remit was very broad and was determined by the Union Government. It was very clear that the Planning Commission, though advisory in nature, covered significantly larger policy space than fiscal transfers.

There are elements of overlap or duplication between the Planning Commission and Finance Commissions in regard to the transfer of resources. The Constitution specifies two distinct modes for resource transfers between the Union and the States. The first is by means of distribution of the net proceeds of taxes. It is the duty of the Finance Commission to make recommendations on the distribution of the net proceeds of taxes between the Union and the States, as well as the inter se allocation of such proceeds among the States. The system of separately recommending the shares of States in the proceeds of income tax and Union excise duties gave way to recommending shares of States in the total net proceeds of all taxes, through an Amendment of the Constitution in 2000.

The second is by means of grants-in-aid. The Finance Commission is mandated to make recommendations on the amounts to be charged on the Consolidated Fund of India as grants-in-aid of the revenues of those States which are determined by the Parliament to be in need of assistance. Through an amendment to the Constitution, it is further mandated to recommend measures needed to augment the Consolidated Fund of a State to supplement the resources of its Panchayats and Municipalities, on the basis of the recommendations made by the State's Finance Commission. The provision relating to the role of the Finance Commission in the finances of local bodies is somewhat confusing. It is a complex arrangement to enable transfer of resources from the Union to local bodies, without violating the Constitutional design of the local bodies, which are solely in the domain of States.

The provisions relevant to the Finance Commission deal specifically with one-way transfers, i.e., transfers from the Union to the States. Article 282, on the other hand, empowers both the Union and the States to make grants out of their revenues for any public purpose, regardless of the purpose being within the legislative competence of the Parliament or the State Legislature.

There had been considerable debate on the Constitutional intent of grants under Article 282, particularly on the aspect of whether those under this provision were meant to be made on an exceptional or regular basis. Regardless of the debate, the factual position is that grants made under Article 282 from the Union to the States have grown over the years and occupy significant fiscal space in the present context.

Grants, whether under Article 275 or Article 282, could be for revenue or capital expenditures, even though the former provision was predominantly used for revenue expenditure and the latter mainly for capital expenditure.

The link between the Planning and Finance Commissions and the overlap in their functions was recognized quite some time ago. Therefore, it became customary to appoint a Member of the Planning Commission as a part-time Member of the Finance Commission from the Sixth Finance Commission onwards. This practice was expected to ensure coordination in their work and to enable the Finance Commission to take into account the considerations that govern the transfers from the Union to States on account of the Plan. A proposal to ensure that the recommendations of the Finance Commission were coterminous with the Five-Year Plans was not acted upon. Similarly, the proposal to make Finance Commission a permanent body was not acted upon.

In the past, grants-in-aid have generally been recommended by Finance Commissions to fill the estimated deficit in the revenue account of States (in particular, non-Plan revenue deficits), in addition to grants relating to disaster management and local bodies. However, the overlap with the Planning Commission arose in respect of sector-specific or project-specific grants to States. Past experience had been varying in terms of sectors covered by grants-in-aid, the conditionalities laid down, and the outcomes achieved. There was also some overlap, as the Planning Commission gave non-Plan revenue-deficit grants on some occasions on the grounds that the norms adopted by the Finance Commissions were unrealistic. Over the years, there was more change than continuity in the sectors identified for grants-in-aid. In terms of the magnitude, the grants provided by the Finance Commission constitute a small part of the total expenditure by the States on the sectors concerned. In some cases, the links between the conditionalities and outcomes had been questioned by some States. If the sector-specific grants of the Finance Commission have not been effective, it may be partly because the evolving circumstances in scheme implementation cannot be captured by a body that is periodic and has a lifespan of about two years. It is also relevant to ponder over the extent of expertise available within the Commission in identifying sectors and designing conditions.

The Planning Commission advised the Union Government and, to some extent, State Governments in regard to several matters of relevance to federal fiscal relations. The most significant of these related to transfers effected by the Union Government to the States. These transfers were additional to those that took place on the recommendations of the Finance Commission. Such transfers could be untied in terms of Central assistance to State Plans, or tied to specific activities or schemes, including CSS. In addition, direct transfers to entities within the State were also done for the implementation of some schemes, and this mode of transfer became the principal component of grant transfers to the States through various flagship CSS. As indicated earlier, this practice was given up in 2014–15.

The grants by the Union to the States outside of the recommendations of the Finance Commission, essentially at the instance of Planning Commission, covered several sectors and specific regions within the States. There has been an increase in non-formula-based fiscal transfers from the Union, particularly through the mechanism of CSS. The States contend that these schemes are often formulated without adequate consultation and without keeping in mind State-specific variations and priorities, and that they have led to a significant burden on their resources.

It can be argued that CSS, implemented with the approval of the NDC, have helped to ensure that Central funds actually flow to critical sectors and have led to a matching contribution of States' funds into these sectors. Transfers outside the mechanism of Finance Commissions are advocated for several legitimate reasons: the need to provide comparable levels of public services across the country, based upon the requirements of a welfare State as per the framework laid down under the Directive Principles of State

Policy; based on norms legislated by the Union Parliament; and based on obligations in social sectors arising out of international commitments. These considerations, which are beyond the scope of the Finance Commission, provide the rationale for nationwide approaches to sectoral policies and the need for providing guidance, incentives, and disincentives to the States.

The issue of overlap with the Finance Commission arose entirely in the context of fiscal transfers from the Union to the States. At one stage, a view was taken that all transfers, barring those done under exceptional circumstances, should take place only on the basis of the recommendations of the Finance Commission. However, as mentioned, the remit of the Finance Commission over a period was restricted to the consideration of non-Plan revenue expenditure requirements of the States, though some grants-in-aid were also recommended for capital works and on specified developmental activities. This, in a way, resulted in the overlap. In the recent past, some transfers on account of grants-in-aid on the basis of the recommendations of the Finance Commission were also treated as Plan funds. Further, as already mentioned, in recent years Finance Commissions have also been incorporating considerations relating to policies of the Union Government in their awards, especially grants-in-aid.

As mentioned, the major concern of the States in regard to this overlap was that the share of the transfers from the Union to the States at the instance of the Planning Commission was increasing, and this was not envisaged in the Constitution. In their view, the Planning Commission undermined the role of the Finance Commission and enabled the encroachment of the States' legitimate fiscal space by the Union. Some of the States felt that in a way the Finance Commission enabled such transfers by allowing the needed excess fiscal space to the Union in their recommendations. At the same time, the Finance Commission was often required to consider non-core items of Union–State fiscal relations that overlapped with the development strategies and policies that were in the legitimate domain of the Planning Commission.

PERFORMANCE OF THE PLANNING COMMISSION

The performance of the Planning Commission towards the promotion of growth is not easy to access. However, its performance relative to promise can be gauged from the outcomes relative to projected growth. Table 12.4 shows that for the major part, the actual performance of the economy felt short of targets.

While the growth performance varies across Plan periods as compared with the targets, there is clear evidence to conclude that income inequalities have been increasing, more particularly in the post-reform era (Figure 12.1).

The issue of growing inequalities has also been analysed by comparing the differentials between the highest-income and lowest-income States in three periods (see Table 12.5).

Table 12.4 Five-Year Plans: GDP Growth Targets and Realization

Five-Year Plan	Growth Target	Growth Realized
First (1951–6)	2.1	3.6
Second (1956–61)	4.5	4.3
Third (1961–6)	5.6	2.8
Fourth (1969–74)	5.7	3.3
Fifth (1974–9)	4.4	4.8
Sixth (1980–5)	5.2	5.7
Seventh (1985–90)	5.0	6.0
Eighth (1992–7)	5.6	6.8
Ninth (1997–2002)	6.5	5.4
Tenth (2002–7)	8.0	7.6
Eleventh (2007–12)	9.0	8.0
Twelfth (2012–17)	8.0	6.9

Source: For the First to Eleventh Five-Year Plans, compiled from the Ministry of Statistics and Programme Implementation, Statistical Year Book—India 2017. For the Twelfth Five-Year Plan, growth rates based on the 2011 series as compiled by the Central Statistical Office have been used.

Note: The period of three years from 1966–9 were covered by Annual Plans; the Fifth Plan was terminated in 1977–8, and the two years 1978–9 were treated as rolling Plans.

Figure 12.1 Inequalities in Per Capita Income of States at Current Prices

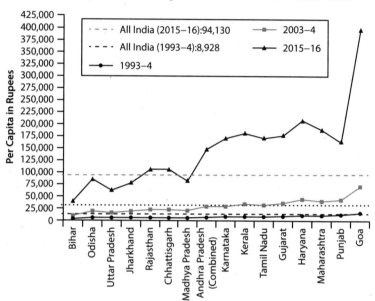

Source: Per capita GSDP of States as given by Central Statistical Office, Ministry of Statistics and Programme Implementation.

Note: The States included in the figure are general-category States, with Andhra Pradesh including Telangana.

Table 12.5 Differential Between the Highest and Lowest Average Per Capita Income State

State	1980–90 (Pre-Reform)	1991–2000 (Post Reform)	2001–14 (Post Reform)
Highest Per-Capita income	4,967 (Punjab)	17,557 (Haryana)	74,031 (Haryana)
Lowest Per-Capita income	1,675 (Bihar)	4,003 (Bihar)	14,806 (Bihar)
Difference	3,292	13,554	59,224
Ratio of Highest to Lowest	2.97	4.39	5.00

Source: Per capita GSDP of States as given by Central Statistical Office, Ministry of Statistics and Programme Implementation.

Note: Goa, being an outlier, has been excluded for the purpose of working out the differential.

THE PLANNING COMMISSION UNDER ATTACK

There were, as already mentioned, reservations about the appropriateness of the design of the Planning Commission since its inception. There was also dissatisfaction with the outcomes. Milton Friedman stated in 1963 that he was not against good planning, but rather against bad planning, as practised by the Planning Commission. Similar views were expressed by Sukhamoy Chakravarty when he referred to Plan weariness, and by Raj Krishna when he said that a Five-Year Plan was a new edition of the first Plan. In the context of fiscal federalism, the Planning Commission was faulted for encroaching upon the policy space of the States, especially through the grants-in-aid that it had been dispensing with significant discretion.

Some of the Chairmen of the Planning Commission had also expressed dissatisfaction with regard to the functioning of the institution. Pandit Nehru was one of the earliest to express his sense of discomfort with excessive bureaucratization, in 1963. Rajiv Gandhi was reported to have expressed his lack of respect for the Planning Commission, and more recently, in 2009, Manmohan Singh pleaded for its reform.

There is also an opinion that the Planning Commission did not adapt itself to the changing economic requirements. While a planned development strategy was needed to meet the challenges of low levels of saving and investment, poor infrastructure, and pessimism in regard to the country's capacity to export to pay for its imports, the practice of employing the consistency framework continued even after market-based reforms were introduced in 1991. More importantly, centralized planning is the negation of federalism, and the practice of according approvals to individual State Plans by the Planning Commission, even after the market-based economic reforms were introduced, strained the federal spirit in some sense.

The general feeling was that reform had not taken place given the way the planning function was performed by the Planning Commission and the manner in which the institution was organized.

Prime Minister Modi announced the decision to wind up the Planning Commission in August 2014. In its place, the National Institution for Transforming India (NITI Aayog) was set up on 1 January 2015.

▼▲▼

The Planning Commission was established at a time when there was an intellectual consensus in favour of planned development. As an institution, it played a critical role in influencing the debates in the country. It also provided a forum of interaction between the Union and the States. In a way, it was a meeting ground for the politics and economics as well as for the generalist and subject-matter specialists at the Union and State levels. This was critical at a time when public investments were determining factors in the process of development. However, over time, technological developments and institutional dynamics resulted in significant scepticism in regard to planning as an instrument of development. In India, there was a delayed recognition of the importance of a changed approach to Central intervention in the economy.

While there can be differences of opinion with reference to the performance of the economy under the aegis of the Planning Commission, the evidence in regard to growing inter-State inequalities in the growth of per capita income is compelling. However, the fact remains that the Planning Commission was the only forum for the exchange of views between the Union and the States. One of the main reasons for winding up the Planning Commission was the resentment of the Chief Ministers. When a serving Chief Minister became the Prime Minister, the Planning Commission was abolished, and NITI Aayog was appointed in its place. The critical point is whether NITI Aayog would be a better forum for interaction between the Union and the States in matters of fiscal federalism.

13

NITI AAYOG
PROMISE AND PERFORMANCE

ON 1 JANUARY 2015, THE Government of India announced its decision to set up National Institution for Transforming India (NITI Aayog) in place of the Planning Commission. The decision was ostensibly meant to bring about institutional changes reflecting the changed dynamics of new India and the dynamic policy shifts that could nurture large-scale changes to better serve the needs and aspirations of the people. The origins of NITI Aayog could be traced to the disenchantment with the Planning Commission on two important fronts: the perception that it was not able to capture the new realities of macroeconomic management at the national level, and that it had not been conducive to sound fiscal relations between the Union and the States.

PREMISE OF NITI AAYOG

The new realities of macroeconomic management that the Planning Commission reportedly failed to address related to the increased role of the private sector; the increasing role of financial markets in the allocation of resources; the nature and process of development being increasingly influenced by independent regulators in a market-oriented economy; global factors influencing the national economy; the need to allow States to formulate and implement their plans on functions assigned to them in the Constitution without having to get them 'approved' by the Planning Commission; and the role of not only promoting investment but putting in place institutions and incentives for improving productivity and promoting overall economic development.

The official notification of the Cabinet Resolution establishing NITI Aayog explained that '[t]he one-size-fits-all approach, often inherent in central planning, has the potential of creating needless tensions and undermining the harmony needed for national effort' (Cabinet Secretariat). The Resolution noted that India had changed dramatically at multiple levels and across varied scales. It identified the biggest forces of transformation. These were the development of the industry and service sectors and their operations on a global scale; increase in the traditional strength of agriculture; greater integration of India with the global economy; the growing middle class and its purchasing power; a rich pool of entrepreneurial, scientific, and intellectual human capital; spread of non-resident Indians across more than 200 countries; and irreversible increasing urbanization. The major challenges referred to in the Resolution were leveraging India's demographic dividend fruitfully; eliminating poverty; integrating villages into the development process; developing small businesses; skill development; and maintaining environmentally sustainable development. It was explained that these warranted overhauling the planning process to align with the shifts in the economy.

The official notification recognized that the States of the Union of India had evolved from being mere appendages of the Centre to being the actual drivers of national development. The Resolution listed out the functions of NITI Aayog under 13 heads. The important ones among these are: evolving a shared vision of national priories with the active involvement of States; fostering cooperative federalism; developing mechanisms to formulate credible plans; designing strategic and long-term policy and programme frameworks and monitoring their implementation; providing expertise as a think tank; providing a platform for the resolution of inter-sectoral and inter-departmental issues to accelerate the implementation of programmes; and maintaining a state-of-the-art resource centre. As articulated by NITI Aayog, at the core of its creation are two hubs, 'the Team India Hub', to engage the States with the Central Government, and the 'Knowledge and Innovation Hub', to build a think tank.

A SUCCESSOR WITH SOME DIFFERENCE

NITI Aayog's Governing Council is similar to the NDC in its composition. It is chaired by the Prime Minister, as in the case of Planning Commission, with a Vice Chairman corresponding to the Deputy Chairman of the Planning Commission. The members of the Governing Council are a few Cabinet Ministers of the Union (ex-officio), full-time members of NITI Aayog appointed by the Union Government, Chief Ministers of all States and Union Territories with legislatures, Lieutenant Governors of Union Territories without Legislatures, and special invitees nominated by the Prime Minister. The composition of NITI Aayog is more or less similar to that of its predecessor.

Though the nomenclature of NITI Aayog is different, the process of setting up is similar to the Planning Commission, through a Cabinet Resolution based on the initiative of Prime Minister. The NDC has been replaced with a Governing Council but with a more or less similar composition. However, NITI Aayog has the additional option of creating Regional Councils to address specific issues and contingencies impacting more than one State or region. NITI Aayog's composition and structure remain similar to the Planning Commission in terms of its being coterminous with the political cycles of the Union Government. It essentially remains an advisory body, but unlike the Planning Commission, does not play an active role in the allocation of funds to States or Ministries.

NITI Aayog is supposed to be different from the Planning Commission in terms of articulating the new realities, with its work style fashioned to capture them. Further, its approach is contended to go beyond the limited sphere of the public sector and the Government of India, and it is intended be a catalyst to the developmental process. Finally, the articulation in favour of NITI Aayog also emphasizes that States have been co-opted as partners and will be consulted in the formulation of policies.

PERFORMANCE OF NITI AAYOG

The first meeting of NITI Aayog's Governing Council was held in February 2015. Thereafter, three Sub-Groups of Chief Ministers were constituted by the Prime Minister, one each on rationalization of centrally sponsored schemes, skill development, and Swacch Bharat, with NITI Aayog acting as the secretariat. During its first three months, it initiated the work relating to the Mid-Term Appraisal of the Twelfth Five-Year Plan.

All the three Sub-Groups of Chief Ministers submitted their reports during the year 2015–16. In the finalization of these reports, the officials of NITI Aayog seemed to have played their role more as agents of the Central Government than as technical advisers. This was evident from the fact that just a day after the presentation of the report of the Sub-Group of Chief Ministers on Rationalisation of Centrally Sponsored Schemes, the Ministry of Finance issued a notification without taking on board most of its recommendations. The fate of the reports by the other two Sub-Groups seems to have been similar.

In the second year of its operation, a second meeting of the Governing Council was held, which emphasized the shift in focus from planning to policy to influence the decisions of the private as well as the public sectors. The conference also emphasized the need for greater interaction between the Centre and the States. In this context, it was suggested that NITI Aayog should act as a repository of best practices for States and provide them advocacy support in resolving matters pending with the Union Ministries.

The Aayog took up the pending cases of the State of Telangana with the Union Ministries concerned while requesting other States to make use of its intermediation. But in retrospect, this role was more recommendatory and most of its suggestions were not acted upon by the Union Ministries concerned.

The Aayog also held a conference in July 2017 with the States to discuss their role in transforming India. However, the actions taken on the suggestions made by the States are still not known. It also published a number of papers on sectors like agriculture, health, education, skill development, managing urbanization, power, infrastructure, social justice, etc. In the area of policy advocacy, it prepared a draft bill on agricultural land leasing and one on regulatory reforms, and completed the appraisal of the Twelfth Five-Year Plan suggesting policy correction in a number of areas. Most of these areas are in the domain of States. During the year 2016–17, the Aayog included, under the label of 'notable initiatives', the constitution of a Committee of Chief Ministers on Digital Payments and initiated the process to develop identified islands for maritime trade, shipping, and fisheries, all areas identified as priority by Central Government.

The Aayog prepared the first-ever indices measuring States' performance in health, education, and water management. It also discussed issues relating to the removal of distinction between Plan and non-Plan expenditure, and the attainment of targets set under Sustainable Development Goals (SDGs) with State officials. Further, it took up the formulation of a Fifteen-Year Vision document as well as a Seven-Year Strategy and a Three-Year Action Agenda to ensure implementation of the Vision. Of these, the Three-Year Action Agenda has already been released and placed in the public domain. There is no evidence that the States have participated in the preparation of this Vision.

The Aayog's Annual Report gives a detailed account of its work during the year 2017–18. Of relevance to Union–State relations is the draft roadmap for the development of the Northeastern and Eastern States, which is laudable. There is a separate section devoted to cooperative federalism. The report highlights two key aspects, and these relate to the joint development of the national developmental agenda by the Centre and the States, and the advocacy of State perspectives with Central Ministries. It also lists a series of initiatives to ensure that 'States are equal partners in the policy-making and implementing process'. Among the items listed are the third meeting of the Governing Council, the National Conference of Chief Secretaries on drivers for transforming India, and several initiatives relating to agriculture.

To sum up, the activities of the Aayog since its inception have mainly been confined to bringing out reports and occasional papers on various sectors of the economy; preparing draft legislations and policy notes for the consideration of the Central Government; evaluating Central Government schemes and bringing out a compilation of best practices in certain sectors; holding conferences with State officials; and working as a secretariat for the Sub-Groups of Chief Ministers.

The singular achievement of NITI Aayog is that it has not irritated the States, as it has dispensed with the Annual Plan approval and the practice of giving grants.

AN INITIAL ASSESSMENT

It is clear that NITI Aayog is meant to be a replacement of the Planning Commission. In many ways, it is a new incarnation that warrants an initial assessment. It is intended to address the observed weaknesses in the functioning of the Planning Commission. It is also expected to give a new orientation to the manner in which the developmental process is managed. It seeks to address the most important aspect of the weaknesses in the working of the erstwhile Planning Commission, viz., the management of Union–State relations.

NITI Aayog's mandate is very broad and sweeping. It has inherited the physical infrastructure as well as the manpower from the erstwhile Planning Commission. (It has, however, taken a number of experts/advisers laterally.) Yet, the underlying ecosystem that governs the thinking has not changed demonstrably. Above all, the Planning Commission had a special stature by virtue of its Deputy Chairman being invited to the Cabinet meetings of the Union Government. The Vice Chairman of NITI Aayog has not been extended such a courtesy. In a way, therefore, NITI Aayog started with some disadvantages.

The Aayog's performance can be assessed with reference to what was promised when it was established. NITI Aayog was expected to address new realities of macroeconomic management that were missed by the Planning Commission. The stated objective was that the States would be allowed to implement their plans or functions assigned to them in the Constitution without having to get them approved. To this limited extent of giving up the practice of formal approval of the State plans, NITI Aayog has delivered.

The official notification establishing NITI Aayog recognized the pitfalls of the one-size-fits-all approach inherent in Central Planning. It is not very clear in what manner this has been changed. The notification also explained that the nature of the Planning process would be changed to align with the shifts in the economy. From the Annual Reports available, it is not very clear in what manner the process has been improved.

The notification also mentions the importance of making States the actual drivers of national development. However, most of the programmes initiated in the recent past were conceived and initiated by the Prime Minister and the Central Government, and the States have been more or less persuaded to implement them. It is difficult to find evidence that policies and programmes have evolved out of consultations between the Union and the States. On the contrary, many flagship schemes carry the 'prefix' 'Pradhan Mantri', and are declared as Central Government schemes.

The major complaints of States in regard to the functioning of the Planning Commission remain unaddressed. The complaints have largely been on the perception that the Centre is encroaching upon the States' responsibilities; imposing its own priorities while funding; assuming, without basis, that governance in States is weak despite the Union's own dismal record in administering Union Territories; taking credit for schemes that are jointly funded; and continuing to advocate a one-size-fits-all approach in administration.

The Aayog has missed some opportunities to make a qualitative difference. The CSS had to be reformed in the light of the recommendations of the Fourteenth Finance Commission. Though the Niti Aayog was involved in the process, the manner in which these schemes were modified shows that the effort was only to shift greater responsibility onto States in terms of financing. The reform does not in any manner reflect the qualitative change in the design and implementation of the Central schemes that was promised when the Planning Commission was wound up.

A second opportunity arose when the distinction between Plan and non-Plan was removed. At that point, the organization had an opportunity to insist on taking a sector-wise comprehensive view of capital and revenue expenditures. However, that has not been done.

COMPLEMENTING THE FINANCE COMMISSION

The primary objective of the arrangement for fiscal transfers is to correct the horizontal and vertical imbalances in fiscal management at the Union and State levels. The First Finance Commission confined itself to the revenue account, leaving the capital needs to be met out of borrowings. Consequently, the Planning Commission had to deal with fiscal transfers on account of capital needs, and access to borrowings by States and loans to them from the Centre became part of the remit of the Planning Commission. With the abolition of the Planning Commission, there is no evidence that its successor, NITI Aayog, is performing this role.

Successive Finance Commissions have recognized the fact that the budgetary situation of the Union Government had a direct bearing on State finances, but could not impose any conditions for its reform. They also could not evolve a system under which the Union Government adhered to its commitment to fiscal responsibility. As revenue account transfers from the Union to the States constitute more than one-third of the total revenue resources of the States, if the Union's revenue performance declines, States also get affected. To ensure prudent management of State finances, the Eleventh Finance Commission had suggested the creation of an incentive fund; the twelfth Commission had proposed the linking of States' debt relief to fiscal responsibility; and the thirteenth Commission had recommended incentive grants. Currently, the challenges of fiscal consolidation predominantly relate to Union finances. The Fourteenth Finance Commission emphasized the importance of establishing fiscal councils with a mandate to make ex-ante assessments of budget proposals. A weak fiscal position of the Union not only affects macroeconomic management and stability, but also has bearing on State finances. NITI Aayog has an opportunity and, indeed, an obligation to contribute to fiscal responsibility in both the Union and State Governments consistent with developmental priorities and sound fiscal federal relations. It is in a position to contribute to these objectives, as it is a continuing body and can play a critical, though advisory, role in regard to Union finances, State finances, and transfers from Union to States on a continuous basis.

The Fourteenth Finance Commission suggested a new institutional mechanism for transfers outside the recommendations of the Finance Commission in the interest of sound fiscal federalism. NITI Aayog could take advantage of the underlying logic of such institutional mechanisms and devise its methods in a manner consistent with the spirit of the recommendations. For sectors and activities for which Union transfers to States should take place, the design of schemes and the distribution of resources among the States will have to be worked out in a forum that has representation from the Union, the States, and domain experts.

The Fourteenth Finance Commission has eschewed prescribing conditionalities or policies that are considered desirable at a national level. It has addressed some of the overlap between the Finance Commission and the Planning Commission by relinquishing most of the State-specific or project-specific grants-in-aid and associated conditionalities in its recommendations. By relinquishing its marginal role as promoter of economic reforms, the Finance Commission has put additional responsibility on NITI Aayog to promote appropriate policies and schemes both in the Union and among States on a continuous basis.

Areas under Schedule VI of the Constitution in the northeastern States remain outside the ambit of the measures recommended by Finance Commissions for Panchayats and Municipalities and have been excluded from its ToR. This was necessitated by the fact that the Constitution mandates the Union Government to play a direct role in supporting the development of these areas. However, the quantum of assistance given over the years to these regions by Ministries in the Union Government has been very limited. NITI Aayog could consider larger assistance and more effective intervention for the upgrade of administration as well as the development of these areas.

The ToR, barring the core ones, of the Finance Commission, have been expanding over a period and have also been varying. Many of them had overlap with the work of the Planning Commission, while a few others related to tax reforms, expenditure reforms, public enterprise reforms, pricing of public utilities, etc. Further, the recommendations in regard to other ToR have often been treated as mere suggestions and seldom acted upon vigorously. At the same time, the other ToR reduce the focus and the attention that the Finance Commission could give to its core ToR. NITI Aayog may legitimately address on a continuous basis the undeniably important policy issues often incorporated in other ToR of the Finance Commission, thus reducing its need to address such issues in an ad hoc and often arbitrary manner. This initiative will relieve the burden on the Finance Commission in meeting some of the controversial ToR.

▼▲▼

It may be fair to conclude that many irritants in Union–State relations that arose in the functioning of the Planning Commission have been removed with its abolition. However, NITI Aayog has not been able to come forward with anything positive in that sphere. The scope and the remit of NITI Aayog has been expanded and its stature reduced, with the result that there is little evidence of a focus in its working. This has resulted in a vacuum of institutional and procedural arrangements for interaction between Union and States. That vacuum has been unfortunately occupied by the Ministries in the Union Government.

SELECT REFERENCES

1. Alagh, Yoginder K. 2018, 'The Next Stage of Planning in India', *Economic and Political Weekly*, 53(26–27), 30 June.

2. Cabinet Secretariat. 2015. 'Cabinet Resolution', *Gazette of India: Extraordinary*, 1 January. New Delhi: Government of India.

3. Patnaik, Prabhat. 2015. 'From the Planning Commission to the NITI Aayog', *Economic and Political Weekly*, 50(4), 24 January.

4. NITI Aayog. 2018. *Annual Report 2017–18*. New Delhi: Government of India.

5. Rao, M. Govinda. 2015. 'Role and functions of NITI Aayog', *Economic and Political Weekly*, 50(4), 24 January.

6. Reddy, Y.V. 2014. 'A Tale of Two Commissions and Missing Links', Presidential Address, 97th Annual Conference of Indian Economic Association, 24 December, Udaipur, Rajasthan.

14

PUBLIC DEBT AND FINANCE COMMISSIONS

THE FIRST FINANCE COMMISSION MADE it clear that it was primarily concerned with the distribution of revenues between the Centre and the States and the determination of grants-in-aid of State revenues (which came from Central revenues), and that the capital needs of both the Centre and States had to be met largely from borrowed funds. Until 2004–5, fiscal transfers under the Plan account had both loan and grant components. Thus, a part of the fiscal transfers to States outside the Finance Commission awards was in the form of loans. In addition, until 1998–9, small savings collections by the Centre were directly lent to the States concerned. It is, therefore, not surprising that over a period, the ToR of the Finance Commissions included issues relating to the assessment of the outstanding debt of States and, in particular, the debt owed by the States to the Centre. The remit of the Finance Commissions with respect to the debt burden and its sustainability evolved with the changing interface between the Centre and the States in regard to borrowings.

EVOLUTION OF INTERFACE IN BORROWINGS

The Constitution enables both the Union and the States to borrow, but within the limits prescribed by their respective legislatures. However, the Union and the States are not on par in their ability to access debt. Borrowings by a State need the approval of the Union as long as it is in debt to the Union. Further, States cannot borrow externally as per the Constitution. Hence, the Union is an intermediary for external flows to State Governments. The aggregate debt of the Central and State Governments net of inter-governmental debt is the total public debt of the country.

The sustainable levels of aggregate debt and the relative shares of public debt of the Union and States, and of each State, are to a large extent determined by the Union Government. Access to debt is a resource available today but should be serviced in the future. Hence, the interface between Union and States on matters relating to public debt is of significance in their fiscal relations.

The policies and procedures adopted by the Centre over the years in regard to determining States' access to debt can be divided into certain phases. In the first phase, which may be called the pre-Gadgil formula phase, the dominant source of debt of the States was the Central Government, but the amount of debt was a result of mainly cumulative loan components of different schemes. This was one of the issues that was addressed by D.R. Gadgil in determining the formula in the allocation of Central Plan assistance to States and suggesting that the loan and grant component of such assistance may be 70:30. The amount of Plan assistance that each State would get was also subject to a formula largely based on population. However, for special-category States, the proportion of grant assistance was 90 per cent. In addition to the loan component of Plan assistance, States were permitted access to market borrowings as determined by the Centre in the Plan process.

The procedure adopted for the approval of the Plan consisted of determining the surplus of revenues; additional resource mobilization; Central assistance; and market borrowings. The market borrowings component, however, was determined as a result of discussions between the Planning Commission and the Union Ministry of Finance incrementally every year. The level of borrowings permitted under the Plan included borrowings by power utility, transport utility, and promotional industrial organizations. In other words, the States' access to debt was determined partly as a result of the Gadgil formula and partly as a result of the continuing negotiations. The grant of access to borrowings by the Union Government meant that they could take place smoothly for all States. This was enabled by the fact that the RBI was the debt manager for the Union and the States.

The access to borrowings by the government was smooth, partly because banks were nationalized in 1969 and provided a captive source, and partly because of the extensive recourse to automatic monetization since 1957. Automatic monetization meant that the RBI was obliged to make available the amounts required to the Government of India virtually as a loan in perpetuity at low interest rates. This continued until the reforms in the 1990s, when the fiscal profligacy of both the Centre and States played a hand in the balance-of-payments crisis in 1991.

The reforms that were initiated as a consequence of the crisis in 1991 included fiscal consolidation. In order to achieve this objective, the RBI initiated the process of estimating the aggregate public debt and an optimal borrowing programme consistent with macro stability, and recommending the same to the Government of India. The Government of India, in consultation with the Planning Commission, decided the allocation of such debt between the Centre and States and among the States. There was no particular formula governing the distribution of debt among the States, except that a policy of proportional increase to the States over the previous year was adopted as a matter of convenience. There have been many occasions where individual States were permitted additional borrowings at the discretion of the Union Government. The access to market borrowings under the procedure was part of the Plan process. In brief, the access of State Governments' debt was partly derived from formula and partly ad hoc, with a few exceptions.

As part of the reforms, the Central Government took increasing recourse to market borrowings, with the interest rates increasingly determined by market conditions. This period marked the move to encourage States to take recourse to borrowings on a stand-alone basis, replacing the tranche approach. (In a tranche approach, the borrowing programmes of the States were pooled and securities were issued to them at a uniform rate and maturity.) When States' borrowing programmes are funded on a stand-alone basis, interest rates may be varied reflecting the market perception in regard to the fiscal position of individual States. This did not, however, change the access to debt accorded by the Union Government.

In 2003, fiscal responsibility legislation virtually put a ceiling to the borrowing programme of the Centre. State Governments were also encouraged to put a limit on fiscal deficits as well as guarantees. This was enforced through the requirement of approval of the States' borrowing programme by the Union Government.

As a result of the recommendation of the Twelfth Finance Commission, the Government of India decided to put a stop to the intermediation of loans to States by the Centre. In other words, Plan assistance from the States would no longer contain a loan component, and all amounts transferred would be grants. The States were, therefore, required to access debt mostly through market-borrowing programmes. They were also given the flexibility to pre-pay some debt or restructure it. During this period, a State's access to debt was determined by its GSDP, from which the level of permissible borrowings was determined.

In practice, the Central Government breached the limits imposed on the borrowings. On some occasions, the States could also breach the fiscal-deficit limits. This was possible for several reasons. The States had access to a share of the net National Small Savings raised in their jurisdictions. They could also circumvent the rules by creating special-purpose vehicles for budgetary support. Some breach of the limits was also tolerated at the instance of the Union Government in connection with reforms in the power sector. Another way in which they breached the limit was by having State enterprises borrow while the State Government stood as guarantor and later took over the loan to avoid default.

In addition to the National Small Savings and special-purpose vehicles influencing the access to debt, there have been occasions in the past where the Government of India extended loans to give relief to States from persistent large overdrafts drawn on the RBI. Debt was written off by the Central Government in select cases, and was also restructured as per the recommendations of the Finance Commission.

FINANCE COMMISSIONS AND RECOMMENDATIONS ON PUBLIC DEBT

The Sixth Finance Commission was the first to be associated in a substantive manner with issues of debt. It was asked to undertake a general review of the States' debt position, with particular reference to Central loans advanced to them, and suggest changes in the terms of repayment, keeping in view the overall non-Plan capital gaps of States, arrived at on a uniform and comparable basis. The Commission arrived at the non-Plan capital gap/surplus of each State and recommended the write-off of pre-autonomy outstanding loans (loans dating back from 1937 extended to Provinces in pre-Independent India and later allocated to States). It also made a general review of the debt position of the States, with particular reference to the Central loans advanced to them and likely to be outstanding at the end of 1973–4, and recommended changes in the terms of repayment having regard to the non-Plan capital gaps of States.

The Seventh Finance Commission's ToR was more or less the same, with the exception that it was asked to suggest appropriate measures to deal with the non-Plan capital gaps. After working them out, it categorized the loans advanced by the Centre to States on the basis of their deemed utilization as non-productive, semi-productive, and productive. The Commission recommended different periods for the repayment of outstanding loans at the end of 1978–9 based on the categorization.

The eighth Commission's mandate on this subject was similar to that of the seventh. It excluded loans against overdrafts and small savings loans while working out the non-Plan capital gaps of States and recommended no relief in respect of these loans. It also recommended that loans for the relief and rehabilitation of displaced persons be written off. For the outstanding pre-1979 loans consolidated by its immediate predecessor, the Commission recommended their consolidation and repayment in 25 years for a few States and 30 years for others. For other loans (excluding those to clear overdrafts and small savings loans) extended by the Centre in 1979–84 that were outstanding at the end of March 1984, the Commission recommended their consolidation into a single loan whose repayment ranged from 15 to 30 years for different States.

The Ninth Finance Commission's ToR differed significantly from those of the last three Commissions. It was asked to make an assessment of the debt position of the States as on 31 March 1989 and suggest such corrective measures as deemed necessary, keeping in view the financial requirements of the Centre. There was no reference to non-Plan capital gaps. The Commission recommended relief for Plan loans to States extended during 1984–9 outstanding at the end of March 1990 linked to the States' performance in respect of their investments in the power and transport sectors. For this purpose, the States were divided into categories.

The Tenth Finance Commission's mandate was similar to that of the ninth. It was asked to make an assessment of the debt position of the States as on 31 March 1994 and suggest such corrective measures as were deemed necessary, keeping in view the financial requirements of the Centre. There was no reference to non-Plan capital gaps of States. The scheme for debt relief recommended by the tenth Commission had two parts: general debt relief for all the States linked to fiscal performance, and specific relief for States with higher fiscal stress and for special-category States. It measured fiscal performance by comparing the ratio of total revenue receipts to total revenue expenditure in a given year with the average corresponding ratio in the three immediately preceding years. The Commission recommended double the excess of the ratio over the average ratio of fiscal improvement in the preceding three years as relief in respect of the Central loans contracted during 1989–95 and due for repayment after 31 March 1995. However, the relief was limited to 10 per cent of the amount due for repayment in a year.

The Tenth Finance Commission was the first to link debt relief to performance. In addition, it recommended debt relief to the highly debt-stressed States and special-category States. It also recommended relief in respect of the special term loans advanced to Punjab to fight militancy and insurgency.

The ToR of the Eleventh Finance Commission was entirely different from those of the previous Commissions in regard to the debt position of the States, perhaps reflecting the deteriorating fiscal health of the country as a whole. The ToR stipulated that the Commission shall review the state of finances of the Union and the States and suggest ways and means by which governments, collectively and severally, might bring about a restructuring of the public finances so as to restore budgetary balance and maintain macroeconomic stability. The Commission was also asked to review the debt position of States and suggest remedial measures keeping in view long-term sustainability for them as well as for the Centre. The Commission took the stand that any scheme of debt relief should be guided by the objective of initiating corrective measures leading to debt sustainability. In this context, it felt that performance-linked relief recommended by the tenth Commission, with some modifications, was the most suitable. It expressed the view that a higher quantum of relief linked to performance would act as an incentive for better performance. The Commission increased the extent of relief from the factor of 2 on the improvement in the ratio of total revenue receipts (excluding deficit grants) to total expenditure recommended by its predecessor to 5 and increased the relief which was limited to 10 per cent of repayments in a year to 25 per cent. It further recommended limits on guarantees given by the Central and State Governments and the establishment of a sinking fund in each State for amortization of debt.

The Eleventh Finance Commission recommended a detailed plan of restructuring the finances of the Centre and States. It recommended, in a Supplementary Report, the setting up of an Incentive Fund consisting of 15 per cent of withheld revenue-deficit grants and an equal contribution by the Centre. The eligibility of a State for incentive grants would depend on the adherence to State-specific monitorable reforms programme. The Commission identified five indicators of performance and assigned indicative weightage to them:

growth of tax revenue (30 per cent), growth of non-tax revenue (20 per cent), non-Plan revenue expenditure on salaries and allowances (30 per cent), interest payments (10 per cent), and reduction of subsidies (10 per cent). The ToR of the Twelfth Finance Commission was extended further to include suggesting a plan for debt reduction along with equitable growth. The Commission was also mandated to review the debt position of States and recommend corrective measures giving due weightage to their performance with regard to human development and investment climate. It made significant recommendations by making debt relief conditional on States enacting fiscal responsibility legislations. It recommended the consolidation of Central loans and write-off linked to the reduction of the States' revenue deficit. The Commission recommended the termination of the Centre acting as an intermediary in lending to States and passing on external assistance on a back-to-back basis. It also recommended a fiscal adjustment path.

The thirteenth Commission was required to review the state of finances of the Union and States, keeping in view, in particular, the operation of the States' Debt Consolidation and Relief Facility 2005–2010, introduced by the Central Government on the basis of the recommendations of the Twelfth Finance Commission, and suggest measures for maintaining a stable and sustainable fiscal environment consistent with equitable growth. By an additional ToR, the Commission was asked to review the roadmap of fiscal adjustment with a view to maintaining the gains of fiscal consolidation through 2010–15, keeping in mind the need to bring the liabilities of the Central Government on account of oil, food, and fertilizer bonds into fiscal accounting and the impact of its various other obligations on the deficit targets.

The thirteenth Commission recommended the write-off of loans for CSS and Central Plan schemes outstanding at the end of 2009–10. The Commission further recommended a revised roadmap for fiscal consolidation by progressive reduction and elimination of the Centre's revenue deficit by 2014–15 and prescribed a target of 68 per cent of GDP for the combined debt of the Centre and the States by 2014–15 (45 per cent for the Centre and less than 25 per cent for the States).

It recommended different roadmaps for different States depending on their levels of deficits.

The scope of the ToR of the Fourteenth Finance Commission was extended further in regard to debt levels. The Commission was mandated to review the state of the finances and the deficit and debt levels of the Union and the States, keeping in view, in particular, the fiscal consolidation roadmap recommended by the Thirteenth Finance Commission. It was also tasked with suggesting measures for maintaining a stable and sustainable fiscal environment consistent with equitable growth, including suggestions to amend the FRBM Acts which were in force. While doing so, the Commission was asked to take into consideration the effect of the receipts and expenditure in the form of grants for the creation of capital assets on the deficits; and to recommend incentives and disincentives for States for observing the obligations laid down in the FRBM Acts.

The Fourteenth Finance Commission felt that a uniform and rigid fiscal rule would not only undermine the fiscal autonomy of the States, but would also result in undesirable cuts in development expenditure to comply with numerical targets. It recommended different fiscal consolidation paths for revenue-deficit and revenue-surplus States. Finally, it attempted to consider the governments' risk exposure to its public sector in the form of guarantees, off-budget borrowings, and accumulated losses of financially weak public sector enterprises (PSEs). In this context, it explored the concept of extended debt, analysing different indicators, including the debt of PSEs, guarantees to them, and a risk-weighted combination of the guarantees. However, its analysis was constrained by the non-availability of comprehensive audited data.

THE CURRENT STATUS

In sum, the access of States to debt was initially predominantly ad hoc. Over a period, it became more formula based. More recently, fiscal rules determine States' access to debt, subject to the approval of the Central Government. In the process, the share of market borrowings has increased, and the share of the Centre as a source of debt to States has declined. The current system has two implications. First, the ceiling on access to borrowings is predominantly determined by the GSDP. Second, the terms and conditions under which public borrowings can be raised in the market tend to be favourable to the richer States.

The relative allocation of debt between the Union and States was addressed formally and explicitly by the N.K. Singh Committee (FRBM Review Committee). The Committee, in its report submitted in January 2017, recommended the enactment of a new Debt and Fiscal Responsibility Act and the adoption of a medium-term ceiling of general government debt of 60 per cent of the GDP to be achieved by no later than 2022–3 (with a ceiling of 40 per cent for the Centre and 20 per cent for the States). It recommended the adoption of fiscal deficit as the key operational target, consistent with achieving the medium-term debt ceiling. Accordingly, the Committee recommended the reduction of fiscal deficit to 2.5 per cent of the GDP and that of revenue deficit to 0.8 per cent in a phased manner by fiscal year 2023. These recommendations, if implemented, will change the relative shares of the Union and States in their access to public debt and the fiscal reform path contemplated by the Fourteenth Finance Commission. Currently, FRBM Acts of the Union and States are consistent with the fiscal reform paths recommended by the fourteenth Commission.

▼▲▼

To conclude, the role of the Finance Commission as contemplated in the Constitution relates to the sharing of Central tax revenue and grants from the Centre to States. However, the initiation of planned economic development through the institution of the Planning Commission resulted in the transfer of resources from the Centre to the States in the form of both grants and loans. With the increase in the debt burden of the States, issues relating to debt were added to the remit of the Finance Commission from the sixth Commission onwards. The initiation of economic reforms brought to the fore the sustainability of general government debt (that of the Centre and States combined) and the debt sustainability of the Centre as well as individual States. The focus, therefore, shifted to fiscal sustainability compatible with macroeconomic stability. Another development was the Centre giving up the practice of additional borrowings for on-lending to States, except in the case of EAPs. The role of the Finance Commission accordingly shifted from recommending debt restructuring to rule-based fiscal regimes and roadmaps for fiscal consolidation.

SELECT REFERENCES

1. RBI. Various Years. *Annual Reports*. Mumbai: RBI.
2. RBI. Various Years. *State Finances: A Study of Budgets*. Mumbai: RBI.
3. RBI. 2017. *Statistical Tables Relating to Indian Economy*. Mumbai: RBI.

15

AGGREGATE CENTRAL TRANSFERS TO STATES

THE CORE OF FISCAL FEDERALISM in India relates to transfers from the Union to the States. Transfers are predominantly based on the recommendations of the Finance Commission, and consist of tax devolution and grants. With the initiation of planned economic development and the Centre's interventions in a number of subjects in the State List in the form of CSS, a significant number of transfers are taking place outside the recommendations of the Finance Commission. Therefore, to get a comprehensive view of Central transfers, it becomes necessary to analyse the aggregate transfers, i.e., those recommended by the Finance Commission and those made outside of it. A study of these shows that vertical as well as horizontal balances recommended by the Finance Commission can be counterbalanced to some extent by the Union through the levy of cesses and surcharges and through non-Finance Commission transfers.

AGGREGATE TRANSFERS: MAGNITUDES

The aggregate transfers to States as a percentage of GDP increased from around 2 per cent in the early 1960s to 6.35 per cent in 2016–17.

Within the overall transfers, the share of tax devolution started increasing, and by 2016–17, tax devolution as a percentage of GDP increased to 4 per cent. This was mainly because of the following: increase in tax devolution recommended by successive Finance Commissions; the subsuming of some Plan grants in tax devolution; and the absence of sector-specific grants in the award of the Fourteenth Finance Commission. The trends in the aggregate Central transfers to States are presented in Figure 15.1.

When we examine the aggregate transfers to States as a share in the gross revenue of the Centre, the trends are not as favourable as they appear. As a percentage of Central gross revenues they ranged between 33 and 42 per cent from 1990–1 to 2013–14, excluding direct transfers to implementing agencies in the States. The spike to over 46 per cent in 2014–15 and around 50 per cent in 2018–19 (BE) was on account of the termination of direct transfers to implementing agencies and the marginal increase in tax devolution (see Table 16.2 for recent trends). This is because the Centre's revenue outside the divisible pool had increased significantly through the levy of cesses and surcharges (these are exclusively earmarked for the Centre's use).

Figure 15.1 Trends in Aggregate Central Transfers to States (As Percentage of GDP)

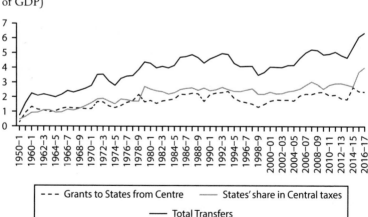

Source: Derived from Union Budgets and Union Finance Accounts, various years.

There was a also a significant increase in the non-tax revenues of the Centre (which are outside the divisible pool for the purpose of tax devolution).

RELATIVE SHARES OF THE UNION AND STATES IN COMBINED REVENUE AND EXPENDITURE

A remarkable feature of Indian fiscal federalism is the near stability in the shares of the Centre and the States in the combined revenue receipts both before and after transfers (see Table 15.1). At the pre-transfer stage, these mainly consist of their respective tax and non-tax revenues. In the post-transfer scenario, the revenue receipts of States are inclusive of own tax and non-tax revenues, tax devolution, and grants from the Centre.

The share of revenue receipts of the Centre (pre-transfer) in the combined revenue receipts ranged between 58.50 per cent and 64.75 per cent from 1984–2017. Transfers from the Centre, both statutory and non-statutory, remained stable at around 25 per cent of its total revenue receipts until 2013–14. The spike in the transfers to States in 2014–15 was more from a change in accounting than from any real increase in transfers. In 2014–15, the Centre dispensed with the practice of transferring money directly to the implementing agencies, bypassing the States. Since then, transfers to implementing agencies are routed through the State Governments for more accountability.

Though the Fourteenth Finance Commission increased tax devolution, it was essentially a compositional shift from tied to untied transfers. Also, the tax devolution recommended by the Commission subsumed some of the Plan transfers to States and covered both Plan and non-Plan revenue expenditure.

The shares of the Centre and States in the combined total expenditure (revenue and capital) post transfers remained stable at about 45 per cent and 55 per cent respectively till 2014–15. From 2014–15, there was an increase in the share of States in the combined total expenditure, mainly because direct transfers to them were terminated (see Table 15.2). A similar trend is noticed in regard to the shares of the Centre and the States in the combined revenue

Table 15.1 Relative Shares of the Union and States in the Combined Revenue Receipts

(Per Cent)

Period	Union			States		
*Finance Commission = FC	Revenue Receipts Before Transfers	Transfers (Statutory and Non-Statutory)	Revenue Receipts After Transfers	Revenue Receipts Before Transfers	Transfers (Statutory and Non-Statutory)	Revenue Receipts After Transfers
FC-VIII (1984–9)	65.40	26.70	38.70	34.60	26.70	61.30
FC-IX (1989–95)	62.80	27.50	35.30	37.20	27.50	64.70
FC-X (1995–2000)	60.80	24.50	36.30	39.20	24.50	63.70
FC-XI (2000–5)	58.50	25.20	33.30	41.50	25.20	66.70
FC-XII (2005–10)	63.81	25.36	38.45	36.19	25.36	61.55
2010–11	64.68	24.49	40.20	35.32	24.49	59.80
2011–12	60.63	26.51	34.12	39.37	26.51	65.88
2012–13	60.33	24.68	35.64	39.67	24.68	64.36
2013–14	61.10	23.64	37.46	38.90	23.64	62.54
2014–15	60.99	28.26	32.72	39.01	28.26	67.28
2015–16	63.04	30.73	32.31	36.96	30.73	67.69
2016–17	64.75	31.39	33.37	35.25	31.39	66.63

Source: Compiled from *Fourteenth Finance Commission, 2015–2020* (Volume I) for data up to the Twelfth Finance Commission, and for 2010–11 to 2016–17, *Receipt Budget, 2018–19*, and *State Finances: A Study of Budgets,* various issues.

Table 15.2 Relative Shares of the Union and States in Revenue
and Total Expenditure

Finance Commission (FC) Periods	Total Expenditure		Revenue Expenditure	
	Union	States	Union	States
FC-I (1952–7)	43.83	56.17	40.77	59.23
FC-II (1957–62)	49.47	50.53	41.83	58.17
FC-III (1962–6)	50.51	49.49	46.10	53.90
FC-IV (1966–9)	47.69	52.31	41.77	58.23
FC-V (1969–74)	43.14	56.86	40.00	60.00
FC-VI (1974–9)	47.35	52.65	44.19	55.81
FC-VII (1979–84)	44.79	55.21	41.98	58.02
FC-VIII (1984–9)	47.86	52.14	44.22	55.78
FC-IX (1989–95)	45.58	54.42	43.45	56.55
FC-X (1995–2000)	43.35	56.65	43.18	56.82
FC-XI (2000–5)	43.77	56.23	44.03	55.97
FC-XII (2005–10)	46.08	53.92	47.59	52.41
2010–11	48.47	51.53	48.67	51.33
2011–12	47.11	52.89	47.51	52.49
2012–13	45.46	54.54	46.24	53.76
2013–14	45.29	54.71	45.95	54.05
2014–15	41.14	58.86	41.24	58.76

Source: Report of Fourteenth Finance Commission for data up to Twelfth Finance Commission, and from 2010–11 to 2014–15, *Indian Public Finance Statistics 2016–17*.

expenditure post transfers. In the period covered by the First Finance Commission (1952–7), the relative shares of the Centre and States were 41 per cent and 59 per cent respectively. It was a similar situation in 2014–15.

COMPOSITION OF TRANSFERS

From 1995–6 until 2013–14, transfers from the Finance Commission ranged between 68 per cent and 73 per cent of the total transfers (see Table 15.3). In the year 2014–15, there was a drop in the share of Finance Commission transfers to 60.15 per cent, and a corresponding

Table 15.3 Percentage Shares of Finance Commission Transfers and Other Transfers (Accounts)

Years	Finance Commission (FC) Transfers			Other Transfers			Total Transfers (Total Finance Commission Transfers + Total Other Transfers)
	Share in Central Taxes	Grants	Total Finance Commission Transfers (Share in Central Taxes + Grants)	Plan Grants	Non-Plan Grants	Total Other Transfers (Plan + Non-Plan Grants)	
FC-VIII (1984–9)	53.48	6.65	60.13	35.80	4.07	39.87	100.00
FC-IX (1989–5)	52.98	8.48	61.46	35.91	2.63	38.54	100.00
FC-X (1995–2000)	62.06	6.55	68.61	29.52	1.87	31.39	100.00
FC-XI (2000–5)	58.38	11.00	69.38	28.65	1.97	30.62	100.00
2005–6	56.98	14.95	71.93	25.37	2.70	28.07	100.00
2006–7	57.92	13.47	71.39	25.56	3.05	28.61	100.00
2007–8	59.09	10.14	69.23	27.51	3.26	30.77	100.00
2008–9	57.08	9.61	66.69	29.87	3.44	33.31	100.00
2009–10	55.08	9.74	64.82	30.19	4.99	35.18	100.00
2010–11	59.03	8.33	67.36	28.03	4.61	32.64	100.00
2011–12	59.67	10.11	69.78	28.69	1.53	30.22	100.00
2012–13	62.69	9.64	72.33	27.27	0.40	27.67	100.00
2013–14	62.75	10.48	73.23	25.54	1.23	26.77	100.00
2014–15	50.75	9.40	60.15	37.69	2.15	39.84	100.00
2015–16	62.37	10.65	73.02	24.80	2.18	26.98	100.00
2016–17	66.86	11.67	78.53	19.96	1.52	21.48	100.00

Source: Thirteenth Finance Commission, 2010–2015 (Volume II) for data up to the Eleventh Finance Commission and from 2005–6 to 2016–17, *Finance Accounts of Government of India*, various issues.

Note: Because these figures have been rounded off, the totals may not add exactly up to 100.

increase in other transfers, to about 40 per cent, mainly on account of the termination of direct transfers to implementing agencies. From 2015–16 onwards, there was an increase in the share of Finance Commission transfers, to 78 per cent in 2016–17, with a corresponding drop in the share of other transfers. As already indicated, from 2015–16, transfers from the Finance Commission subsumed some of the Plan transfers.

One noteworthy development consequent upon the acceptance of the recommendations of the Fourteenth Finance Commission is the decline in discretionary transfers since 2015–16 from the Centre. With the removal of distinction between Plan and non-Plan, the predominant share of the Finance Commission transfers in total transfers is likely to continue, if the Centre does not use its fiscal headroom to introduce more schemes funded by the Centre.

EQUITY IN TRANSFERS

The per capita Finance Commission transfers during the period 2010–15 were found to be more equitable than other transfers, as seen from Figures 15.2 and 15.3.

Figure 15.2 Average Per Capita Finance Commission Transfers and Per Capita Income in 2010–15

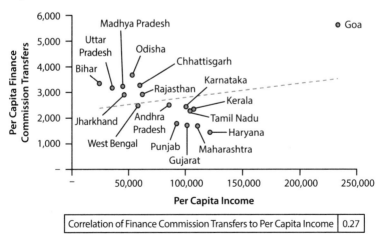

| Correlation of Finance Commission Transfers to Per Capita Income | 0.27 |

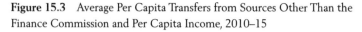

Figure 15.3 Average Per Capita Transfers from Sources Other Than the Finance Commission and Per Capita Income, 2010–15

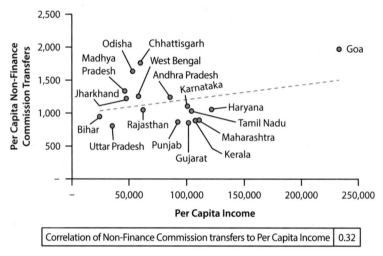

| Correlation of Non-Finance Commission transfers to Per Capita Income | 0.32 |

EQUITY IN SOCIAL SECTOR EXPENDITURE

Though there is no distinct trend, by and large, the per capita expenditure of the high per capita income States on social sectors tended to be higher (see Figure 15.4). The differential in the per capita expenditure across States widened between 2006–7 and 2016–17.

EQUITY IN CAPITAL EXPENDITURE

The per capita capital expenditure by States also shows a mixed trend, but on the whole, high-income States are able to incur more capital expenditure on a per capita basis (see Figure 15.5). But a clear trend that is discernible is the growing inequalities in the per capita capital expenditure across States between 2006–7 and 2016–17.

Since the capital requirements of States are outside the remit of the Finance Commissions, a new institutional mechanism may be needed to address this issue for backward States. Alternatively, NITI Aayog has to be empowered to consider the issue of equity in capital expenditure in States.

Figure 15.4 Per Capita Expenditure of Major States on Social Services, 2006–7 and 2016–17

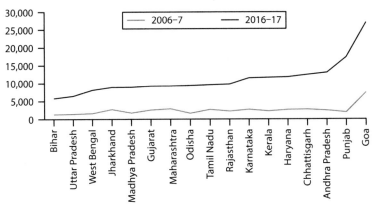

Source: *State Finances: A Study of Budgets,* 2008–9 and 2018–19.
Note: 1. The 2016–17 figures for Telangana and Andhra Pradesh are combined for the purpose of comparison.

2. These States belong to the general category and are relatively larger in terms of both population and area as compared with special-category States.

Figure 15.5 Per Capita Capital Expenditure of Major States, 2006–7 and 2016–17

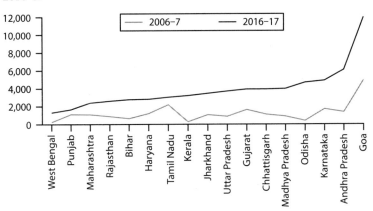

Source: *RBI States Finances,* 2008–09 and 2018–19.
Note: 2016–17 figures for Telangana and Andhra Pradesh are combined for the purpose of comparison.

TAX DEVOLUTION RELATIVE TO GROSS TAX REVENUE

Despite the increase in tax devolution recommended by successive Finance Commissions, the share of tax devolution in the gross tax revenue of the Centre remained between 26 and 28 per cent until 2014–15 (see Table 15.4).

The relative stability is almost wholly because of the levy of cesses and surcharges, which are outside the divisible pool of Central taxes. These neutralized the increase in tax devolution recommended by the successive Finance Commissions. The extent to which the Centre has pre-empted tax revenue for its own use through increased recourse to these is evident from Table 15.5.

The proceeds of cesses and surcharges, which constituted only 2.3 per cent of the gross tax revenue of the Centre, increased to 11.3 per cent by 2012–13, and then to more than 14 per cent in recent years.

Table 15.4 Tax Devolution to States Relative to Gross Tax Revenue of the Union

(Rs in Crore)

Year	Tax Devolution	Gross Tax Revenue of the Centre	% of Tax Devolution to Gross Tax Revenue
1980–1	3,790	13,149	28.8
1990–1	14,241	57,576	24.7
2000–1	50,737	188,603	26.9
2010–11	219,489	793,072	27.7
2011–12	255,592	889,177	28.7
2012–13	291,530	1,036,235	28.1
2013–14	311,572	1,138,733	27.4
2014–15	337,807	1,244,886	27.1
2015–16	506,193	1,455,648	34.8
2016–17	607,860	1,715,822	35.4
2017–18 (RE)	693,420	1,946,119	35.6
2018–19 (BE)	814,660	2,271,242	35.9

Source: State Finances: A Study of Budgets, various years, and Gross Tax Revenue as per Budget Documents of Ministry of Finance, Government of India.

Table 15.5 Shares of Revenue from Cesses and Surcharges in the Gross Tax
Revenue of the Centre

(Rs in Crore)

Year	Gross Tax Revenue of the Centre	Cesses and Surcharges	Cesses and Surcharges as % of GTR of the Centre
1980–1	13,149	298	2.3
1990–1	57,576	3,334	5.8
2000–1	188,603	5,655	3.0
2012–13	1,036,235	117,399	11.3
2013–14	1,138,733	135,800	11.9
2014–15	1,244,886	179,643	14.4
2015–16	1,455,648	239,777	16.5
2016–17	1,715,822	255,591	14.9
2017–18 RE	1,946,119	284,768	14.6
2018–19 BE	2,271,242	324,622	14.3

Source: Report of Twelfth Finance Commission for Data up to 2001–2 and from
2011–12 to 2018–19 Union Budget, various issues.

The hope that the share of cesses and surcharges will reduce with
the roll-out of GST has been belied for now. The Union Government
introduced new cesses on imports to make up for the cesses subsumed
under GST.

▼▲▼

There has been relative stability in the shares of the Union and the
States in revenues in the combined revenue and the (combined)
revenue expenditure. One of the main reasons for this is the levy
of cesses and surcharges by the Union. State Governments have
been pleading before successive Finance Commissions to include the
proceeds of cesses and surcharges in the divisible pool of Central
taxes. The Finance Commissions, though sympathetic to the pleas
of the States, were handicapped because the proceeds of cesses
and surcharges do not form part of the divisible pool as per the
Constitutional provisions. So, a number of Commissions exhorted

the Centre to review the policy with regard to the levy of cesses and keep them at the barest minimum.

A similar trend is observed in the case of the relative shares of the Centre and States in the combined total expenditure.

Another remarkable trend is the relative stability in the shares of the Finance Commission and non-Finance Commission transfers from 1984–5 to 2014–15. With the fourteenth Commission taking into consideration the entire revenue account and subsuming some of the Plan transfers in tax devolution, there has been an increase in the share of Finance Commission transfers post 2014–15.

SELECT REFERENCES

1. Controller General of Accounts. *Union Finance Accounts*, Various Issues. New Delhi: Government of India.

2. Ministry of Finance. Various Years. Report of the Finance Commission, XII–XIV. New Delhi: Government of India.

3. RBI. *State Finances: A Study of Budgets*, Various Issues. Mumbai: RBI.

4. Srivastava, D.K. and Bhujanga Rao. 2009. 'Review of Trends in Fiscal Transfers in India', Report Submitted to the Thirteenth Finance Commission, July. New Delhi: Government of India.

16

THE FIFTEENTH
FINANCE COMMISSION
NEW CHALLENGES

THE APPOINTMENT OF THE FIFTEENTH FINANCE COMMISSION on 27 November 2017 has come at a time of momentous changes in India's fiscal federalism. Since the Fourteenth Finance Commission submitted its report in 2014, the Planning Commission, an iconic institution, was wound up, and the NITI Aayog established in January 2015 in its place. The classification of expenditure into Plan and non-Plan was dispensed with from 2017–18. The introduction of the much-awaited GST in July 2017 fundamentally altered the relative roles of the Union and the States in regard to indirect taxes, and the GST Council, a forum of Finance Ministers at the Union–State level, was set up on a permanent basis. The Fifteenth Finance Commission has the onerous task of addressing these and other domestic developments amid an uncertain global geopolitical and economic outlook, making its responsibilities all the more challenging. The task has been made particularly difficult because of the unprecedented controversies surrounding its ToR (see Annexure 16A.1) and associated considerations.

The controversies relate to revenue-deficit grants; use of the 2011 population figures; review of tax devolution recommended by the fourteenth Commission; the imperative of the national development programme, including New India 2022; imposition of conditions by the Union while providing consent to the borrowings of States; performance-based incentives; and the assessment of resources and matters relating to GST.

REVENUE-DEFICIT GRANTS

One of the core functions entrusted to the Finance Commissions and included in their ToR, starting from the Second to the Fourteenth Finance Commission (2014), is to make recommendations on:

> the principles which should govern the grants-in-aid of the revenues of States out of the Consolidated Fund of India and the sums to be paid to the States which are in need of assistance by way of grants-in-aid of their revenues under article 275 of the Constitution for purposes other than those specified in the provisos to clause (1) of that article.

In the ToR of the Fifteenth Finance Commission, the words 'which are in need of assistance' have been omitted.

The ToR may thus be viewed as a violation of Articles 275 and 280 of the Constitution according to some critics, as it is tantamount to asking the Commission to ignore Articles 275 (1) and 280 (3) (b).

In favour of the ToR, it is argued that there is no need for gap grants because, following the enactment of Fiscal Responsibility and Budget Management Act (FRBM), all States are statutorily liable to balance their revenue accounts. However, this argument is countered by clarifying that States are under an obligation to balance their revenue accounts after factoring the revenue-deficit grants recommended by the Finance Commissions.

Another argument against revenue-deficit grants is the moral hazard or the perverse incentive to remain profligate. This argument also ignores the fact that the Finance Commissions arrive at the post-devolution gaps based on a normative approach. One of the options suggested is to compare the projections of revenue and expenditure of all States with the actuals next year and release revenue-deficit grants only if the State has not adhered to the projections of its own volition. It can be argued that if any dispensation to a State is to be based on actuals vis-à-vis estimates, similar annual assessments should be made regarding the outcome for the Union Government as well.

The reference in previous ToR to States in need of assistance has logic behind it. Tax devolution and grants-in-aid together constitute a package that help maintain vertical and horizontal balance. Horizontal balance is sought to be achieved through a formula-based approach. No formula, however, will be able to address all the needs of all the States. Grants-in-aid are meant precisely to take care of the inherent inadequacies of formula-based solutions. If the tax devolution is such that no State has revenue deficit, then such grants-in-aid become superfluous. Yet, tax devolution cannot be made so large or progressive enough to ensure that no State has post-devolution revenue deficit.

The States genuinely fear that in the absence of need-based revenue-deficit grants, discretionary powers will be conferred on the Union, contrary to what is intended in the Constitution. The Commission is well advised to take cognizance of the concerns of the States and not undermine valuable and guiding Constitutional provisions, in both letter and spirit.

THE 2011 POPULATION FIGURES

A consideration included in the ToR of the Fifteenth Finance Commission that has generated a lot of heat is the use of the 2011 population figures. The seventh to the thirteenth Commissions were asked to take into account population figures from 1971 in all cases where population was a factor to determine the devolution of taxes and duties and grants-in-aid. This was because the 1971 census had become a benchmark (on account of the National Family Welfare Policy 1977) and a resolution was passed in Parliament to this effect.

For the Fourteenth Finance Commission (2014), the criterion regarding the use of the 1971 population figures was diluted, with the consideration in its ToR stipulating that 'the Commission shall generally take the base of population figures as of 1971 in all cases where population is a factor for determination of taxes and duties and grants-in-aid: however, the Commission may also take into account the demographic changes that have taken place subsequent to 1971'.

Taking this into account, the Fourteenth Finance Commission assigned a weight of 17.5 per cent to the 1971 population and 10 per cent weight to the 2011 population figures in its tax-devolution formula. The interesting issues are: what was the justification given by the Commission for taking the 2011 population figures? And what was the Commission's view on the appropriate population? The report of the Commission clarified that the 2011 population figures were taken to represent the 'demographic changes' that it was required to take into account as per the ToR. The Report (2014) clearly preferred the population relevant to the period for which the award was recommended. It said:

> We have taken the view that the weight assigned to population should be decided first and an indicator for demographic changes be introduced separately. Though we are of the view that the use of dated population data is unfair, we are bound by our ToR and have assigned a 17.5 per cent weight to the 1971 population. On the basis of the exercises conducted, we concluded that a weight to the 2011 population would capture the demographic changes since 1971, both in terms of migration and age structure. We, therefore, assigned a 10 per cent weight to the 2011 population.

The ToR of the Fifteenth Finance Commission mandates the use of the 2011 population figures while making its recommendations. The apprehensions of the southern States are that the replacement of the 1971 population figures with those of 2011 could have a large impact, and they will lose out when population is used as a separate criterion for tax devolution and also when it is used as a scaling factor in criteria like income distance. An impression has gained ground that the use of the 2011 population numbers will result in a north–south divide and that it has become almost untenable for Tamil Nadu and Kerala to thrive in the Indian Union. Such impressions are far-fetched. It is not only the south Indian States (with the exception of Telangana) which witnessed a decline in their share in population between 1971 and 2011. Such States include Odisha, West Bengal, Punjab, Assam, Himachal Pradesh, and Goa, though to a much lesser extent. Table 16.1 presents the differences between the population in these two years. The adoption of the 1971 population numbers was ostensibly to incentivize the States to take effective steps to moderate the growth of their populations. By 2011, the scenario had changed significantly. The growth of population had come down from 24.8 per cent in 1961–71 to 17.7 per cent in 2001–11. As many as 18 States had reached replacement rates of population. In a large country like India, there are bound to be divergences. The adoption of the 1971 population figures for transfer of resources to States has not resulted in the moderation of population growth in north Indian States. Similarly, even without the use of the 1971 population numbers, there would have been a

Table 16.1 Relative Shares of States Based on the 1971 and 2011 Population Figures

		States with Lower Share in 2011 Population Figures				
	State	**1971**		**2011**		**Percentage Difference in Shares**
		Population in Lakhs	**% Share**	**Population in Lakhs**	**% Share**	
1	Tamil Nadu	411.99	7.586	721.47	6.059	–1.527
2	Kerala	213.47	3.931	334.06	2.806	–1.125
3	Andhra Pradesh	276.85	5.098	495.77	4.164	–0.934
4	Odisha	219.45	4.041	419.74	3.525	–0.516
5	West Bengal	443.12	8.159	912.76	7.666	–0.494
6	Karnataka	292.99	5.395	610.95	5.131	–0.264
7	Punjab	135.51	2.495	277.43	2.330	–0.165
8	Assam	146.25	2.693	312.06	2.621	–0.072
9	Himachal Pradesh	34.60	0.637	68.65	0.577	–0.061
10	Goa	7.96	0.147	14.59	0.122	–0.024

(*Cont'd*)

Table 16.1 (Cont'd)

States with Higher Share in 2011 Population Figures

	State	1971		2011		Percentage Difference in Shares
		Population in Lakhs	% Share	Population in Lakhs	% Share	
1	Uttar Pradesh	838.50	15.439	1998.12	16.781	1.341
2	Rajasthan	257.66	4.744	685.48	5.757	1.013
3	Bihar	421.27	7.757	1040.99	8.742	0.986
4	Madhya Pradesh	300.17	5.527	726.27	6.099	0.572
5	Haryana	100.36	1.848	253.51	2.129	0.281
6	Jammu & Kashmir	46.17	0.850	125.41	1.053	0.203
7	Gujarat	266.97	4.916	604.40	5.076	0.160
8	Maharashtra	504.12	9.283	1123.74	9.437	0.155
9	Jharkhand	142.27	2.620	329.88	2.770	0.151
10	Nagaland	5.16	0.095	19.79	0.166	0.071
11	Meghalaya	10.12	0.186	29.67	0.249	0.063
12	Manipur	10.74	0.198	28.56	0.240	0.042
13	Mizoram	3.32	0.061	10.97	0.092	0.031
14	Arunachal Pradesh	4.69	0.086	13.84	0.116	0.030
15	Telangana	158.18	2.913	350.04	2.940	0.027
16	Tripura	15.56	0.287	36.74	0.309	0.022
17	Uttarakhand	44.94	0.827	100.86	0.847	0.020
18	Sikkim	2.10	0.039	6.11	0.051	0.013
19	Chhattisgarh	116.37	2.143	255.45	2.146	0.003

Source: Registrar General of India, Populations Census 1971 and 2011.

reduction in the growth of population of the southern States because of their higher literacy and income levels.

The link between population growth and incentives or rewards to States through Finance Commission transfers does not appear to be obvious. Fundamentally, the needs of the future cannot be assessed on the basis of the population of the past. In fact, the Fourteenth Finance Commission expressed the view that the use of dated population figures is unfair. Hence, the use of the 2011 census is less unfair than of the 1971 census. In any case, the ToR of the Fifteenth Finance Commission (Ministry of Finance) is unequivocal when it says: 'The Commission shall use the population data of 2011 while making its recommendations.' However, the tradition has been to ensure that the relative shares of States are not drastically altered. The Commission may wisely adopt a pragmatic approach to the use of the population criterion as a part of the package in order to moderate the adverse impact on certain States.

REVIEW OF TAX DEVOLUTION

The Fifteenth Finance Commission has been asked to take into account the impact of the 'substantial increase' in the tax devolution recommended by the previous Commission. This is the first time that any Finance Commission has been asked to review the recommendations of its immediate predecessor on which the President has given a sanction, and Parliament has been informed of the action taken. Every Finance Commission has to take into account the prevalent state of affairs, which is a cumulative effect of all factors including the effects of the recommendations of the previous Commission(s) acted upon and not acted upon.

As Govinda Rao (2017) has explained:

> increasing devolution from 32% to 42% is not as generous as it looks. To cover the requirements under both Plan and Non-Plan accounts, 5.5% of the divisible pool was needed. The 14th [Finance Commission] avoided giving discretionary sectoral grants amounting to 1.5% of the divisible pool previously. Thus, the legitimate comparison should be between 39% and 42%.

Thus, the increase in tax devolution is not large enough to be described as 'substantial' because of non-comparability of the tax devolution by the fourteenth Commission with that recommended by the previous Commissions.

Further, the overall transfers on revenue account increased only marginally, as evident from Table 16.2.

Table 16.2 Revenue Account Transfers to States as Percentage of Gross Revenue Receipts of the Centre

(Rs in Crore)

	2014–15	2015–16	2016–17	2017–18 (RE)	2018–19 (BE)
I. Gross Revenue Receipts	**1,442,743**	**1,706,908**	**1,988,653**	**2,182,093**	**2,516,331**
a) Gross Tax Revenue	1,244,886	1,455,648	1,715,822	1,946,119	2,271,242
b) Non-Tax Revenue	197,857	251,260	272,831	235,974	245,089
Growth Rate of Gross Revenue Receipts		18.31%	16.51%	9.73%	15.32%
II. Revenue Account Transfers to States	**667,542**	**797,344**	**958,597**	**1,088,929**	**1,237,388**
Growth Rate of Revenue Account Transfers to States		19.44%	20.22%	13.60%	13.63%
a) Tax Devolution	337,808	506,193	608,000	673,005	788,093
b) Revenue-Deficit Grants	10,724	48,905	41,307	35,819	34,582
c) Grants to Local Bodies	–	26,917	45,868	56,288	64,939
d) State Disaster Response Fund	–	8,756	8,375	9,383	9,852
e) National Disaster Response Fund	–	12,452	11,441	7,167	10,000
f) CSS	–	175,736	225,848	263,783	277,754
g) Central Sector Schemes	–	2,606	2,407	31,765	32,186
h) Other Transfers	–	15,779	15,351	11,719	19,982
i) Non-Plan (Finance Commission and others)	65,561	–	–	–	–
j) Plan (State Plan, CSS, Central Sector)	252,846	–	–	–	–
III. Revenue Account Transfers to States as Percentage of Gross Revenue Receipts of the Centre	**46.27**	**46.71**	**48.20**	**49.90**	**49.17**

Sources: The figures for the year 2014–15 relating to revenue account transfers to States are compiled from the Union Finance Accounts and Budget Briefs of relevant years.

Note: Non-tax revenues are net of receipts from commercial operations of the Departments of the Union Government.

While implementing the recommendations of the Fourteenth Finance Commission, the CSS were restructured by grouping the then existing schemes. While there is no change in the funding pattern for the core schemes, the matching contribution of States in respect of other schemes has been increased. This restructuring has not resulted in any change in the number of CSS except in their grouping under certain umbrella heads.

Retaining the existing number of CSS and increasing the matching contribution of States in respect of a number of such schemes has more or less neutralized the intended benefits of untied transfers through higher devolution.

In brief, the Fifteenth Finance Commission could analyse the nature and extent of increase in overall transfers and not confine itself to tax devolution in isolation.

A NEW INDIA

The imperative of the National Development Programme, including New India 2022, has been mentioned as a consideration for the Finance Commission. This could be construed as seeking support for a particular programme formulated by the Union Government of the day in allocating resources between Union and States. As the Finance Commission has to treat the Union and the States symmetrically, similar programmes by individual States should also be considered.

New India 2022 is described as a model for the world. It consists of resolutions to have a poverty-free, dirt- and squalor-free, corruption-free, terrorism-free, casteism-free, and communalism-free India. There is also a reference to looking ahead, where the country has embraced the fourth industrial revolution; is on the high table of global governance; has a demographic dividend; and has a new governance paradigm.

It can be argued that these are desirable. But the transfers from the Union outside the recommendations of Finance Commission have been used precisely for such policy purposes. Should the Finance Commission become another instrument for such policies, undermining its role as arbiter of competing demands from the Union and the States and as one that assures the predictability of transfers?

The Fifteenth Finance Commission cannot avoid being perceived to be an instrument of political or economic agenda if it takes the goals for New India 2022 in its considerations too seriously.

CONSENT OF THE UNION

The Commission has been mandated to take into consideration the conditions that the Government of India may impose while providing consent under Article 293(3) of the Constitution. This is the first time that such a reference has been made to 'conditions'.

A State cannot raise any loan without the consent of the Union if there is any part of an outstanding loan from the Union to the State under Article 293(3). Under clause (4) of the Article, the Union may stipulate conditions as it may deem fit while giving consent to States to borrow. The approval is required only as long as a State is indebted to the Government of India. It is obviously meant for protecting the interests of the Union as a lender and cannot conceivably be meant for any other purpose.

The borrowing may be for supporting the State's budgetary resources, or for a specific project. The issue of conditions would arise only if the borrowing is for a specific project, and in such cases, the lender should take care of the conditions. In any case, the need for consent is diminishing, as consent is needed only if the State has outstanding loans to the Centre.

It is interesting to speculate why this consideration has been included in the ToR for the first time. The share of Central loans in outstanding debt of the States has dropped, and quite drastically, following the termination of on-lending by the Centre, from 2005–6: at the end of 2016–17, loans from the Centre constituted less than 5 per cent of the outstanding loans of States. So even as the possibility of all States liquidating their outstanding loans from the Centre is remote (for the Centre continues to pass on assistance under the externally assisted projects on a back-to-back basis), the possibility of a few States liquidating their outstanding debt to the Centre exists. With the FRBM Act in place, States are required to balance their revenue accounts. As most States have been adhering to this stipulation, the quantum of borrowings being diverted for revenue expenditure is likely to be negligible. In any case, the borrowing limits of States are fixed by the Union. Therefore, while the purpose of imposing those conditions is not clear, the potential for shifting the balance of power in favour of the Centre by subjecting the access to debt to conditionalities is enormous.

The Fifteenth Finance Commission can legitimately take the stand that the well-established policies and procedures have served us well and need not be disturbed.

PERFORMANCE-BASED INCENTIVES

Paragraph 7 of the ToR (see Annexure 16A.1) lists out as many as nine areas for proposing measurable performance-based incentives. The list reads like a chart to a subordinate office from headquarters, if not a student's marksheet. At best, it is applicable to a sanctioning authority. But, tax devolution is, in reality, sharing and not transfer, as Pinaki Chakraborty (2018) has expressed eloquently:

> Finally, the policy on resource sharing needs to make a distinction between tax sharing and grants. Tax sharing is to correct the vertical and horizontal imbalances arising due to constitutional assignment of tax powers and expenditure responsibilities between the Union and states. Also, as per the Article 270 of the Indian Constitution, tax share recommended by the Finance Commission does not form part of the consolidated fund of the Union government, implying this is not a component of Union budget. This distinction should not be ignored in any policy debate on transfers to states. This also implies incentive or reward should be done through a grant mechanism instead of horizontal tax sharing. Probably it is time to change the term tax devolution to national tax sharing to clear ambiguities!

An important issue within the rubric of a performance-based approach is the consideration relating to achievements in implementing the flagship programmes of the Government of India. These may not be of equal priority to States. Most are one-size-fits-all programmes with too many conditionalities and sub-programmes. Adhering to all these conditionalities is a big drag on their implementation. It can even be argued that through these schemes, the Union has intruded into State subjects.

Another consideration which has resulted in a lot of resentment from the States is the control—or lack of it—in incurring expenditure on 'populist' measures. There are no objective criteria to categorize schemes into populist and non-populist. In a vast and diverse country like India, the requirements differ from State to State, and even within a State, from district to district. A populist measure in one State may be a necessity in another. When the Government of Tamil Nadu introduced the Midday Meal Scheme, it was dubbed populist. Similarly, the Employment Guarantee Scheme introduced by the Government of Maharashtra was castigated. The same schemes were adopted by the Union Government subsequently. States are now mature enough to decide what is good for their people as they are closer and more answerable to them. It can be also argued that the Centre is equally at fault for running a number of populist schemes.

The Commission has to reckon with three basic questions. First, do performance-based indicators in determining the shares in tax devolution or grants work as incentives? Second, should such indicators be equally applicable to the Centre and States? Third, who decides on appropriate indicators? The Commission should have no difficulty in explaining the serious adverse consequences of using performance indicators.

ASSESSMENT OF RESOURCES

The Fifteenth Finance Commission has been asked to take into consideration the resources of the Central and State Governments for the five years commencing 1 April 2020 on the basis of the levels of tax and non-tax revenue likely to be reached by 2024–5. This is in total contrast to the consideration given to the previous Finance Commissions, which were asked to assess the resources of the Centre and States on the basis of the levels of tax and non-tax revenues prevailing in a base year, generally the year preceding the award period of a Commission. The concern is that assessing the resources for the five-year period on the basis of the levels of tax and non-tax revenue likely to be reached in the terminal year of the award without any reference to a base year has the potential to be arbitrary.

THE GOODS AND SERVICES TAX

There are other matters in the ToR over which there are concerns. One such consideration is the impact of GST and the abolition of a number of cesses and other reform programmes on the finances of the Centre and the States, including payment of compensation for possible loss of revenue for five years. The matters relating to GST concern the GSTC on which the Centre and the States are represented. The consideration to take into account the impact of GST encroaches upon the role of the Council. As far as the question of cesses is concerned, their abolition and inclusion in the basic rates was long overdue. But the Centre has again resorted to the levy of more cesses on direct taxes and custom duties. The Union Budget 2018–19 increased the rates of education and health cesses, and imposed a social welfare surcharge on a number of imported goods.

The Fifteenth Finance Commission's ToR are heavily tilted in favour of the Centre, but these are not insurmountable constraints on its working. For example, when the ToR of the Ninth Finance Commission stipulated that it should adopt a normative approach, the Chairman wrote to all Chief Ministers that the Commission would consider, inter alia, adopting a normative approach wherever appropriate in the interests of sound finance and, in doing so, would apply a uniform, just, and equitable yardstick both to the Centre and the States. Similarly, when the Thirteenth Finance Commission was asked to take into account the demands on the resources of the Central Government, in particular, on account of the projected gross budgetary support (GBS) to the Central and State Plans while making its recommendations, the Commission observed in its Report (2009):

> In the dispensation of recent Finance Commissions, GBS emerged as a residual after fully providing for the requirements of the Centre on non-plan

account. If the GBS is taken upfront as a demand on the Centre's resources, the Finance Commission transfers will have to be tailored accordingly. This, in a way, reverses the current practice of arriving at the GBS residually and alters the basic character of the Finance Commission transfers.... After examining all these aspects, we are of the view that there are far too many practical difficulties in taking the GBS for plan as a demand on the resources of the Centre and that the balance of advantage clearly lies in arriving at the GBS residually, as has been the practice in the past.

The Fifteenth Finance Commission has a major task ahead in addressing the various contentious issues against the backdrop of the recent momentous changes in Indian fiscal federalism. Going by the stand taken by the previous Finance Commissions, the fifteenth Commission is not bound by all the considerations listed out in the ToR. However, in some other cases, like in the choice of population figures, it may not have the freedom or flexibility that its predecessor enjoyed.

It is hoped that the Fifteenth Finance Commission would have the courage and wisdom to be guided by the letter and spirit of Constitutional provisions in discharging its responsibility and upholding the sanctity of the institution.

SELECT REFERENCES

1. Aiyar, S.A. 2018. 'North India Deserves Credit for Demographic Dividend', *Times of India*, 15 April.

2. Bhaskar, V. 2018. 'Challenges before the Fifteenth Finance Commission', *Economic and Political Weekly*, 53(19), 10 March.

3. Chakraborty, Pinaki. 2018. '15th Finance Commission: Is It Just a South India vs North India Debate? *Mint*, 10 April.

4. Ministry of Finance. 2017. 'Notification', *Gazette of India: Extraordinary*, 27 November. New Delhi: Government of India.

5. Ministry of Finance. Various Years. *Report of the Finance Commission*, II–XIV. New Delhi: Government of India.

6. Rangarajan, C., and D.K. Srivastava. 2018. 'Balancing Conflicting Claims', *The Hindu*, 19 May.

7. Rao, M. Govinda. 2017. '15th Finance Commission: To Realise the Goals under New India 2022, Here is What Centre Must Remember', *Financial Express*, 5 December.

8. Rao, M. Govinda. 2018. 'Mandate and Allocations', *The Hindu*, 16 April.

9. Rao, M. Govinda. 2018. 'Finance Commission: Redefining the Federal Fiscal Landscape?', *Financial Express*, 1 May.

10. Reddy, G.R. 2018. 'Upholding Fiscal Federalism—Terms of Reference of the Fifteenth Finance Commission', *Economic and Political Weekly*, 53(10), 10 March.

11. Reddy, Y.V. 2015. 'Fourteenth Finance Commission: Continuity, Change and Way Forward', Second Raja Chelliah Memorial Lecture, Madras School of Economics, Chennai, 16 March.

12. Roy, Ratin. 2018. '15th Finance Commission: Moving on', *Business Standard*, 18 April.

ANNEXURE 16A.1: FIFTEENTH FINANCE COMMISSION, TERMS OF REFERENCE

Terms of Reference and the matters that shall be taken into consideration by the Fifteenth Finance Commission in making the recommendations are as under:

(i) The distribution between the Union and the States of the net proceeds of taxes which are to be, or may be, divided between them under Chapter I, Part XII of the Constitution and the allocation between the States of the respective shares of such proceeds;

(ii) The principles which should govern the grants-in-aid of the revenues of the States out of the Consolidated Fund of India and the sums to be paid to the States by way of grants-in-aid of their revenues under Article 275 of the Constitution for purposes other than those specified in the provisos to clause (1) of that article; and

(iii) The measures needed to augment the Consolidated Fund of a State to supplement the resources of the Panchayats and Municipalities in the State on the basis of the recommendations made by the Finance Commission of the State.

2. The Commission shall review the current status of the finance, deficit, debt levels, cash balances and fiscal discipline efforts of the Union and the States, and recommend a fiscal consolidation roadmap for sound fiscal management, taking into account the responsibility of the Central Government and State Governments to adhere to appropriate levels of general and consolidated government debt and deficit levels, while fostering higher inclusive growth in the country, guided by the principles of equity, efficiency and transparency. The Commission may also examine whether revenue deficit grants be provided at all.

3. While making its recommendations, the Commission shall have regard, among other considerations, to:

(i) The resources of the Central Government and the State Governments for the five years commencing on 1st April 2020 on the basis of the levels of tax and the non-tax revenues likely to be reached by 2024–25. In the context of both tax and non-tax revenues, the Commission will also take into consideration their potential and fiscal capacity;

(ii) The demand on the resources of the Central Government particularly on account of defence, internal security, infrastructure, railways, climate change, commitments towards administration of Union Territories without legislature, and other committed expenditure and liabilities;

(iii) The demand on the resources of the State Governments, particularly on account of financing socioeconomic development and critical infrastructure, assets maintenance expenditure, balanced regional development and impact of the debt and liabilities of their public utilities;

(iv) The impact on the fiscal situation of the Union Government of substantially enhanced tax devolution to States following recommendations of the 14th Finance Commission, coupled with the continuing imperative of the national development programme including New India–2022;

(v) The impact of the GST, including payment of compensation for possible loss of revenues for 5 years, and abolition of a number of cesses, earmarking thereof for compensation and other structural reforms programme, on the finances of Centre and States; and

(vi) The conditions that Government of India may impose on the States while providing consent under Article 293(3) of the Constitution.

4. The Commission may consider proposing measurable performance-based incentives for States, at the appropriate level of government, in following areas:

(i) Efforts made by the States in expansion and deepening of tax net under GST;

(ii) Efforts and Progress made in moving towards replacement rate of population growth;

(iii) Achievements in implementation of flagship schemes of Government of India, disaster resilient infrastructure, sustainable development goals, and quality of expenditure;

(iv) Progress made in increasing capital expenditure, eliminating losses of power sector, and improving the quality of such expenditure in generating future income streams;

(v) Progress made in increasing tax/non-tax revenues, promoting savings by adoption of Direct Benefit Transfers and Public Finance Management System, promoting digital economy and removing layers between the government and the beneficiaries;

(vi) Progress made in promoting ease of doing business by effecting related policy and regulatory changes and promoting labour intensive growth;

(vii) Provision of grants in aid to local bodies for basic services, including quality human resources, and implementation of performance grant system in improving delivery of services;

(viii) Control or lack of it in incurring expenditure on populist measures; and

(ix) Progress made in sanitation, solid waste management and bringing in behavioural change to end open defecation.

5. The Commission shall use the population data of 2011 while making its recommendations.

6. The Commission may review the present arrangements on financing Disaster Management initiatives, with reference to the funds constituted under the Disaster Management Act, 2005 (53 of 2005), and make appropriate recommendations thereon.

7. The Commission shall indicate the basis on which it has arrived at its findings and make available the State wise estimates of receipts and expenditure.

8. The Commission shall make its report available by 30th October, 2019, covering a period of five years commencing 1st April, 2020.

AFTERWORD
THE WAY FORWARD

INDIA'S FISCAL FEDERALISM, WHICH HAS withstood the test of times, is at a crossroads because of momentous changes since 2014. These include the transformative recommendations of the Fourteenth Finance Commission; the replacement of the Planning Commission by NITI Aayog; and the dispensation of the classification of expenditure into Plan and non-Plan. The introduction of the much-awaited GST in July 2017 fundamentally altered the relative roles of the Union and States in regard to indirect taxes, while the establishment of the GSTC has added a new institutional mechanism in Union–State fiscal relations.

Five years ago, there was a euphoria about competing models of development from different States, more particularly the Gujarat and the Kerala models of development. Now, the Central Government seems to be advocating a one-nation-one-policy format. This is a contrast.

There are some immediate concerns with regard to Union–State fiscal relations, in addition to the persistent ones. The immediate concern is the discomfort with regard to the ToR of the Fifteenth Finance

Commission. The persistent concerns relate to centrally sponsored schemes; discretionary transfers outside the Finance Commission; equity compatible with efficiency in Central transfers; and perceptions about relative efficiencies of the Centre and States.

Fiscal relations are also conditioned by beliefs and assumptions in regard to centralization and decentralization. Which of the two is good depends on the current status as against the desired ideal. In terms of a multilevel decision-making framework, the optimal level is determined by functional efficiency and externalities. For example, while in revenue raising, centralization has a clear advantage, decentralization of expenditure is more efficient in improving the delivery of services and accountability. So the basis for advocating centralization or decentralization should be on the appropriate level in respect of different functions.

The debate on Centre–State relations, in particular fiscal relations, is often conditioned by a presumption about the relative efficiencies of the Centre and the States. There is an impression that States are fiscally imprudent and profligate relative to the Centre. However, the revenue and fiscal deficit indicators do not support this view. Similarly, some believe that the States, relative to the Centre, do not adequately emphasize social expenditures. Here again there can be varying assessments of the level and usefulness of social expenditures. A search for empirical evidence would help validate assumptions on relative efficiencies.

There has been more competition between the Centre and States to provide private goods, or subsidized private goods, than for public goods such as roads and law and order. Further, there are inappropriate electoral promises in the sense that the Central leadership promises to deliver on subjects entirely in the State List. At times, political leadership expands the Concurrent List, or takes extensive recourse to its provisions, to discharge its electoral promises. The political and intellectual debate also does not distinguish between the respective jurisdictions of the Centre and the States, or of the electoral promises that are made. The concern of the States is that their administrative machinery and funds are used as instruments to implement the Centre's programmes. The institutional framework needs to be reviewed in order to address, even if partially, these complex issues.

THE FINANCE COMMISSION

The recommendations of the Finance Commission relating to core ToR have been relatively non-controversial until recently. The main task of the Commission relates to the sharing of taxes and grants. However, over the years, some of the tasks that have been and are being assigned to the Commission go beyond what could be achieved by changing the relative shares of taxes and some grants. In other words, the instruments available to the Finance Commission are often inadequate to cater to the tasks and considerations assigned to it. There is a need to redefine objectives and restrict the scope of its work appropriate to the instruments available to it. The Union Government has a dominant role in this regard.

Ideally, the ToR of the Finance Commission should be decided by the President in a forum or through a process in which both the Union and the States are represented. Similarly, there should be an opportunity for such a forum or process to note the action taken on the recommendations.

Several issues are referred to the Finance Commission in the interests of 'sound finance', but many of the recommendations are seldom acted upon. The examples of its expanded list include matters relating to public enterprises and expenditure management. The elimination of these references would add to the Commission's efficient functioning and timeliness.

In regard to vertical distribution, the main issue has been in relation to the fiscal space available to the Central Government that enabled it to expand fiscal transfers to States outside the recommendations of the Finance Commissions. The interface between the Union and the States in this area is easily the most contentious. Since its remit is restricted to revenue account, transfers outside the Finance Commission become inevitable. The Commission itself recognized this and ceded space for such transfers.

The considerations that govern horizontal distribution are also contentious. In general, a continuing controversy has been regarding the relative weightage to be given to the need, equity, and performance of States. More often than not, giving higher weightage to two competing objectives may as well nullify the advantages to both and become ineffective. Further, the effectiveness of incentives and rewards being built into the criteria is uncertain.

Transfers outside the Finance Commission should be viewed as supplementing, and not undermining, its functioning and authority. Further, developmental and equity objectives can be met through continuity in collaboration between the Union and States. An institution with which the Union and States are equally involved is necessary for this. The Planning Commission was meant to perform this function, while NITI Aayog is not yet designed to discharge it. This has created a vacuum, one that has been occupied by the Ministries in the Union Government.

Finally, the extent to which the Finance Commission should be an instrument of policy of the Union Government of the day is another thorny issue that has come up now. The predictability of transfers over the medium term, cutting across the political spectrum assured by it, is the strength of the Finance Commission. Any condition for a State availing transfers through the Finance Commission undermines such predictability.

NITI AAYOG

NITI Aayog suffers from a wide mandate and diffused focus. The organization should ideally be the focal point for all transfers from the Centre to States outside the recommendations of the Finance Commission. As a continuing body, it could also ensure implementation of the Finance Commissions' recommendations. In order to achieve this, it requires significant technical support from experts and, at the same time, substantial political support. The latter requires an institutional arrangement, and this should ideally be in the ambit of the ISC.

It is advisable to specify the tasks of NITI Aayog that are most relevant for Centre–State relations: identifying the sectors in the States that should be eligible for grants from the Union; indicating criteria for inter-State distribution; helping design schemes with appropriate flexibility accorded to States regarding implementation; and identifying and providing area-specific grants.

Ideally, the scope of Central transfers outside the Finance Commission should be considered by a forum consisting of the Union and the States. Further, since all aspects of implementation as well as consequences of CSS (except for partial funding) are borne by the States, they should be called Centre–State projects so as to reflect the joint effort and ensure shared ownership.

In brief, wisdom lies in refocusing the scope of the Finance Commission to maintain the trust of all stakeholders in the institution as a pillar of fiscal federalism. To fill the existing institutional vacuum for other Central transfers to States and related matters, it is necessary to reinvent NITI Aayog. This organization should be endowed with appropriate stature and expertise and have the benefit of Constitutional legitimacy, possibly by linking it to the ISC.

It should be recognized that the dominant objective of federal transfers is moderating the fiscal-capacity differential across States to provide comparable levels of public services at comparable levels of taxation. The complex issue of reducing inequalities in development among States should be addressed by the cooperative efforts of both Union and the States on several policy fronts as this should be a matter of national concern.

INDEX

ABOUT THE AUTHORS

Y.V. Reddy was Chairman, Fourteenth Finance Commission (2013–14), and Governor, Reserve Bank of India (2003–8). He belongs to the Indian Administrative Service (1964) and was Secretary (Finance and Planning) in the Government of Andhra Pradesh and Secretary in the Union Ministry of Finance. His memoirs, *Advice and Dissent: My Life in Public Service*, were published in 2017. He is currently honorary Professor at the Centre for Economic and Social Studies, Hyderabad, and Professor of Practice at the Indian Institute of Management Ahmedabad.

G.R. Reddy has been Adviser (Finance) to the Government of Telangana since 2014 and belongs to the Indian Economic Service (1971). He served the Government of India and Government of Andhra Pradesh mainly in the area of public finance and Union–State relations. He was Adviser to the Thirteenth Finance Commission and consulted for the World Bank, Government of Karnataka, the Punchhi Commission on Centre–State Relations, and the Centre for Good Governance.